A Thankless Child

The Life and times of
Georgiana Jane Henderson (1771-1850)

by

SUSAN BENNETT MA

© the author 2020

Front cover image: *Georgiana Jane Keate* by Angelica Kauffman, 1779
Private Collection, UK. Photograph courtesy of Richard Green Gallery, London

ISBN: 978-1-71668-984-0
Imprint: Lulu.co

To my son Sam

	Introduction	7
1.	With a heart aching	9
2.	So much sunshine and happiness	13
3.	A very excellent LEASEHOLD DWELLING	17
4.	Who can my ill form'd house restore	19
5.	The Blossom might ripen into future Fruit	21
6.	Bard, his child and wife…They scaped with life	24
7.	In verse record his case	27
8.	A luminous wonder	29
9.	The pattern of her honoured life	32
10.	Three or four leagues distant	35
11.	Are you friend or enemy	38
12.	Sparkling on the bosom of the ocean	41
13.	So much virtue	44
14.	She has a beard	47
15.	To ride in the air like a bird	50
16.	This trophy's thine	54
17.	I've got a new madness	58
18.	Dear Pretty Pretty Plotty	61
19.	Is the stage clear?	65
20.	Still speaks of your rapturous kisses	69
21.	Everything she touches turns to gold	73
22.	Rage for music	76
23.	Good news about Mr de Sade	79
24.	Pure and salubrious air	82
25.	Whose high and bending head	85
26.	HKM	89
27.	Never having a child	92
28.	Rent asunder every tie	96
29.	Any other husband	99
30.	Rather a brilliance of talents	103
31.	Retiring into the country	109
32.	Breathing tranquillity	112
33.	I am related to Kings	116
34.	Elixir of life	119
35.	One of the finest	123
36.	A most useful lesson to youth	127
37.	The sailors came for our luggage	130
38.	High walk towards Egypt	134

39. A plan for living	137
40. In testimony of my forgiveness	140
41. Prior to going to Bath	144
42. Took possession of our lodgings	147
43. Taking the waters	151
44. Opened the door out of their bedroom	156
45. Slept with Henderson again	159
46. To be churched	162
47. Charles Cooper	167
48. Inoculated Charles for cowpock	172
49. The Defence and Security of the Realm	175
50. Quit Chertsey	178
51. An excellent one	182
52. Much grown and improved	186
53. In a capital style	189
54. Every mark of loyalty and respect	192
55. Took the least notice	196
56. Getting close to Cooper	200
57. Not possible to refuse	204
58. Vulgar and disagreeable as usual	209
59. She might have the pleasure	213
60. Nothing unpleasant makes a lasting impression	218
61. A canary in a cage	221
62. Beyond the power of description	225
63. The entire field of art	228
Acknowledgements	233
About the author	233

Introduction

The contents of a recorded delivery package addressed to me, as Curator/Archivist of the Royal Society of Arts, started me on a long journey that has led to this story of *A Thankless Child*.

Two small red leather diaries, measuring 5" x 3" (12cm x 8cm), protected in bubble wrap arrived on my desk on a grey morning in April 2000. They had been found by the then navigation officer on Concorde. She came across them as she sorted out her late mother's effects. She didn't know if they had been written by a family member or, more likely, her mother had found them in the local secondhand bookshop, where she often acquired items of interest. The closely written entries had been a struggle to read but when she came across the name Captain William Bligh, of 'Mutiny on the Bounty' fame, she thought they might have some historical value. It was this entry, written on 27th May 1794, that bought the diaries to my notice as the writer records attending the Society of Arts ceremony where Bligh received a gold medal for successfully transporting breadfruit and other plants from the East to the West Indies'.

Curious to know if there were any further references to the Society I asked to see the diary and to my surprise two diaries, one for 1794 and the other 1802, arrived unannounced. They proved to be more a record of daily activity rather than the author's innermost thoughts. She records daily walks, the people she met, the plays she attended but no comments on the performance or the actors. One name does appear quite frequently in both diaries – Mr Henderson. He appears to be a welcome guest at the dinner table and attends the family when they visit Dover for a holiday in 1794. During the eight year gap between the diaries she has obviously married Henderson and started a family. This, together with the transcript of a third diary dated 1803, which came to light from another source, surviving correspondence and secondary sources made it possible for me to identify the author as the much loved only child of amateur artist and poet George Keate, and wife of amateur artist John Henderson. Her name was Georgiana Jane Henderson (nee Keate). Through the kindness of George and Amanda Rosenberg, who had provided me with transcripts of some surviving nineteenth century diaries by one of their ancestors, Fanny

Chapman, a member of Georgiana's friendship circle, a circle that included Mrs Delany, David Garrick, Dorothy Jordan, Prince Lee Boo and James Smithson, I was able to discover more of Georgiana's character – even though it was through the jaundiced eye of Fanny, who considered her a rival for the affections of Dr John Hutton Cooper.

Georgiana was an accomplished amateur artist whose skill was recognised by Angelica Kauffmann. Two of her watercolours were turned into fashion satires by James Gillray and can now be seen in the British Museum.

What drew me to discover more about Georgiana was the fact that her father, in his will, had described her as 'a thankless child' for marrying a man 'whose manners and principles she knew I detested'. This was the same man, Henderson, who had been a welcome guest at their home in 1794. What could be the reason for this vehement response? And so my long quest began. Unlike her namesake, the Duchess of Devonshire who made quite a splash in eighteenth century society, Georgiana is rarely mentioned in the records of the day. It was only as a result of her father's Shakespearean response to her marriage that her name appeared in the public press.

During her lifetime decades of internal strife had come to an end. Wondrous goods arrived from exotic places through the trading activities of the East India, Levant, Turkey and Russia companies. Almost daily the papers reported new discoveries, ideas and innovations. Increasingly wealthy industrialists, entrepreneurs and merchants were making their own way in society. She also witnessed the loss of the American colonies, the terrors of the French Revolution, the madness and death of George III, the extravagance of George IV and the coronation of Queen Victoria.

The marriage appears to have been a happy one and both died in their late 70s of natural causes. Due to the paucity of material this book is not a biography but rather a story of the times, the people and the events Georgiana witnessed and, it is hoped, will lead the reader to want to find out more about England's rich history.

1. With a heart aching

Twenty-four year old Georgiana Keate wrote to her godfather in 1795 that she found 'it hard to be obliged to Joke and appear in spirits with a heart aching' yet, she told him that she must appear so for 'the prospect of mentioning the least affair of consequence' to her mother was 'more distant than ever', and to speak to her father was 'impossible'. The reason for her low spirits was her parents' reaction to the news that she wished to marry John Henderson.

Financially independent, he was a family friend of some years standing and she loved him. She found it hard to accept their disapproval of his proposal when their own marriage had been a love match. Even her paternal grandparents had lived 'for many years in perfect harmony', although this idyll was cut short when her grandfather died in 1738 and was buried at Greenwich 'without any pomp', as he decreed in his will. Unusually he had named his widow as his executor, a role usually undertaken by a male member of the family, or a close friend. He had also stipulated that his estate be left to his wife in her maiden name, Rachel Cowalsky, as he was concerned that unkind persons would ask for proof of their marriage, 'which after this length of time may be a difficulty'. The couple had three young sons. The eldest, nine-year-old George had been named, as was the custom, after his father; next was five-year-old Henry and then the baby, John who had just turned one, when their father died. Five years later Rachel married for a second time. However, she protected her sons' inheritance by putting her late husband's estate into a trust for their benefit. Sadly only George appears to have survived childhood, and Rachel ensured that he received the type of education appropriate for the son of a gentleman. She sent him to one of the finest small schools of the time, the 'Free Grammar School' at Kingston-upon-Thames. Under the tutelage of the school's headmaster, the Revd Richard Woodeson, he learnt to 'revere nature or nature polished but by classic art'. His memories of this time were so happy that he instructed his executors to inter him 'in the chancel of the church of Kingston-upon-Thames, the place of his education', if there was no space for him in the church at Isleworth, the town where he was born.

On completion of his education Georgiana's father secured the position of articled clerk to the 4th Duke of Bedford's agent and steward, Robert Palmer. No doubt he owed this opportunity to his father's support, many years earlier, for the Duke of Bedford's election to the Board charged with the drainage of a fen in eastern England known as the 'Bedford Level'. After several years learning the mysteries of estate management Georgiana's father entered the Honourable Society of the Inner Temple, like his father before him, to study law. However, he remained friends with Palmer for the rest of his life. Untangling the machinations of the legal system did not suit the poetic heart of George Keate:

> Quite jaded out, I march to Nando's
> And look as grave as any man does
> Shake hands with friends I wish to see
> And take my sober pot of tea

Here, much more to his liking, he would sit by the fire and read the daily newspapers provided by the coffee house, or join in the conversations going on around him. Perhaps they discussed the progress of the latest war, exchanged gossip or enthused about the latest inventions or experiments they had recently witnessed. Or he may have attended one of the many clubs and societies that were springing up in this new environment. Meanwhile the waiting staff refilled empty coffee cups or provided tea for those, like Keate, who preferred this beverage, said to make 'the body active and lusty' and preserve 'perfect health until extreme old age'. Another distraction from his studies was provided by Bernard Lintot's bookshop next door to Nando's, but eventually he could delay no longer:

> So back to Chambers I return
> More patience and more Law to learn

In spite of the tedium he successfully completed his studies and was called to the Bar. Then his mother died. At the age of twenty-five George Keate, as the only surviving son, inherited the whole of his late father's estate. Now a man 'of independent fortune, of good connections and good family', as the playwright George Colman the elder described him, Keate settled happily into the life of a man of leisure. Firstly, he decided to see something of the world. In 1754 he set out on a 'Grand Tour' that would take him three years. Thanks to his skill with a paintbrush he was able to retrace his journey through the series of watercolours he had painted of the people and the various countries he passed through, from the vineyards of France to the romantic ruins of Italy. They include a view of *The Manner of passing Mount Cenis* in 1755. We see the artist sitting in a small open chair suspended on poles, like a sedan chair, as the porters carry him through the Alps where 'there was scarce room for a cloven foot', as one terrified tourist wrote. Keate took a particular interest in the Swiss and their culture, spending a year in the capital writing a *Short Account of the Ancient History, Present Government and Laws of the Republic of Geneva*. The area was also home to the famous French philosopher Voltaire, who lived at Ferney near the French/Swiss border. With their shared interest in literary and theatrical matters the two men soon became firm friends, in spite of a thirty-five-year age gap. In surviving correspondence Keate acknowledged the role that Voltaire had played in literature, a cause he had 'for so long a series of years so gloriously protected, by rooting up all the weeds of false Taste, and embellishing with the fairest Flowers the Garden of the Arts'. Sadly, Voltaire died before Keate had the opportunity of seeing his kind 'Friend at Ferney, and renewing some of those agreeable hours', he had formerly enjoyed in the great man's company. These letters from Voltaire remained treasured family possessions until the late 19th century when they were donated to the British Museum.

When Keate returned to London in 1757 he, like many of his contemporaries, rented rooms in the Temple, where he was in easy reach of the coffee house, the theatre, and the homes of his friends, who regularly invited him to dine. 'A man of business', Keate once said, 'should not indulge in much reading if he wished to make money', however he now had no such worries. Keate had always enjoyed reading and his inheritance allowed him to buy many fine editions for his library shelves including *The Pleasures of the Imagination* by the poet Mark Akenside, various editions of the works of Shakespeare, the published *Letters* written by Lady Mary Montague as well as printed volumes of his own poetry. He acquired a reputation as an amiable eccentric who had a particular fondness for talking about his own work. As a 'Gentleman well known to the Public by his Writings & a Lover of Philosophical Learning' it is not surprising to find that he was elected a Fellow of both the prestigious Royal Society and the Society of Antiquaries when he was thirty-seven years old. It was also around this time that this seemingly confirmed bachelor met the woman who would become his wife.

2. So much sunshine and happiness

We don't know when Georgiana's father first met the woman who was to change his life, but it was most probably during the late 1760s at her brother's home in Arundel Street. As the Crown and Anchor tavern nearby was a favourite haunt for literary figures, like Dr Samuel Johnson and James Boswell, we can imagine that Keate also frequented its rooms and may have met Charles Grave Hudson here. We know the two men were friends by 1765 as Hudson proposed his future brother-in-law to the Fellowship of the Royal Society in this year. However, it would appear that Keate did not meet Jane for another three years, possibly at the christening of her nephew, Stevenson Charles Hudson, born in 1768.

Like her brother, Jane had been born in Tunis where their father, Joseph Hudson, had established himself as a merchant. While Charles would have been sent to England for his education Jane remained behind with her parents among the bright colours and exotic scents of this Mediterranean port for the first twenty-four years of her life. Her mother came from a similar background as she had been born in the Italian port of Livorno (or Leghorn as the British called it). Hudson was in his early sixties when he married the thirty seven year old Sarah Plowman. Perhaps he sought to give her a better life following her father's behaviour. According to gossip the successful trader William Plowman, had left his wife and seven children (including Sarah) to bigamously marry the daughter of a worthy family from Essex. Plowman had already damaged his reputation when, in 1697, he ignored the orders of the Grand Duke of Tuscany, sailed out of the port and took all the French ships he met by force. Imprisoned by Cosimo de Medici on charges of piracy he was finally released three years later after signing a confession to his illegal acts. His fellow merchants appealed to the Duke against the damages imposed against them for Plowman's piracy as they were not responsible for his actions and, they added 'no Man in Christendom, or out of it, that hath ever known him, will venture to say, He [Plowman] is an Honest Man'.

When Joseph Hudson died at the age of eighty-six in 1754 Sarah, with Jane, left Tunis to join her son in England. The two women disembarked at one of the coastal ports just as Keate left on his Grand Tour. Three years later he returned to his lodgings in the Temple but after seven months of 'sitting still' he 'had so much the itch of travelling' on him that he decided to undertake a tour covering the length and breadth of England 'rambling where curiosity prompts'. His journey took him 'thro many of the Midland counties, and all round that of York'. In Scarborough he enjoyed 'the pleasure of sea-bathing' before turning to the southwest, where he traversed Dorset's chalk downs and limestone hills, before travelling through the open moorland and wooded valleys of Devon to reach the furthest south-western point of England's coastline, Land's End in Cornwall.

While Keate was away Charles had found suitable accommodation for his mother and sister in the fashionable riverside village of Chelsea. There was much to amuse and entertain the two women at the nearby Ranelagh Gardens. They could walk around the ornamental lake or attend musical performances in the Rotunda. They may have been in the audience when the nine-year-old Mozart played his own compositions on the harpsichord. The nearby Bun shop provided an opportunity to socialise or they could admire the collection of curiosities, models, paintings, statues and clocks, as they bought some Chelsea buns for their tea, so they had little reason to make the journey into town except on special occasions.

When Georgiana's father first set eyes on Jane it appears to have been love at first sight. He gave her the poetical name of 'Ardelia' and published a number of poems praising her qualities. In *To the Thames* he asks the river:

>Should'st thou haply see my Fair
>Lure her to thy view awhile
>Tidings of my Welfare bear
>Waft a Sigh, and steal a Smile

In another he tells the reader that 'a mutual passion reigns, in Ardelia's breast and mine'. A present of a finely decorated ivory fan was accompanied by a verse in which Keate imagined his gift unfolding 'with the touch of her hands' as his 'breast, when I muse on my Fair, with each wish of affection expands'. He just couldn't stop thinking about her and during a visit to Margate he wrote it was now 'time that life's tumult should cease', and added, 'with thy Sunshine Ardelia...no Storms can my Steadiness move; your bosom's my Harbour of Rest and the Anchor that holds me, your Love'. Six months later, on 7th February 1769, the couple were married in St Luke's Church at Chelsea. Georgiana's father then took his new bride to the West Country to meet his relatives. To his horror Jane was struck down with a fever as they neared Exeter. She lost both weight and strength. 'Death's dark shade o'er Life's gay prospect cast, Twas Horror, almost bordering on Despair!' 'Could it be less?' he asked, 'When all I held most dear...shook by Disease, alarmed by every Fear'. Thankfully her fever broke as she responded to rest and whatever medical care was available. Not surprisingly Georgiana's father recorded his feelings in verse:

> My Breast to throb with sufferings long prepared
> Once more feels Peace, nor throbs but with delight.

He also wrote to his cousin, Mrs Blake, in Wiltshire to tell her that 'Mrs Keate is much mended since her journey to this place' and, he added, he planned to cut short their trip in order for the acclaimed Dr William Heberden of Pall Mall to examine his wife. A year later he wrote to Mrs Blake to tell her that, 'Mrs Keate has been pronounced to be with child and is so near her time that she expects to be summoned to bed in the course of next week'. His wife was in very good spirits and he thanked 'God [had] an excellent good constitution', he told her, but his own health had been affected by the 'dreadful anxiety and suspense [he] had endured for almost nine months'. We can imagine that Keate would have sought the services of the best man midwife available, Dr William Hunter, to oversee the birth, particularly as Jane was 38 years old at this time. In spite of concerns over possible complications all appears to have gone well and their baby daughter was born on 26th February 1771. They named her Georgiana Jane.

Georgiana's father found himself reflecting that at the age of 40 he had not only met and married the 'best of Women, and steadiest Friend' who had 'spread so much sunshine and happiness' over his life but she had also presented him with a child, something which had been beyond his imagination.

3 A Very excellent LEASEHOLD DWELLING

Although his rooms in the Temple had suited his bachelor lifestyle Georgiana's father now sought more appropriate accommodation for his married state. Through his old mentor Robert Palmer he heard about a recent development of seventeen houses, on the Duke of Bedford's land on the newly established Charlotte Street, designed by the architect Stiff Leadbetter, who had established a reputation for himself as the builder of Fulham Palace and other fine houses.

Keate agreed to pay the Duke £13 10s a year (the equivalent of the annual wage bill for a housekeeper) for an 83 year lease on no 9 located within easy walking distance of fashionable Bloomsbury Square, and just around the corner from the pleasures of the British Museum. Georgiana's father commissioned a team of builders and carpenters to fit out the interior of this three storey house which then had 'nothing but bare walls in view'. When he visited the building to see how the work was progressing Keate discovered the workmen sitting 'idling by the unfinish'd Chimney's side' whilst 'empty Porter Pots bestrew the floor' instead of making the building habitable. There was a lot to do. The kitchen and domestic offices were in the basement to service the dining room and breakfast parlour on the ground floor. A simple stone staircase in the centre of the building led to the reception and drawing rooms on the first floor and then to the bedrooms and Georgiana's nursery on the second level. The servants sleeping quarters were at the top under the eaves. On one visit to see how the work was progressing Keate noticed that, not only were the workmen lazy, they were not particularly accomplished in their work. He saw that 'the Shelf's awry, the Door's too wide' but before he could say anything one of the masons came rushing into the room announcing that he had just seen the most sorry sight:

> Thro' St Giles moving slowly
> (All the gaping Crowd intent)
> Jack with looks that pictured sorrow
> Sucked an Orange as he went.
> High and low
> Above, below
> From Garret Tops

Down to the Shops
Twas all one staring Face to view the mournful Show.

A carpenter, who 'knew well his trade', Jack was 'both given to drinking and raking' but, the mason continued, he had been arrested when he 'mistook for House building, House breaking'. Georgiana's father noticed the look of 'terror in every workman's face' on hearing about Jack's fate:

..when to Tyburn he came
How he changed Colour often
As he looked at his Coffin
...
As he stood in the Cart
It quite pierced my Heart
To see him so tremble and snivel
Soon the Slip-Knot was tied
So he prayed, sang and cryed

When this morbid tale was complete 'all busy once again' the men, with 'error guiding all their Motions. Hurry, hurry, bustle, bustle…with sounds that split the Ear…and jagged Saws [that] set all one's Teeth on Edge!', were back at work and finally, Keate wrote, he could 'close the door' on them.

Although he was glad that the men had left he saw that the house was not yet a fit place for his wife and child. As he lamented the quality of the workmanship he wondered 'who can my ill-formed House restore? Heal its Defects? Its Faults amend?'

4 Who can my ill-form'd House restore?

Georgiana's father first made the acquaintance of Robert Adam in Rome fifteen years earlier. The two men probably met in the historical centre of the city in the warehouse managed by Thomas Jenkins, who also acted as a banker for the grand tourists. Jenkins had first come to Rome to paint but quickly realised that he could make a better living as a guide and a dealer. Georgiana's father would have made use of his services and, like Adam, would have been interested in Jenkins' stock of antiquities, sculpture and salvaged architectural details. Alternatively, they could have met at the nearby Caffe Inglese – as its name suggests this was a favourite haunt for English visitors. Wherever they met they soon discovered they shared a mutual acquaintance in the figure of the Scottish advocate and politician Sir Adam Fergusson. The two visitors spent many happy hours together sketching the city's 'mouldering fragments and tottering arches' as well as the 'stately ruins that from various shores attract the traveller'.

On his return to England Adam sought funding for the publication of the survey he had undertaken of the ancient palace of the Emperor Diocletian. On 10th January 1760 Keate wrote to Fergusson to tell him that 'we toasted you last night at Bob Adam's who is a very ingenious Fellow', and he added that Adam is 'about publishing by Subscription the Views of Spalettra (I don't believe I spell it well'), he added. Keate subscribed towards the cost of this book on Diocletian's palace, which had been built at Spalatro, or Split as we call it today, in the former Roman province of Dalmatia (modern day Croatia). Adam responded by designing a title page and frontispiece for Keate's watercolours of his Grand Tour. Georgiana's father then had both his paintings and Adam's book on the *Ruins of the Palace of the Emperor Diocletian* bound in the same red Russia leather with gold tooling. No doubt these matching volumes would have made a fine impression on visitors to Keate's library at Charlotte Street. Certainly the album of watercolours became a family heirloom that Georgiana passed on to her children.

As Adam had established a reputation for his lightness of touch in producing well proportioned and convenient spaces it is not surprising, therefore, to find Georgiana's father inviting the architect to 'round my Walls your Graces fling'. Influenced by his studies in antiquity Adam had received many commissions for his fine interior designs, and his busy architectural practice was also engaged in a speculative scheme on the north bank of the Thames near the Strand. Although he was fully stretched Adam managed to find time to respond to his friend's call. Georgiana grew up in a house with an elegant neo-classical interior decorated in the 'Etruscan' style of painted motifs linked by chains. From decorative plaster ceilings, carved fireplaces, cabinets and commodes to fine mirror frames and ornate girandoles, or wall candleholders, Georgiana was surrounded by fashionable good taste. With his sense of unity and balance Adam also designed a symmetrical octagonal interior for Keate's museum that he had built on an irregular piece of land adjoining the house, measuring 9'3" by 6'6". The ceiling decoration featured different animals in seven of the eight roundels, from a lion, a sea-lion, a stag, a camel, an elephant and a sphinx to a horse ridden by a female figure. The eighth roundel had the same female figure leaning on a globe. Normally details in Adam's ceilings would be picked out in fashionable black, terracotta or white but, perhaps to link with the natural world, shades of green were used in the decorative scheme at Charlotte Street. This room would prove a treasure trove for the young Georgiana. She could admire the beautifully painted frescoes of birds and fruits on the lids of the six specially glazed cabinets designed by Adam to hold her father's natural history collections. Then she could open one or more of the individually numbered drawers or shelves within to see the various minerals, shells and gems that her father had acquired. The cabinets were on stands that had been elaborately decorated with gilded metal swags and winged griffins, and Adam had also designed a similar seventh cabinet to house Keate's collection of medals and tokens.

These improvements cost Keate £1200 (around £75k today) and he had to sign a new lease in 1777 to take account of the additional work carried out on no.6 Charlotte Street.

As he stood back and surveyed his elegant home Georgiana's father must have thought that Adam had indeed healed the defects of his house.

5. The Blossom might ripen into future Fruit

Finally, the family could settle into their new home. However, Georgiana's father worried about 'the Insecurity of Streets in a thronged Metropolis' and as his daughter required 'Air and Exercise' so that 'the Blossom might ripen into future fruit' he wrote to his friend, Dr Matthew Maty, Principal Librarian of the British Museum for permission to use the museum's gardens to provide his daughter with both 'the means of Health and security'. To reinforce his request Keate informed Maty that 'all the gardens of the different inns of Court, all the gardens of the different Companies in the City, even the Gardens of Majesty itself have been constantly thrown open at proper hours, for just such a benevolent purpose'. Maty replied that tickets were not issued to children but as long as Georgiana and her maid did not 'meddle with anything that grew' in the garden he saw no reason why she couldn't take her daily walk in their grounds.

For nearly seven years Georgiana enjoyed the pleasures of this garden. We can imagine that she would put on her walking shoes and, if the weather proved to be wet or wintry she would wear a coat over her white cotton gown, a bonnet to protect her hair and gloves for her hands. Then, with her maid, she would make her way to the end of Charlotte Street, turn onto Great Russell Street, with its handsome and well-built houses, and then onto Montagu Street. The walk to the garden would take her pass what was considered one of the grandest private houses of the late 17th century. Montagu House had been built for the 1st Duke of Montagu but was now home to the British Museum. This imposing mansion with its seventeen bays facing onto the street became a familiar sight to Georgiana as she made her way to the garden entrance on the far side of the building. The porter opened the gate allowing Georgiana and her maid to join the other 'persons of fashion and repute' strolling along the gravel walks to admire the 'Philosophic Grove and Physick Garden open to the view of a delightful Country'. Georgiana's father noted that 'so constantly [was she] there that she may be almost said to have grown in it'.

However, this uninterrupted access came to an abrupt end during Georgiana's evening walk on Friday 4th June 1779. The assistant porter approached eight-year-old Georgiana and asked her to leave the garden immediately. She politely requested that she be allowed to finish her walk but the porter was adamant that she should go and, without further ado, he escorted Georgiana and her maid out of the garden.

When Georgiana's father heard this distressing news he immediately put pen to paper to ask the museum trustees why his daughter had been dismissed 'in so hasty a manner'. In a long letter he wrote that he had taken great pains to ensure that Georgiana behaved with the utmost propriety, to such an extent that he 'never in a single Instance permitted his Daughter to carry a Flower in her bosom when she was to walk in the Garden less it should excite the slightest Doubt whether she might not have gathered it in'. Knowing how much pleasure his daughter derived from her regular walks 'was a great source of Happiness and consolation' to him, he added. Georgiana's father concluded with a plea that the trustees reverse their decision and reinstate her access to the gardens.

The rules strictly forbad entrance to servants, the museum secretary replied, and as his daughter was of an age that made it necessary for her to be attended by a maid the porters had no option but to eject the young lady from the grounds. Like any loving father Keate did not leave it there. He wrote again expressing his concern that Georgiana 'may suffer in Health from being cut off from this necessary advantage' and he was convinced that the trustees would be sympathetic to his worries over the 'welfare of an only child'. Keate could not conceive, he continued, that they would wish 'to withdraw that Protection from the Children of Gentlemen residing near their Gardens, which they have for so many years at least tacitly allowed'. 'So many young persons now grown up...possibly ascribe much of their Health to the Indulgence of the Garden granted their Youth', he said. He pleaded that his 'own Happiness' but more particularly that of his daughter, depended on their change of heart on this matter.

His pleas fell on deaf ears. The secretary reiterated that the rules, which had been made sixteen years earlier, stated that no children or servants were to be allowed access. Although this regulation had been established when the garden had been 'differently circumstanced', he added, and the planned grand botanical schemes had never materialised, the trustees were unwilling to rescind their decision.

Georgiana and her family did not have long to dwell on their disappointment. Several months after her expulsion there was a public disturbance that gave them much a graver cause for concern.

6. Bard, his child and wife...They scaped with life

Keate's fears were realised the following summer. On 2nd June 1780 nearly 60,000 Protestants, waving flags and carrying banners, had answered Lord George Gordon's call to march on Parliament to demand the repeal of the Papists Act of 1778. Inflamed by fears of Papism and unable to force their way into the House of Commons they turned their attention to several Catholic churches, which they proceeded to destroy. This mob then broke into breweries and distilleries and, with their passions further inflamed by the consumption of large amounts of alcohol, they freed prisoners from the Clink, Fleet and Newgate prisons. Others unsuccessfully besieged the Bank of England.

When he heard that men with clubs were roaming the streets looking for trouble Georgiana's father took action. He bundled his wife and child into his coach and directed the coachman to drive to their friend, Mr Franks at The Butts, Brentford. Indeed such was the speed of their flight that Georgiana's mother sent word to her maid to send her the 'two or three odd things' she 'forgot in her hurry yesterday'. At this time Brentford, a pleasant airy space was considered 'almost a garden' with its many orchards and said to resemble 'the seat of paradise'.

Keate had been torn between concern for his family's safety and the security of his home in Charlotte Street but thankfully his old friend, and Georgiana's godfather, John Plott had agreed to stay and look after the house. He wrote to Plott on 7th June to tell him that he intended to stay in Brentford for another three or four days as 'Mrs K is...poorly being much harried' and, he added, he would be 'infinitely obliged' if Plott would continue to stay at Charlotte Street as his presence would keep the servants 'who are all Strangers almost' together. He also asked Plott to instruct the handmaid not to open the window shutters of the Museum or Gallery, even better Keate wrote, would be for Plott to lock them both shut and to keep the key. Georgiana's father was particularly anxious about security as he had read that the rioters had broken windows to enter the houses of Catholic families and, once inside, torn down panels, taken doors off their hinges and windows out of their frames, before pulling out the frames themselves. These were then dragged out into the street, together with anything else that was portable, such as tables, chairs, clothes, etc. and used to feed the many fires raging in the streets. 'With the flames glaring upon them & the fires between them and us', recorded one eye witness, they 'seemed like so many Infernals & their actions contributed to assist this resemblance...for more fury and rage than they showed in demolishing everything they met with cannot be conceived'. Plott was also to talk with Mr Brinsdon and request him 'to continue to sleep every Night in the House as he is an Honest Man' and someone Keate could trust. Finally he asked Plott to instruct his 'new man Woolf to come down by one of the Brentford stages early on Saturday morning' with a 'shirt or two in his pocket for himself and anything he may want for a day or two'. He added that Georgiana sent her love.

The family then heard that units of the Honourable Artillery Company and the 1st Battalion of the 2nd Regiment of Foot had been called out to quell the riots. To this end the soldiers opened fire on groups of four or more who refused to disperse which resulted in the death of 285 rioters, and wounded several hundred. But it had the desired effect. Georgiana and her parents returned to Charlotte Street and were delighted to find their home had escaped the attention of the mob. They must also have been reassured to discover that the militia had been quartered in the ground of the British Museum. With the 'Gordon Riot' quelled this encampment became a popular tourist attraction. What must Georgiana have felt as, so shortly after her expulsion, she once again visited the museum's gardens to take tea with the 'field officers and the officers of the museum' in the tents erected on the terrace. Neatly laid out in lines on the lawn in front of her Georgiana would have seen the tents for the common soldiers. She may have agreed with the King who, during an inspection visit, described the scene as 'a fairy grove'. After two months, with no indication of further riots, the camp was broken up and life returned to normal, although we don't know if Georgiana was allowed to once more take her daily walk in the museum's gardens. Three years later Georgiana would once again witness ranks of soldiers on London's streets, but this time the men were returning from an unsuccessful campaign that led to the Treaty of Paris in 1783 granting America its independence. As he was a relative of one of their close friends its possible that Georgiana had met William Pitt, appointed in this same year, the youngest ever Prime Minister of England, at a social gathering. Twelve-year-old Georgiana was certainly growing up at an interesting time in England's history.

Visitors to the family home were often welcomed by Georgiana as her mother's poor health, whether real or imaginary, prevented her carrying out her role as hostess. We can imagine that Georgiana would happily show their guests Adam's novel and fashionable designs, such as an elegant commode in the front room which had been 'beautifully inlaid with flowers and expensively fitted up with a profusion of ormolu', or the large 'handsome chimney glass' with an 'arched head ornamented with paintings in a neat gilt and bordered frame' on the wall of the museum room. However, her enjoyment was shaken one day in 1785 when, without warning, the family were disturbed by the sound of an enormous crash coming from the museum. Luckily no one had been in the room when they discovered:

> The ground with beauteous fragments strewing
> Spreading a dusty cloud of ruin
> Whilst the scar'd Bard, his Child and Wife
> Shall blest their stars, They scap'd with life

The beautiful Etruscan ceiling under attack from wet and dry rot had simply collapsed. Keate blamed the architect for this disaster and took Adam to court. After a long and protracted case, which 'from its subject, its peculiarity and its duration, much attracted the Public Notice', Georgiana's father was ordered to pay Adam £163 14s 4d in damages. He consoled himself with the pronouncement of the wife of the King of Israel 'the battle is not always to the strong'.

7. In verse record his case

'Good humour is the Guardian of our health and spirits' Keate told his daughter. In order to pay his lawyer's bill, Georgiana's father said he would 'in Verse record his Case' to show that he 'prosecuted mens actions – not the men'. After all he told Georgiana, although men would laugh with delight at winning their case there was nothing 'which prohibits those who lose to be merry' and the income he made from the sale of his poem would enable him to settle his legal costs. Georgiana's father demonstrated his belief that we should 'laugh at those evils we cannot redress', by publishing his experience in *The Distressed Poet. A serio-comic poem*. Over three cantos he lays the blame for the collapse squarely at the door of the classical goddesses, the Nine Muses. He felt that they had decided to teach 'this apostate creature' a lesson. After all had they not 'taught [him] the dangerous Alps to tread' so that he could continue his Grand Tour to Rome to study classical antiquity at its best. However, two years later they found him paying all his attention to 'Nature!' and to make matters worse 'to her a Temple now he's raising...and all her treasures sparkle round.' As they watched him abandon classical art in order to waste his time with 'frippery taste' the Muses called on the god Apollo to teach their poet a lesson. Apollo decided to 'mark this Edifice for ruin'. He spread a 'most wonder working plaister' over the interior and this 'magick composition', which would never dry, would make the timbers 'rot and slacken. Their heart decay, their surface blacken' and that by 'slow, yet sure degrees, will shake his building and his ease' until 'sudden shall fall the Etruscan Ceiling.'

As they sat 'amidst the Ruins' he told Georgiana that although 'the Journey of Life must inevitably sometimes lead through rugged and difficult roads ', there were those along the way who had 'rendered [the experience] sufficiently pleasurable'. Such a one, he continued, was Gryffydd Price, who had acted as his legal adviser during the court case.

It was well known that Robert Adam was a designer, not a builder. He produced the most wonderful drawings of his various designs but he never made anything, so its curious that Georgiana's father chose to sue the architect, and no surprise that he lost his case. Did the rot that so ignobly destroy his elegant Etruscan ceiling also damage, beyond repair, his friendship with Robert Adam. Georgiana and her parents continued to enjoy the fashionable interiors that Adam had designed for them but there is no record of the architect restoring his acquaintance with his one-time friend, George Keate.

8. A luminous wonder

Now that the dust had settled Keate could once again admire the portraits of his wife and daughter painted by 'the celebrated Paintress', Angelica Kauffmann, which she had completed just before the Gordon Riots.

Georgiana's father most probably met this 'Sweet Mistress of the Mimic Art' through his friend the actor/manager David Garrick. By the age of eleven Swiss-born Angelica had demonstrated a precocious talent for drawing and painting encouraged by her father, who was a skilled painter. By her early 20s her facility for languages meant she was fluent in English, French, Italian and German and she very quickly built up a clientele among the many grand tourists, including Garrick, when she set up a studio in Rome in 1764.

Georgiana's father didn't have to wait too long to meet this 'great female artist'. At the invitation of Lady Wentworth, the wife of the English Ambassador in Rome, Angelica travelled with her to London. Within a week of her arrival on 22nd June 1766 Angelica had set up her studio and made the acquaintance of Joshua Reynolds. The two artists became firm friends. They painted each other's portraits on a number of occasions and Reynolds was instrumental in promoting the career of his 'Miss Angel', who he also made a foundation member of the Royal Academy, only one of the two women to receive this honour until the 20th century.

When King Christian VII of Denmark visited London in 1768 Angelica demonstrated another accomplishment. She played the 'harmonica', a fashionable instrument comprising nested glass bowls that the musician rubbed to produce ethereal sounds, for his entertainment, as well as painting his portrait. So that she could work undisturbed Angelica arranged for her completed paintings to be displayed in a different room from her studio. This became a popular social space and Angelica wrote to her father to tell him that 'the ladies...[are] very kind, of great decency and politeness', and that the gentlemen were also kind, sincere and most sensible'. No doubt she was including Keate in this appreciation. In response he penned an *Epistle to Angelica Kauffmann* in which he praised the 'talents of a lady' who, 'had not her superior Passion for Painting totally engaged her Mind' would surely have been 'one of the first Singers in Europe'. Described as 'a luminous wonder', it was said by many who heard her sweet voice that 'her expression touched the heart [and] her talent was astonishing'.

Did Angelica sing, or perhaps she recited some of her favourite poetry, when the eight-year-old Georgiana sat for her portrait in 1779. The artist was known to favour the *Wanderer's Nightsong* by the German writer, Johann Wolfgang von Goethe although, as the 'burning power of sensibility...[and] depth of artistic sense' would often bring tears to her eyes, she may have chosen a lighter, more humorous piece to amuse her young sitter. In this enchanting painting Angelica has captured, as Keate requested, the 'breathing image [on which they] doat' and shown the 'rosy Blush of virgin Youth, the Smile of Innocence and Truth' on his daughter's face. Her large brown eyes, set in a heart shaped faced framed by dark lustrous hair cut into a short fringe, look out at the viewer. Georgiana gently clasps a ring-necked dove – a symbol employed by Angelica to express the subject's Venus-like beauty and the tender bond of love. Did the artist use 'pounded Mummy' to produce the 'soft transparent shade' of brown in this painting? Angelica had once explained to Georgiana's father that the pulverized bodies of Egyptian mummies, both human and feline, were a key ingredient in producing this pigment which, 'if skilfully used created a very happy effect on some parts of the painting', 'Rich with Gums of Ages past...Makes every shadow clearer show, and every Light more brilliant glow'.

The following year Keate commissioned Angelica to paint a scene demonstrating the love of a father for his daughter to illustrate a dramatic poem, *The Monument in Arcadia*, he was publishing. He was delighted with her depiction of a newly married couple visiting a venerable old man to receive his blessing. When this sage discovers that the young woman standing before him was the long lost daughter, to whom he had dedicated the monument by which he stood, his sorrow quickly turned to joy. Georgiana's father paid the artist fifty guineas (around £7,000 today) for this painting.

When Angelica decided to marry Antonio Zucchi, an artist Keate had used to paint two oils in imitation of drawings to illustrate his *Sketches from Nature taken and coloured in a Journey to Margate*, she asked Georgiana's father, together with the businessman Henry Peter Kuliff and Daniel Braithwaite of the General Post Office, to protect the fortune she had accumulated from her portrait and history painting. Angelica's first marriage had been a disaster as her husband, who she thought was a wealthy Swedish nobleman, turned out to be an imposter and bigamist who stole all her money. However, her second husband was a very different man. Five days after their wedding in 1781 the couple left for the continent. They finally settled in Rome where they remained for the rest of their lives.

Georgiana never forgot her friend. When she was thirteen Georgiana tried her hand at etching on copper and sent her first effort to Angelica in Rome. In a rare survival from their correspondence Angelica wrote in 1794 to thank her 'estimed [sic] Friend...for the valuable present'. She told Georgiana that 'I alweis[sic] admired your Talent, and your first attempt on copper is a new prove[sic] of it. I shall keep the little head [who is real[l]y beautiful] in high estime[sic] being exceedingly well done'. We can imagine that on hearing the sad news of Zucchi's death the following year the family would have written a letter of condolence to Angelica. At least they could see their friend's work as she continued to send over new paintings for the Royal Academy summer exhibitions until 1797. Ten years later Georgiana read the sad news of Angelica's death but would have been pleased to see that she was given a splendid funeral. Two of her paintings were carried aloft during the procession to her tomb, with many important artists paying their respects to this great female painter whose modesty and tenderness of character alike had made 'everyone love and esteem her'.

In his *Epistle* Georgiana's father had foreseen that 'Rome's seven hills your praise resound...Exults such excellence to boast' and Georgiana felt sure that 'TIME shall protect a Name so dear'.

9. The pattern of her honoured life

Another Golden Square resident, 'a lady of singular integrity and politeness', was a member of the Keates' friendship circle. Well read in the classics and English literature, Mrs Mary Delany, could discuss history with authority and converse in fluent French. 'Her manners were faultless, her deportment was of marked elegance, her speech was all sweetness, and her air and address were all dignity', qualities that 'endeared her through life to many noble and excellent persons' and led Keate to advise his daughter to 'try by the pattern of her honoured life to cut out her own'.

While being prepared for her role as a Maid of Honour to the Royal court, the young Mary came into contact with the composer Handel, and the two of them became friends. When the great man came to call, Mary wrote that he gave her 'the best lesson' she ever received. However, she was a little embarrassed that there was no better instrument in the house than her little spinet, but 'the great musician performed wonders'. Even though she had great musical ability Mary would never let anybody 'but her intimate acquaintances hear' her play. However, the death of Queen Anne in 1714 put paid to Mary becoming a maid in waiting, and at the age of seventeen, due to financial necessity, Mary found herself married to a 60-year-old man. Six years later her husband died in his sleep. He had made no provision for Mary in his will so, with no home of her own, she went to stay with relatives and friends. When she was forty-three Mary visited Ireland where she met Dr Patrick Delany, whose wealthy wife had recently died. They discovered that they shared an interest in botany, became fond of each other and before long decided to marry. They married and set up home in Dublin, where they indulged their mutual interest by planting a well-stocked garden. They lived happily together for twenty-five years until, during a visit to Bath in 1768, Delany died. The newly widowed Mary took lodgings in Golden Square and it may have been here that Georgiana first met this 'lady of singular ingenuity'. We know that at the age of ten she went with her parents, the Duchess of Portland, Lady Bute, Miss Hamilton, Mrs Vesey and other ladies to one of Mary's musical evenings. They had gathered to hear the six-year old Miss Stow play minuets and cotillions. Mary had previously told them she plays in exact time and 'perfectly clean' and 'bids fair to be...a wonder'.

Mary also spent a lot of time at the country home of her close friend, the widowed Duchess of Portland. The two women shared a passion for botany and Mary would spend many happy hours at Bulstrode, in Buckinghamshire, in the garden and estate, painting, designing embroideries, cutting silhouettes and making ornaments. Georgiana's father was a regular visitor too. He would bring his young daughter with him when he went to discuss shells with the Duchess who was a keen collector.

Georgiana would have been taken to see the subject of her father's poem, *A Petition from Mrs Delany's Citron-Tree, to Her Grace the Duchess Dowager of Portland*. This told the story of the close friendship between the two women from the plant's viewpoint. While living in Ireland Mary had planted the seeds 'from Citron-Groves on distant shores' in her garden at Dublin. She had carefully nurtured the seedling and by the time she had to leave Ireland it had grown into a very fine specimen. She often spoke of the lovely shape, fine colour and graceful appearance of this tree and lamented its loss. To please her friend the Duchess secretly arranged for the tree to be dug up and transported to Bulstrode, where, once recovered from its journey, it was placed in plain view in one of the greenhouses on the estate for Mary to 'discover'.

While staying at Bulstrode the seventy-four year old Mary developed a 'new way of imitating flowers' by creating a 'painting' using thin strips of paper. She had been so struck by the similarity in colour of a geranium she had seen on the estate and some red paper that she found on the table in the sitting room, that she fetched a pair of scissors and began to cut out petal shapes and then fashioned leaves and stems from some green paper. The Duchess entered the room just as Mary had finished laying out her picture and mistook the finished work for a pressed version of the real flower. So impressed by the skill of her friend the Duchess encouraged her to make more of these life-size 'paintings'. She spent many hours cutting out hundreds of thin strips of paper to provide the fine detail for each flower she depicted. For instance, to accurately produce the spines on the pod of the willow-leaved Dogsbane, she used 114 individual pieces of paper.

When she discovered the citron tree, 'with her artful Scissors' she immediately set about making a faithful representation, comparing it all the while with the one she had left behind in Ireland. We can imagine her delight when the Duchess told her that it was indeed her tree, that she had arranged for it to be brought to Bulstrode so that her friend could once again enjoy its beauty. Mary only stopped when her 'bright eyes of indeterminate colour' started to fail, by which time she had created nearly a thousand of these botanically correct pictures. Georgiana's father wrote that the 'Magic of her Hand' gave these flowers and plants 'A Kind of IMMORTALITY'.

On one of their visits Mary offered to show Georgiana how she produced these paper paintings. Keate recorded the experience in one of his poems. 'Over thee, my Child, the Good Delany bends, directs thy Scissors, and reveals her Art'. 'Mark thy kind Instructress, watch her Hand', he told his daughter, and 'thy Scissors make like her's, a Magic Wand.' She had obviously been an attentive pupil. In June 1779 Mary writes to her niece, Mary Port, that the eight-year old Georgiana had stood at her elbow and cut out 'a figure which, if I can find it, I will enclose it'. Georgiana obviously knew the family well because on learning that, instead of accompanying her aunt on this visit to Charlotte Street, the young Mary had gone to be with her 'dear papa, mama, brothers and sister' away from the heat and dust of London, Georgiana's disappointment at not seeing her quickly turned to happiness at this news.

Although she was seventy when she first met George III and Queen Charlotte their mutual love for Handel, her unaffected piety and politeness, ensured that she quickly became a royal favourite. At one concert Mary wrote, 'The King was so gracious as to make me name the pieces I like best of Mr Handel's music'. When the Duchess of Portland died in 1785 the King provided the eighty-five-year old Mary with a pension of £300 a year and a house at Windsor, where she died three years later.

10. Three or four leagues distant

While Georgiana practised her paper cutting another family friend and his son set sail for the Far East. Captain Henry Wilson had been put in charge of the ninety-six-foot long *Antelope* with orders to return thirteen Chinese citizens to their homeland, and to deliver high priority messages to the East India Company agents in China. Wilson signed up his fifteen-year old son Henry, who joined his uncle Matthias, two officers, a surgeon, eleven sailors and an artist to crew his ship.

When Wilson finally returned to London in 1783 Georgiana heard first hand the whole story about his eventful voyage. All had started well, he told her. He had sailed the ship to Falmouth. While waiting for his sailing orders, he had spent his time organising the purchase and storage of dry goods for the voyage: loaves of bread and boxes of sea biscuits, together with sacks of flour, oatmeal, dried peas and beans; barrels of rum, beer, brandy, vinegar, oil and water. Added to this was a good supply of vitamin C in the form of lime juice to prevent the crew from suffering the effects of scurvy. Lastly, he securely stowed the gunpowder for the six eight-pounder cannon, and the two boxes of trinkets for trading. As English shipping was subject to regular hostile attacks by the French, Spanish and Dutch nations at this time, he was instructed to take the westwards route around Cape Horn. Ten weeks after leaving England's shores they had their first sight of the coast of South America. As the *Antelope* travelled down the coastline of Patagonia men were sent ashore to look for fresh water to replenish their dwindling supply. They returned empty handed so when they reached Tierra del Fuego, near the tip of the continent he decided to personally undertake the search. Not only did he find fresh water he also made contact with the locals, who thankfully, were friendly. He retrieved one of the boxes of 'treasure' from his cabin and proceeded to exchange the trinkets, beads and knives, 'with which they seemed much pleased' for two arrows but, he told her, 'they would not part with the bow'.

After six months at sea he anchored the *Antelope* in the mouth of an unnamed river and, as it was Christmas Day, he told Georgiana, he allowed the crew to celebrate by washing themselves and their clothes. The following morning they continued their voyage. It would be another six weeks before they saw land again. However, they were so eager to get to their destination that, when Eauripik came into view, they paid it little heed, although they later discovered that they were most probably the first Europeans to have seen this Pacific atoll.

They had to make one more stop off the coast of New Guinea as their food and water were running low. The natives came out in their canoes to trade but suddenly, and unexpectedly, they unleashed a flight of arrows. Although one struck the artist in the chest, Arthur William Devis was saved from any serious injury thanks to his flannel-lined double serge waistcoat, although he did suffer a minor cut on his cheek from a second arrow. Wilson gave the order to open fire with the ship's cannon and the natives quickly fled. Concerned that they might return to attack again, and with his ship becalmed, he ordered his men into the tender and told them to row as hard as they could in order to tow the *Antelope* further out to sea. Two months later, with the main topgallant damaged by storms, they finally sailed into the waters off Macao. In total it had taken them nine months and three days to sail from Falmouth to China. Highly suspicious, the Chinese authorities could not understand why a ship with a capacity of 280 tons had no goods to trade for their silk and tea, and would not let the crew disembark until the East Indian agent was able to placate them. Twenty-two days after their arrival the men could finally go ashore. While his crew enjoyed their leave Wilson arranged for the water butts to be repaired and refilled and to supplement their usual foodstuffs, with live geese, ducks, chickens, some 'Chinese' dry cured hams and smoked fish. Sixteen Chinese sailors were recruited to help the crew. Messages delivered, all necessary repairs complete and their stores replenished, he gave the order, on 20 July 1783, to set sail for home.

Thanks to a strong south-easterly, or 'blue dragon' wind as the Chinese called it, he was able to sail in a straight line nearly all the way to Formosa (modern day Taiwan) before he had to change course. It proved a difficult tack and the weather in the region was unpredictable. One day, he said, the sea would be as calm as a millpond and the next there would be mountainous waves. He had to call on all his experience as a seaman to the keep the ship on course, and he was unaware that he was sailing alongside a barely submerged coral reef that stretched for over a hundred miles. The weather worsened. Squalls and thunderstorms raged all evening on the night of the 9th August. The sea was extremely treacherous and although he desperately needed a rest, it was past midnight before he felt able to 'quit the deck'. Wilson left the helm in the charge of the first mate, Mr Benger but he had barely laid down on his bunk when he heard the lookout cry 'Breakers' and heard a terrible noise, the sound of the ship running aground. He 'sprang upon the deck in an instant', looked over the rail and, as the waves receded, he saw the exposed jagged coral he knew that there was no hope for the *Antelope*.

While the storm raged around them he ordered the crew to cut away the three masts to prevent the ship from overturning. Others he instructed to stock the ship's boats with provisions, drinking water, small arms, ammunition and a compass. He then placed two crewmen in each of the boats and told them to keep in the lee of the *Antelope* out of reach of the reef. The rest of the crew gathered on the highest part of the ship – the quarterdeck and waited out the storm. Although their situation was critical it was not hopeless, he told them, provided the men did nothing to further endanger themselves. While they waited for daylight he ordered each man to have a measure of wine and some biscuit for sustenance.

When morning finally dawned they could see that the nearest land was to their south, about 'three or four leagues distant'. There were other islands to the east and to the north of them, but they were much further away.

As Wilson recounted his adventures to his attentive audience Georgiana took solace that at least he was not alone, unlike the fictional Robinson Crusoe. However, she didn't allow herself to be distracted too long by these thoughts as Wilson settled down to tell them the next part of his story.

11. Are you friend or enemy?

Stories of shipwrecks and life lost at sea regularly featured in the newspapers, and no doubt, in letters from friends and relatives, so we can imagine that Georgiana was eager to hear how her friend and his men survived. Did Georgiana sit patiently waiting, or did she in her eagerness ask questions about what happened next? Wilson continued his account.

Now that the sun had risen he could plan a course of action, he told her. They didn't know if the islands were inhabited so he ordered Mr Benger to take enough men to crew the tender and the ship's jolly boat. They were to row to the nearest island and establish a camp and if they encountered any natives they should be treated in a friendly manner. While he and the remaining crew waited for news, he ordered that the booms should be disentangled and the spars used to make a small raft, just in case the small boats didn't return, or the *Antelope* sank before they did.

Mr Benger returned to the ship around 4pm. Not only had they secured a small cove but a search party had found fresh water. This news could not have come a moment too soon, he told Georgiana, for the ship was in imminent danger of breaking up. They lashed the ship's two dogs, five geese and numerous chickens, as well as themselves to the raft. Sadly he had to report that he lost one of his crew. He had told the men to put on all their clothes, in order to save them, but as his Quartermaster, Godfrey Minks, struggled to free the mast of the raft, which had become entangled in the stern of the ship, Minks fell overboard and sadly drowned before anyone could reach him. Having saved his clothes he couldn't save himself.

There was no time to grieve. He put the strongest men in the tender and ordered them to tow the raft clear of the reef. The pull of the current was so strong that they made little headway. The sailors in the ship's jolly boat came to their aid and after about half an hour of sustained effort they finally managed to escape the thrashing sea. He then left the tender to tow the raft to the island while he took the jolly boat to inspect the campsite established by Mr Benger. When night fell and there was no sign of the tender or the raft he went out in the dinghy to look for them. Suddenly the still night air was rent by a terrible noise. Fearing an attack by angry natives he ordered the dinghy round and headed back to the safety of the shore. Thankfully the rest of the crew eventually made landfall and found the camp, drawn by the light from the small fire their shipmates had lit earlier in the day. They explained that the Chinese sailors had become hysterical when they thought the tender was about to be swamped and they would all drown. It had been their shrieks and screams that everyone heard. After a late supper of cheese and biscuits, washed down with fresh water, they settled down for the night. However, he told Georgiana, their clothes were damp, their muscles ached and many of the men suffered from irritating heat and sweat rashes and, to add to their misery, it rained continuously.

They were glad, therefore, when the morning, and better weather, arrived. He ordered some of the crew to go out to the *Antelope* to recover any undamaged foodstuffs that had survived the storm. The men he had sent out to investigate the island returned with disturbing news. On learning that they had discovered ashes from recent fires not far from the campsite, he instructed the men to clean and check their guns in case they had any unwelcome visitors. The foragers returned with equally bad news. The *Antelope* was damaged beyond repair. Another uncomfortable night followed with only the glow of the fire to relieve their feelings of despair.

Early next morning one of the lookouts reported seeing two canoes coming around the point of the island. He immediately told the men to hide until he could establish the intentions of the visitors. Tom Rose, who described himself as a 'linguist' stayed with him and was able to translate when one of the natives called out, 'Who are you and are you friend or enemy?' As Captain Wilson was sitting with her Georgiana knew that his story had a good outcome but she may still have experienced some concern for her friend and his men. At his dictation Rose replied, 'We are unfortunate Englishmen who have lost our ship on the reef and we are your friends'. He told his men it was safe to come out of hiding and, by using gestures, he invited the natives to share their breakfast of tea and sweet biscuits.

Finally their fortunes had turned. He had lost only one man, the unfortunate Godfrey Minks, established a secure base with fresh water and the natives were friendly and he could converse with them through Rose and a Malay castaway, by the name of Soogle, who had been rescued by the natives and had decided to stay with them to learn their culture and language, as they had shown him nothing but kindness.

Now, he told Georgiana, he could make plans to get his men off the island and back to England.

12. Sparkling on the bosom of the ocean

With the camp established, Wilson told Georgiana, he went out in the dinghy to investigate. He returned several hours later with news that, although the reef appeared to encircle the island, he had managed to find a gap just wide enough to allow a small boat to pass through. Encouraged by this news the men went out to sweep the stricken *Antelope* for everything they could salvage before the ship sank, and was completely lost to them. The ship's carpenter was now set the task of building a craft large enough to carry them all but narrow enough to clear the gap.

Eventually the boat was finished. When barrels of fresh water and the remnants of their meagre supplies had been stowed away, Wilson told Georgiana that the Rupack, 'the excellent man who ruled over these sons of Nature', approached him and asked that he take Prince Lee Boo with him. His son, he explained, had heard so much about the country from the crew that he was eager to see it for himself, and learn how to behave like an Englishman. However, the chief added, he must moderate the Prince's youthful eagerness, take personal care of him if he became ill and treat him as if he was his own son. Wilson agreed. Sad as they were to leave their new friends it was with a sense of great excitement that they finally set sail on 12th November 1783.

However, it was not all plain sailing. After they had successfully negotiated their way through the reef they discovered they had sprang a leak. Rather than run the risk of further planks opening up if they tried to carry out repairs at sea, he set two men at a time to work the pump. With great relief they finally limped into Macao seven days later and abandoned their waterlogged craft. The local agents of the East India Company congratulated them on their safe arrival and instructed Wilson to take the men down to the harbour to seek passage to Canton. He was lucky to find Captain Churchill of the *Walpole* willing to carry them on this stage of their journey, but once they arrived at the port he told his men to find their own passage home as there was no ship large enough to take them all and, he added, they should seek compensation from the company for any hardships they might encounter. He was able to find berths for himself and the prince on board an East Indiaman, *The Morse,* and after an uneventful voyage they finally made landfall at Southampton six months later.

Georgiana had already heard from Wilson about the Prince's journey from Southampton to the captain's home in Southwark and how the young visitor had described the coach they travelled in as 'a little house which run away by horses; that he slept but still was going on; and whilst he went one way, the fields, houses and trees, all went another'. Several days later this exotic visitor came to Georgiana's home, accompanied by Captain and Mrs Wilson. She was struck by the affection in which the Prince held his English 'father' and how much he wished to learn how to behave in civilised society. He appeared somewhat embarrassed when Mrs Wilson asked him to pass her some cherries from the bowl at his end of the table and had to be reminded to use a spoon rather than his fingers. Lee Boo presented Georgiana with a gift, a spear from his homeland, which became one of her most treasured objects.

Georgiana's father believed that the chain of events, leading to the discovery of this courteous race and their island home, merited publication. When Wilson told them that he had a new ship and orders to sail to India Keate, 'sensible how soon oral testimony is beyond recovery, and the records of memory effaced by the events or casualties of life', decided to write the book himself. It was important, he told his daughter, to 'rescue these discoveries from sliding into oblivion, and preserve them for the curiosity of the public'. From Wilson's journals and statements taken from the *Antelope*'s crew, who were still in London, Georgiana's father published *An Account of the Pellew Islands* in 1788. So vivid was this picture of South Sea island life that Keate issued a warning telling his readers that there were 'scenes and situations which might startle many'. It was thanks 'solely to the benevolent character of the inhabitants' that Captain Wilson and his crew had all returned home safely, he added. This book was being offered under the double heading of 'Novelty and Authenticity', and 'to prove that good sense, and moral rectitude, may exist in many uncivilised regions, where the prejudices and arrogance of polished life are not always disposed to admit them'. This volume includes an engraving of the fine portrait of Prince Lee Boo that had been painted by Georgiana, from memory, when she was just thirteen years old.

No doubt she joined with her father in expressing the hope that 'if the little cluster of islands...now unveiling to the world (which may truly be regarded as a rich jewel, sparkling on the bosom of the ocean) shall be deemed by the Public an interesting acquisition, Captain WILSON will not have been shipwrecked in vain'.

13. So much virtue

In her charming portrait of their exotic visitor Georgiana has captured something of the character of the twenty-year old Prince Lee Boo. On his island Lee Boo went around in a naked state, but he quickly adapted to wearing the clothes Wilson gave him as they sailed away from the heat of the Pacific to cooler climes. Lee Boo developed such a strong sense of propriety that he would not change his clothing when others were present. It was said that his lively, pleasant manner and politeness, the result of 'good breeding', together with his sensibility and good humour 'instantly prejudiced everyone in his favour'. His clear grey eyes, so quick and intelligent, enabled him to 'announce his thoughts and conceptions without the aid of language'. By combining words and actions Georgiana discovered that she was able to have a 'good deal of conversation' with Lee Boo. He expressed pleasure at everything he saw about him. When he said that it was 'all fine country, fine street, fine coach and house upon house up to the sky', he demonstrated by alternately placing one hand above the other. Wilson explained that up to now Lee Boo had only seen single storey buildings so he must have thought that each floor of a London home was a separate house. Georgiana heard about Lee Boo's amusing reaction to his first encounter with a four-poster bed:

> He jumped in and jumped out again; felt and pulled aside the curtains; got into bed and then got out a second time to admire its exterior form. At length having become acquainted with its use and convenience, he laid himself down to sleep, saying that in England there was a house for everything.

When Lee Boo stood in front of a mirror he stood transfixed thinking this must be the result of magic. On being shown a miniature portrait of Georgiana's father, on one of his visits to her home, the prince declared 'Misser Keate, very nice, very good'. When questioned about what this picture meant Lee Boo replied, 'I understand very well – that Misser Keate die', pointing at the miniature, and 'this Misser Keate live', pointing at Georgiana's father.

True to his word Wilson treated the prince as a member of his own family. He went with them to church services at St Mary's Rotherhithe, although he did not understand what was being said. Wilson enrolled Lee Boo at the academy, near their home in Paradise Row, so that he could learn to read and write. His application was equal to his great desire of learning; and he conducted himself with such propriety, and in a manner so engaging, that he gained not only the esteem of the gentleman under whose tuition he was placed, but also the affection of his young companions'.

Wilson pointed out to Lee Boo many of the city's public buildings, like the Palace of Westminster, as they made their way to visit friends on the other side of the river. The coaches were another source of delight for Lee Boo because, he said, 'people could be carried where they wanted to go and at the same time sit and converse together'. Wilson refrained from taking his young companion to the theatre and other public entertainments until he had enough 'language to be reasoned into the necessity of submitting to the operation' for smallpox inoculation. Sadly, in mid-December 1784 Lee Boo succumbed to the disease. In spite of the best efforts of Dr Carmichael Smyth, later appointed Physician extraordinary to the King, Lee Boo could not be saved. Shortly before his death, on 27th December, the prince asked a friend, who was due to sail to the Pellew Islands, to 'tell Abba Thulle that Lee Boo take much drink to make smallpox go away, but he die: that the Captain and Mother very kind – English very good men; was much sorry he could not speak to the King (his father) the number of things the English had got.' It was noted, that on the day of his funeral, 'a great concourse of parishioners thronged the church' in Rotherhithe. The final lines of the inscription on the tomb of this young man, of 'so much virtue', convey the loss felt by many:

> ...Stop, Reader, stop! – let NATURE claim a Tear
> A Prince of Mine, LEE BOO, lies buried here

Fifteen months after his death, and at her father's request, Georgiana painted a portrait of the Prince, from memory. She has shown him dressed in the English fashion. Over a white shirt he wears a striped waistcoat and a pink jacket with a grey collar. A black cravat completes his outfit. He has brushed his thick black hair into a ponytail. In this half-length portrait we do not see the white stockings that hid the tattoos that decorated both legs from mid-thigh to just above his ankles, or the fine shoes in which, it was said, he walked in a majestic way. Georgiana's portrait was 'acknowledged to be a very striking likeness by everyone who knew him'.

14. She has a beard

We know that Georgiana painted at least one more portrait. She writes in her diary that she spent the morning of 6th October 1794 putting in the background to Mademoiselle D'Eon, a family friend with an interesting story to tell.

A member of the French nobility, D'Eon attended a ball at Versailles in 1755 disguised as a woman. During the course of the evening he claimed that he briefly revealed his masculinity, seduced Madame de Pompadour and then resumed his feminine role and became the object of Louis XV's pressing attention. Because of his court and country connections the twenty-seven-year old D'Eon was recruited by Prince Conti, who sent him to Russia, to work for the spy network he managed for his cousin, the King. On his return to France in 1760 D'Eon served in the dragoons and showed courage in a number of military engagements, but his career was cut short when he was wounded on the battlefield. On his recovery and appointed Secretary to the French Ambassador D'Eon came to London and 'laboured assiduously on the paperwork', but the real mission of this 'audacious…and ambitious' individual, who excelled at languages, was to help with the negotiations to end the Seven Year's War. Already a practised spy, D'Eon took advantage of London's busy social calendar to garner information. By exploiting 'situations and indiscretions' D'Eon was able to achieve a successful conclusion to the task in hand and, in acknowledgement, the French King awarded D'Eon the Cross of St Louis, the title 'Chevalier', and a substantial annuity.

With the war over D'Eon decided to stay in London where Georgiana's father, among others, enjoyed the lavish entertainment he had laid on for them. In fact Keate was so impressed that, in one of his letters to Voltaire, he said that 'every woman in Europe must build to d'Eon an altar for having done so much for the honour of their sex' for she had shown that a woman 'can cultivate all the political arts, acquire the military glory of the conquerors and sustain one's virtues in the midst of the greatest temptations'. While he enjoyed the witty repartee of his host and the gifts, including Burgundian wine from the Chevalier's vineyards, little did Keate realise that D'Eon the spy was once again at work. Angered by the humiliating terms of the peace treaty the French King ordered his spies to gather information that would enable him to invade the British Isles. News that he was to be recalled to Paris led D'Eon to fear that his enemies in the French court wanted him dead. He decided to publish some of the secret diplomatic correspondence, although not the King's invasion plans, with the implicit threat of exposing more secrets if anything should happen to him. Horace Walpole described these letters as full of wit and, he added, 'what makes it more provoking, our ministers know not what to do'. Instead of extraditing D'Eon and imprisoning him in the Bastille the King cancelled his order and instead made the Chevalier an envoy with instructions to carry on spying.

In recompense for his loss of earnings, and for his silence, following the closure of the spy network, in 1774, by the new French King, Louis XVI, who preferred to conduct diplomatic activities through regular channels, D'Eon was given a pension and safe conduct enabling him to return to France. The King also stipulated that D'Eon should continue to live as a woman, and awarded him an additional sum to purchase a new wardrobe of clothes. The Chevalier appears to have been ambivalent about this request but after being jailed for wearing his uniform he accepted the King's terms. Ten years later, on learning that his creditors had designs on the library and collections he had left behind, D'Eon returned to London to sort out his debts. Shortly after his departure Paris erupted. The revolutionaries executed Louis XVI and Marie Antoinette, and a number of D'Eon's relatives were also sent to the guillotine. What did the fourteen year-old Georgiana think about this new visitor to her family home? In spite of possessing small hands and feet, a slender waist, soft fair hair and blue eyes, did she, like the biographer James Boswell, think the Chevalier was 'a man in woman's clothes'? Did she, like Horace Walpole, find D'Eon loud, noisy and vulgar and agree with him that 'her hands and arms seem not to have participated of the change of sexes, but are fitter to carry a chair than a fan'. Even Georgiana's father was heard to say that 'she has a beard & he has seen her shave often'. No doubt Georgiana accompanied her parents when they attended a social event in 1786 at the Surrey home of their friends, Brook Watson and his wife. Another of the guests, the former Chief

Justice of New York, William Smith, saw 'the celebrated Mademoiselle d'Eon' in the company of Mrs Keate during the course of the evening. When Smith attended Watson's home a few months later, he noted in his diary that 'the famous D'Eon' joined Wilberforce and Blackburne, Members of Parliament, Sheriff Sanderson, Mr Keate the Naturalist...and many other Gentleman and Ladies'. No mention is made of Georgiana but she was most probably one of the company that sat down to dinner that evening.

The French revolution had a disastrous effect on D'Eon's life. His annuity fell into arrears, and then was stopped completely. He felt that he could not safely return to his homeland and in order to survive he sold his books and manuscripts in 1791. The following year he was driven to sell his jewellery and plate. To supplement his dwindling income D'Eon, now sixty-five years old and wearing female dress went on stage at The Haymarket theatre and Ranelagh Gardens to demonstrate his skill with a sword. It was reported that he fenced 'as though in vigour of youth'. Two years after Georgiana painted his portrait D'Eon was seriously wounded in the armpit during an assault and could no longer fence. In the end he had to sell his most precious Cross of St Louis to pay for lodgings. His landlady was astounded to discover, following a medical examination after his death in 1810, that her paying guest was in fact a man. The doctors reported that his male organs were 'in every respect perfectly formed'.

D'Eon described himself as 'mad with pride, insolent, obusive, ungrateful and dishonest, in short a complication'. His extraordinary life as a transvestite has overshadowed his remarkable career as a soldier, his skills as a diplomat, informant and secret agent, and his qualities as a scholar and writer. In accordance with his wishes D'Eon was buried in the graveyard at St Pancras Old Church.

15 To ride in the air like a bird

Georgiana encountered another colourful character at this time, Vincenzo Lunardi, Secretary to the Italian ambassador, who introduced London to a wonder of the age – the first manned balloon flight in England. In order to raise funds for this event Lunardi charged 2s 6d for entrance to the exhibition of his newly invented red and white striped balloon, together with its basket, which he had put on display at the Lyceum Theatre near the Strand. Many of the 20,000 visitors were said to be women and they were most probably more interested in viewing the fresh-faced and absurdly handsome Italian, than his balloon. Bubbling with infectious enthusiasm, this incorrigible flirt, with his long unpowdered hair worn loose, bathed in this adulation. He even proposed a toast to himself: 'I give you me, Lunardi – whom all the ladies love'.

Georgiana and her parents may have chosen to pay the guinea entrance fee, which secured a front row seat at the launch and entry to the Lyceum display, as many times as they wished. The great day finally arrived and on 15th September 1784 a huge press of 200,000 people gathered in, and around, the Artillery Ground at Moorfields. Although he shared the public's fascination with ballooning, Dr Samuel Johnson advised a friend not to waste his guinea on paying for a seat as, he said, in 'less than a minute they who gaze at a mile's distance will see all that can be seen'. When the inventor of the newly improved generator to supply the fuel, Dr George Fordyce, visited the site at 4.00am that morning to check on progress he discovered that the workmen were hopelessly drunk, and as a result very little gas had been pumped into the balloon envelope, even though the operation had begun the previous evening. Notoriously addicted to the bottle himself, Fordyce wasn't in a much better state. Georgiana's parents were most probably aware of the gossip about him and the story about the evening he was summoned to the bedside of a prostrate female patient. Fordyce found himself incapable and unable to take her pulse. He muttered to himself 'Drunk by God!' and left. A note he received the following morning, together with a handsome fee, from the patient confessed that his diagnosis had been correct and begged him not to divulge her guilty secret. Even though he got the gas flowing again the balloon was not ready for the advertised 12pm lift-off time. Two hours later, and with the crowd expressing their impatience, Lunardi knew he would have to take action, even though the balloon was not fully inflated. In astonished silence the crowd stood and gazed upwards as he slowly rose into the sky. The men solemnly doffed their hats in acknowledgement and the King, on hearing news of the successful launch, broke off a cabinet meeting with his Prime Minister, William Pitt, to watch Lunardi pass overhead.

As the balloon travelled northerly Lunardi sustained himself with chicken legs and champagne. He spoke to workers in the fields below by means of a silver speaking trumpet and threw out letters tied with long streamers. Although he had to leave his friend Mr Biggin behind at the launch as the balloon didn't have enough gas to carry them both, Lunardi was not alone in the basket, he had a cat, dog and bird in a cage with him. He became concerned for the cat's welfare when it appeared to be suffering from the the cold and when the basket came down low enough over a field near Welham, Lunardi handed the animal out to a spectator before continuing on his way. Twenty four miles and two hours after he rose graciously above Moorfields the young aeronaut landed, somewhat unceremoniously, near Ware in Hertfordshire. He called out for help as he bumped heavily and inelegantly across the fields but a milkmaid was the only person to come to his aid. The farm workers would have nothing to do with one who came in the 'Devil's Horse'.

Georgiana and her parents called at the home of Captain Wilson as they were curious about Prince Lee Boo's reaction to this spectacle, which he had witnessed at a distance. They found that although this 'had excited so much curiosity...it did not appear to have engaged him in the least'. In fact he 'thought it a very foolish thing to ride in the air like a bird, when a man could travel so much more pleasantly on horseback, or in a coach'. It would appear that the prince had not understood the difficulty, and the hazards involved, in such an enterprise, and may even have considered it a common occurrence, 'in a country which is perpetually spreading before him so many objects of surprise'.

There were many, however, who celebrated the Italian's success. His name was eulogised everywhere, from columns in newspapers to popular songs. Modest ladies wore a Lunardi bonnet – a balloon shaped hat about two feet tall, or Lunardi skirts decorated with balloon motifs, while others sported a Lunardi garter. Meanwhile the young aeronaut immediately put the balloon, together with the cat and dog, on display at the Pantheon in Oxford Street. Such was his celebrity that Lunardi wrote to his guardian, 'I am the idol of a whole nation...All the country adores me, every newspaper honours me in prose and verse. Tomorrow I shall put two thousand crowns into the Bank of England'. Amongst all this praise the connoisseur Horace Walpole raised a dissenting voice. He was very angry with Lunardi for putting his cat at risk in such a foolhardy venture.

Delighted by his success and celebrity Lunardi decided to build a bigger and better balloon in order to carry passengers. In her charming watercolour of the launch at St George's Fields, Southwark on 29th June 1785, Georgiana presents a scene of great excitement. The men on the platform have removed their hats in salute as the balloon successfully rises with its two occupants into the air, while the crowd watch on with delight, some from the comfort of their carriages. We see the balloon envelope decorated with the Union Jack as Lunardi wished to show 'his regard and attachment to everything that is English'. Lunardi originally planned to make the ascent with three others, but he had not taken into consideration the rather ample charms of Mrs Sage, an acknowledged beauty of the day. By her own admission she weighed over fourteen stone. The balloon struggled to lift their combined weight. Lunardi decided that it would be better to leave the gondola and allow Mrs Sage and George Biggin, who had missed out on the maiden voyage, to take to the skies. To the crowd's delight the balloon finally started to rise into the sky, and this is the moment that Georgiana captured in her painting.

Spectators were treated to the curious sight of Mrs Sage on all fours, with Mr Biggin standing behind her, as the balloon passed over Piccadilly. They wondered if she had fainted and he was giving her some kind of intimate first aid. In fact, Mrs Sage was doing up the laces on the door which Lunardi, in his haste, had forgotten to secure. Her task complete Mrs Sage stood up, and in so doing she trod on, and broke, the barometer. Mr Biggin now had no means of establishing their altitude. As they drifted along they ate cold chicken and drank sparkling Italian wine, the empties they just threw over the side. The balloon came down in a field near Harrow and before they had gathered their thoughts an irate farmer came over and berated them for damaging his crops. Thankfully they were rescued by the timely arrival of a group of boys from the nearby Harrow School. Mrs Sage delighted in her reputation as the first woman to have experienced balloon flight, while the wealthy young Etonian, Mr Biggin, found himself at the centre of speculation as to whether he had been the first man to board a female aeronaut. Ever the gentleman he refused to comment. A fourteen year old Georgiana is unlikely to have known about these claims, or that the members at Brooks' club were laying bets as to which of them would be the first to have an amorous encounter in a balloon. Colourful characters, exotic visitors, strange novelties and new discoveries were commonplace occurrences during Georgiana's formative years.

16 This trophy's thine

A few years after all the excitement of the manned balloon flight Georgiana found that the main subject of conversation concerned a mutiny on the far side of the world. The captain of the *Bounty* had the sea in his blood. At the tender age of seven William Bligh signed up to be a captain's servant, and over the following years he learned how to read maps, navigate and to behave like a gentleman. Twenty-year-old Bligh's skill as a cartographer led Captain James Cook to appoint him Master of the Resolution for Cook's third, and as it turned out final, expedition to the south Pacific. Following the explorer's death at the hands of the Hawaiians Bligh returned to London to await orders. Shortly afterwards he met and married the pretty and intelligent twenty-seven-year old Elizabeth Bentham in 1781 and the Admiralty raised Bligh to the rank of Lieutenant in recognition of his service and conduct. However, Britain was enjoying a period of peace and, with only his basic navy pay of two shillings a day, and no opportunities for prize money his wife's uncle offered a means of improving his income. A wealthy merchant, who had made his fortune from the West Indies rum and sugar trade, Duncan Campbell needed a trustworthy captain and in Bligh he found his man in this disciplinarian with firm ideas on leadership who had acquired a reputation for running a tight ship.

When the eminent naturalist Sir Joseph Banks had sought to enhance his elaborate scheme to promote British trade, to provide a staple food for slaves, and to enlarge the collection of exotics at Kew he put the thirty-three-year old Bligh in charge of a botanical mission to collect breadfruit and other plants from Tahiti and transport them to the West Indies. The Royal Navy provided a small merchant vessel, *HMS Bounty*, for this voyage but first Bligh had to oversee major alterations on every deck to accommodate the many plant cases and boxes. By the time this work had been completed and they were ready to sail the weather had deteriorated to such an extent that Bligh could not take the shortest route around Cape Horn. Instead it took them ten long months to finally reach their destination, by which time the crew were eager to leave their cramped quarters and take shore leave on the tropical island. Many of the men succumbed to the charms of the Tahitian girls who were fascinated by these white skinned men from faraway. Bligh did not allow himself to be distracted. Instead he spent his days arranging the collection and cultivation of over 1000 breadfruit trees, and other exotic plants, in preparation for their transportation to the West Indies, and to Kew.

It is perhaps not surprising to find that after five months ashore many of the crew were reluctant to leave this tropical paradise but eventually they set sail. One night, three weeks later, armed members of the crew, led by his former friend and first mate, Fletcher Christian, woke Bligh and forced him up on deck. All was noise as some of the men pleaded with the mutineers while others mocked their captain, dressed only in his nightshirt, and with a bayonet pointed at his chest. At first Bligh was at a loss to understand what was going on. He called out 'Murder' and was immediately warned 'not a word sir, or you are Dead'. Christian ordered Bligh, with three of the crew who did not support the mutiny, into the launch, which had already been lowered. To Christian's surprise a further fifteen men squeezed themselves into a boat meant to hold ten. By the time they had loaded the meagre rations and navigational aids supplied by the mutineers their twenty-three-foot long boat sat a mere eight inches above the water. The eighteen occupants had to maintain a certain balance to ensure that the stern did not slip under the waves. Soaked by continual rain, unable to stretch their cramped limbs or lie down to sleep, while pangs of hungry gnawed at their insides as Bligh had to impose strict rationing to eke out their supplies, their discomfort was constant. 'Far from every friendly shore' the men were certain that they would 'meet through lingering Death, a certain grave', but they had not reckoned on Bligh's exceptional skill and determination. Without access to maps Bligh relied on his memory of these waters to plot a course to a safe haven in the Dutch East Indies, over 3,000 miles away. Using only a sextant and a pocket watch Bligh navigated their small open boat through the Pacific Ocean for forty-seven days. Finally they arrived at the port of Timor. As soon as he landed he wrote to his wife. 'I am now...in a part of the world I never expected, it is however a place that has afforded me relief and saved my life, and I have the happiness to assure you that I am in perfect health', but he added, 'Dear Betsy...I have lost the Bounty'.

While Bligh completed his epic voyage the mutineers had sailed to Pitcairn Island and set up camp in this remote part of the world. After all useful material had been scavenged Christian had the ship destroyed so that the authorities could never find them. Bligh meanwhile returned to London, and a court martial. However, after hearing his version of events the board dismissed all the charges against him.

Inspired by *A Narrative of the Mutiny on Board His Majesty's Ship Bounty, and the Subsequent Voyage of Part of the Crew, in the Ship's Boat, from Tofoa, one of the Friendly Islands, to Timor, a Dutch Settlement in the East Indies* which Bligh published in 1790, Georgiana's father penned a poem *To Captain Bligh (On reading his Narrative of the Mutiny on Board the Bounty, and of his Passage (in an open boat) across the Pacific Ocean.* 'This Gallant sailor', he wrote, whose 'wonderful escape at sea' demonstrated his qualities as equal to those of another intrepid navigator, said that 'what Cook was, hereafter Bligh may be'. As a sign of their friendship and mutual respect Bligh and Keate presented each other with personally inscribed copies of their books. While waiting for new orders Bligh published *A Voyage to the South Seas* in order to correct some of the errors that had appeared in his *Narrative*. We don't know whether Georgiana had met Bligh before the mutiny but we do know from her diary for 1794 that the captain and his wife were family friends. On Tuesday 27th May, 'a little before twelve', Georgiana, accompanied by her parents and John Henderson, went to the Society of Arts in the Adelphi to see 'Captain Bligh receive his gold medal' from the hands of the Society's President, the Duke of Norfolk. This award had been given as a result of Bligh's second, and this time, successful voyage, in the *Providence*. 'Yes, my respected friend, this trophy's thine', wrote Georgiana's father in his second laudatory verse about his friend's achievements. He added that 'where with their weight of fruit thy BREAD TREES bend, AFRICA's dark sons shall in their shade recline...and conscious whence they came, teach children yet unborn to venerate thy name'.

However, the stigma of the mutiny clung to Bligh and, even though Lord Nelson had personally thanked him for his bravery during the Battle of Copenhagen in 1801 and he had been elected a Fellow of the

Royal Society in the same year, Bligh found many doors firmly shut against him. At least Georgiana and her family remained loyal friends. Keate had encouraged his daughter to emulate Mrs Bligh, a woman of 'superior abilities and attainments, and a rare example of every virtue and amiable quality'. Mrs Bligh must have been grateful for the female companionship Georgiana provided during the long periods her husband was away at sea, particularly when she had to bear the loss of their twin sons, who died shortly after birth.

Georgiana's father dispelled the myth that Betsy was her husband's only ally as he left, as a 'memorial of the regard we had for each other', a bequest of £50 to his 'esteemed friend', and a further £300 (worth around £15,000 today) to Bligh after the death of Mrs Keate. With six daughters to bring up Bligh must have appreciated this supplement to his annual pay of £150.

17. I've got a new madness

Bligh returned from his voyages to the other side of the world with rare shells for his wife to admire, and although many of them could be found in most European cabinets of curiosities by the time she died, Elizabeth Bligh's collection was of such high quality that it still sold 'for a valuable consideration' in 1812.

Shells were considered to be literally a gift from God. Only 'the excellent artisan of the universe', it was said, could have created such an intricate object as the wentletrap - a pale, white spiral shell enclosed by slender vertical ribs. Such was the frenzy for rare and exotic shells at this time that the trade in them had been likened to 'Tulipmania' in Holland some years earlier, when fortunes were won and lost over a single bulb. Seeing an opportunity to enhance their wages the sailors, returning from the South Seas, stowed shells into every available space in their cramped quarters, ready to sell to the dealers who waited for them as they disembarked at the docks. George Humphrey paid £150 (around £12,000 today) for the bulk of shells brought back from Captain Cook's second voyage, while Thomas Martyn paid the equivalent of £28,000 to the men who had sailed with Cook on his third voyage. Rarity was everything. A Glory of the Seas cone shell (*Conus gloriamaris*) sold for three times the value of a painting, *Woman in Blue Reading a Letter* by Vermeer, while in 1792 a collector brought a very rare shell only to immediately destroy it in order to maintain the value of the example he already owned.

Although he obviously saved the best shells for his wife Bligh very generously gave Georgiana's father a number of specimens, including a bright red organ pipe coral (Tubipora musica), which Bligh had collected off the coast of New Zealand. It sounds like there was much to delight Georgiana as she helped her father add these new specimens to his collection. Visitors to Charlotte Street expressed their appreciation. One wrote that 'for elegance and brilliancy of effect perhaps no museum exceeds that of George Keate, Esq, in which all varieties of shells, corallines, gems and minerals, with a rich assortment of every species of semi-transparent or opake [sic] fossil bodies...are...most effectually and beautifully displayed'. The

President of the Royal Society, Sir Joseph Banks, told the American artist and naturalist, Charles Wilson Peale, that he had visited 'Mr Keate of Charlotte Street, whose principal Object is the Shells of Land snails', and Mrs Delany wrote that she had been 'much entertained in their museum'.

Mrs Delany told Georgiana that she had been 'struck by the beauty of the shells' from an early age, when she used to pick them up from the beach near her childhood home in Falmouth, Cornwall. Her interest was rekindled in 1734 when Mrs Delany wrote to her sister to tell her that she had 'got a new madness, I am running wild after shells'. This fascination would prove enduring. As well as ornamenting her own home Mrs Delany produced decorative shellwork, often in floral patterns, for many of her friends, which might have included Georgiana and her parents. Georgiana had an opportunity to see another artistic use for shells when she visited, with her father, the country home of the Duchess of Portland. As they walked through the park at Bulstrode they came upon a cave, dug out of a hill. Its cavernous mouth had been edged with an irregular pattern of shells, rather like a row of broken teeth. The entrance was so large that Georgiana could see some way inside, and the light from the small windows near the opening illuminated an interior decorated with more shells. This grotto absorbed such a huge number of shells that the Duchess ordered her men to kill a thousand snails in order to complete the project. Like her father, the Duchess had a museum for her own and her visitor's amusement, however, as the richest woman in England she could afford to buy the finest and the best. Keate wrote that the Duchess 'calls every shell from every shore, nor can the o'erwhelming deep, its coral beds, or treasures keep, For Portland's Art unlinks the chain, that bound them in their wild domain'. The Duchess was a compulsive collector of 'amazing objects'. Following her death in 1785 it took eight days to auction the china, snuff boxes, drawings, coins and medals. However, it took another thirty days to dispose of all the shells, ores, fossils, bird eggs and other natural history items in her museum. Georgiana's father came away with an extremely rare example of a shell from Guinea commonly known as the Green Music Volute (*Voluta virescens*), what was said to be the only known perfect specimen of a very curious species of snail from

Mauritius together with a delicate and beautiful specimen of a form of copper ore which had a velvety green colour.

Both the Duchess and Georgiana's father had subscribed to *The Universal Conchologist*, a beautifully illustrated guide to seashells published by Thomas Martyn in 1789. When he discovered that only miniaturists had the necessary skill for applying the fine detail to the plates in the guide, and they proved very expensive to employ, Martyn had to revise his plans. He opened his own academy and trained boys, 'born of good but humble parents', who had a natural talent but 'could not from their means aspire to the cultivation of any liberal art' to paint the illustrations. Although he was unable to complete his avowed intent of publishing a guide to all known seashells, Martyn was able, thanks to the success of his academy, to publish four volumes of what has been described as one of the most beautifully illustrated books produced on this subject. In the accompanying text Martyn praised the surgeon Dr John Hunter and the collector Sir Ashton Lever, but it was Georgiana's father who received the highest praise for his collection. As Martyn's book did not appear in the sale catalogue of Keate's library perhaps Georgiana kept it for her children to enjoy.

The Times 'lamented that the valuable choice Museum of the late George Keate, author of the Pelew Islands, which will begin selling at Kings in Covent Garden on Monday next was not disposed of altogether, for although it will enrich the cabinets of the first collectors in Europe, it certainly ought to have become a national purchase'. The collection was certainly substantial. Georgiana spent many hours preparing the specimens and ordering them into 1,440 lots for sale at an auction that ran over twelve days in April 1802. Perhaps she and Henderson did not share her father's enthusiasm for shells or, with their growing family, they simply didn't have the space for it, or maybe the pain of her parents' reaction to Georgiana's marriage to Henderson was still too raw for her to entertain the idea of maintaining her father's legacy. I wonder if, while sorting the specimens, she slipped one or two into her pocket in memory of happier times.

18 Dear Pretty, Pretty Plotty

Her father's collections provided Georgiana with interesting objects to paint. By the time she drew 'a couple of shells' in 1794 'to send to Jamaica' Georgiana had demonstrated that she had acquired this accomplishment as a sign of her gentility. Her father, as an amateur artist of some skill, employed tutors to develop her natural ability and the instruction she received from one of her father's oldest friends, the skilled portrait painter John Plott, enabled her to paint the very fine portrait of Prince Lee Boo. Many who saw her work, and knew the Prince, said she had captured his character.

There is no record of when her father and the artist first met, but it was most probably around the 1760s. Keate had returned from his Grand Tour and Plott had left his native Winchester and travelled to London to learn the art of landscape painting from Richard Wilson. However, Plott quickly realised that he was more suited to portraiture and was able to secure an apprenticeship with miniature painter Nathaniel Hone, before setting up very successfully on his own in London and Winchester, where his sister still lived. Keate sat for his friend. Although the portrait is now lost Keate presented an engraved version to the Inner Temple in 1792, in thanks for being made a Bencher the previous year.

Plott became a trusted friend of the family. When Keate took his wife and child to Barnes during the Gordon Riots, he asked Plott to guard his house in Charlotte Street. He also turned to his old friend to copy the relevant correspondence relating to his court case against Robert Adam for the collapse of the ceiling in his museum room.

Ten year old Georgiana sent 'Dear Mr Plott' a 'shell and a tea lady', on 28th March 1781, as she was concerned that 'he should be set out to the best advantage' for the rout, or fashionable gathering, he was holding that afternoon. Georgiana had a great affection for this old family friend and soon dispensed with all formality in her correspondence. She called him her 'Dear Pretty, Pretty, Plotty', and he in term would address her as 'Dear Pretty'.

On 15th December 1789 Georgiana wrote to Plott about 'the many perils that had attended his expedition to Southampton'. She had heard that at first his horse would not pull the gig and, when it finally moved, he 'drove over a calf and broke five or six of its legs', before running into one of the 'posts of the Common gate' and tipping himself over. Even more worrying was the news that, just outside Otterbourne, Hampshire, he had been 'robbed of four shillings and eight pence halfpenny and put in bodily fear by a Boy of thirteen'. All these accumulated misfortunes, she said, must have shook his nerves and shattered his spirits, and in light of 'the manifold dangers...he had miraculously escaped, and the many tumbles ...which...had it not been for the thick covering of flesh, have broken every bone' must have been the cause for his latest fit of gout. So, she added, she expected that her dear Plott would not leave Winchester till he had eaten his way through every Christmas dinner that he had been invited to', and all this food, she supposed, would bring on yet another fit of gout. 'Take a Gun and some clever lad', she advised Plott, 'and shoot my Daddy some Pheasants or partridges'. She felt this would be 'much better [for him] than sitting by the fireside', but she added, 'hold fast by a five barred gate or anything that may be near at hand and shut your Eyes while the Gun is fired off'. Five weeks later Georgiana finally heard from Plott. He had been waiting until he could leave off his 'large Shoes' and go shooting for her Daddy, as she had instructed. 'I am not a little proud and pleased', he added as her old schoolmaster, 'to find that you write and indite so well'.

It would appear that Plott was a lazy correspondent and Georgiana would often castigate him for his tardiness in writing to her, and for neglecting his affairs in London. Exasperated she came up with a plan to get his attention. In a detailed letter she wrote to him in January 1790, that an artist, capable of 'taking portraits and also painting in natural history, such as birds, fishes, plants, etc.', was being sought for a proposed second expedition to the Pelew Islands that would leave in March 1791. It immediately struck her 'Papa' that this would be a 'very advantageous' opportunity for Plott, and that his permission would be required before he could recommend his old friend for the position. In a postscript Georgiana asked Plott 'not to mention the contents of the letter, nor shew it to anybody till you hear further from my Papa'. She added, 'have the goodness to let him know your determination as quickly as you can'. He didn't take the bait and five days later Georgiana writes to him again to tell him that her father needs to know 'whether he is at Liberty to name him...by the return of the post'. Plott did eventually reply. He explained that he had been so busy disposing of his late brother's stock in trade, as well as dealing with the arrangements for his sister's wedding that he had not had a moment to write a letter to her. 'I never knew till now the difficulties and the preparations necessary for such an Event', he told her. He would arrange for his luggage to be sent to Charlotte Street within the next three weeks, and could then 'immediately begin the voyage to the Pelew Islands in the course of which history', he wrote, 'I intend to place you a most conspicuous figure'. Plott wished 'a thousand happy new Years' to Georgiana and her 'two good and constant companions', her parents.

Georgiana replied that his 'fiddle faddle manner which makes you fidget about,' had let this 'opportunity slip by' as the ship had sailed on the very day they finally heard from him. But, she added, 'I rejoice, as we shall not now be without a Plott in Charlotte Street'. Georgiana couldn't close this letter without admitting that everything about the proposed expedition was 'intirely an Invention of my Own' which she had concocted as 'Civility could not procure a Young Lady an Answer to her Letter to try how far Interest could, and twas with much difficulty and from a great Effort' by the artist that she finally received a letter from him. She emphasised this point by adding that as 'you see your giddy pupil (as you used to call her) would not have alarmed her Old Schoolmaster for an instant had she not been certain that in the End it would all terminate in his good'.

Although he was seven years older than her father Georgiana enjoyed his company and often tried to chivvy him to write when they were apart. On 15th January 1794 she sent a letter to her 'Dear Plotty', 'in great haste...I have yet to breakfast', to say how they were all disappointed that he had not joined them for Sunday dinner. 'If you are not engaged today and will take your mutton with us...you will very much oblige us'. 'Come if you can, and you can I know if you please' she wrote to her 'good pretty creature'. In a postscript Georgiana instructs him to 'put your spectacles in your pocket. We have not seen you for near a week and where is the fun of making yourself so rare to old friends - do come'. On another occasion she asks him 'what can you say for yourself – not to answer my hurry hurry letter, that I wrote to you, even before I had taken my feed of corn after my journey'. Georgiana feared that Plott was 'born to be hanged or beheaded – for if there were not some such fate pending over you –if you had had as many lives as a Cat, you must ere have given up the game – for what with fire escapes, water escapes, tumbles, overturns, over-roastings and undertakings, beside the many dangers you suffer, owing to the weak state of your nerves – you really are a wonder of a man to be so fat and well liked as you are...Oh! Plotty! Plotty!' She told him that she would be going, with her parents to Dover, and hoped that he would come and visit them. As it was a time of war they could go cruising in one of the King's Cutters, in case they should chance to come alongside a Frenchman, who might try to attack them in their usual small boat. Or she could show him 'such prospects from the Heights as will make your head giddy'.

For over thirty-two years Georgiana and Plott enjoyed a close friendship then the dreadful news arrived that he 'was dangerously ill'. Before she could write he succumbed to his final illness and died on 27th October 1803 at the age of seventy-one. Georgiana had lost one of her closest friends.

19 Is the stage clear?

Georgiana also painted at least one theatrical performance. Keate had taken his daughter to see a very popular play at the time, Shakespeare's *King John*. Georgiana had been so impressed by Sarah Siddons' portrayal of Constance, when she confronts the King on behalf of her son Arthur, who she believes is the rightful heir to England's throne, that Georgiana went home and painted this scene in watercolour. Although her character only appeared three times in the play Siddons reordered the text to make Constance the dominant force. The actress left her dressing room door open between appearances so that she could hear events on stage to help her muster the 'bitter tears of rage, disappointment, betrayed confidence, baffled ambition, and above all, the agonizing feelings of maternal …tenderness desperate and ferocious as a hunted tigress in defence of her young' for her performance. Georgiana has captured the moment when 'Constance', in her purple robes and a headdress of three feathers, grabs the hand of 'King John' as he steps towards the edge of the stage. Perhaps it was due to the intensity of this performance that Georgiana did not record any scenery, but only the memory of one of Siddons' most memorable roles. On seeing Georgiana's watercolour at the Society of Artists exhibition in 1791 the connoisseur, Horace Walpole, noted in his catalogue that he thought it 'pretty'.

When the new Drury Lane theatre re-opened in 1794 Georgiana and her father went to see Sarah Siddons perform her most famous role, Lady Macbeth. Even though the actress was seven months pregnant at the time, it was said that her powerfully expressive eyes and solemn dignity expressed the character's murderous passions with such force that the 3,600 strong audience were spellbound. Rather than her impression of this performance Georgiana writes in her diary that Henderson joined them in their box for the duration of the play and then waited until they were ready to leave in order to escort her to her father's coach.

Although Georgiana regularly visited the West End to see the latest plays, operas and pantomimes her diary only records her attendance, not her reaction to the performances. However, she did go to see *The*

Children in the Wood at the Haymarket, Piccadilly, on three separate occasions in 1794. This story of two children abandoned in the depths of the forest by their wicked uncle, only to survive the experience and be reunited with their parents, appears to have grabbed Georgiana's imagination. Perhaps, like one of the reviewers, her 'conscience was stirred', even though the boy child Walter, was played by the thirty-four year old actor John Bannister, in one of his favourite roles.

Like many in the audience Georgiana would have been as interested in the spectators as the players. Eighteenth century audiences could be quite lively, catcalling, crisscrossing the floor to visit friends, and talking loudly during the performance. Mr Lovel confesses to *Evelina*, in Fanny Burney's novel, that he seldom listens to the players: 'one has so much to do, in looking about and finding out one's acquaintance, that, really, one has no time to mind the stage'. When the Royal Family attended the theatre it was not unknown for the whole audience to turn their backs to the stage to watch them instead.

On another occasion Captain Bligh and his wife joined Georgiana and her parents for a performance staged for the benefit of the actor/manager, Thomas Hull, who had been acting for over forty years. Fully committed to the profession Hull had also been instrumental in setting up the Covent Garden Theatrical Fund in 1765 to provide pensions for old or ill actors and actresses. Keate had been able to secure half a stage box for his family and friends, who included 'Henderson, Mr Lambert, Mr Nichol & William Nichol'. The translator and playwright John Hoole 'came over the stage' to join them. Most probably this 'gentle, unassuming and affectionate' man 'of middling stature and of athletic make' first met Georgiana's father through their mutual friendship with Dr Samuel Johnson. The evening began with a one-act musical drama, *British Fortitude and Hibernian Friendship, or an escape from France*. Then Mrs Yates played Mandane, the Chinese orphan in the tragedy *Cyrus*. Georgiana had witnessed Mrs Yates 'first night of acting' two months earlier at the Haymarket. Her London debut as 'Euphrasia' in *The Grecian Daughter* had so impressed Georgiana and her father that they called on her the following morning to wish her 'joy'. Hull's benefit evening concluded with a comic opera, *Sprigs of Laurel*. All that Georgiana tells us about this evening is that Henderson 'stayed to see us out'.

In July that same year she went to see *Mogul Tale, or The Descent of the Balloon* by Mrs Inchbald. This two-act farce told the story of a couple from Wapping who went ballooning, got blown off course and landed on an Ottoman palace. A hot air balloon landed on the stage, eunuchs and elaborately dressed women from the palace harem graced an Indian garden but Georgiana tells us nothing of her experience. Or indeed of the sight of a review of the British fleet with French prizes entering an illuminated Portsmouth Harbour on the stage at the Haymarket, in the autumn, for a performance of *Rule Britannia*. This play had been written to celebrate Britain's defeat of the French on 'The Glorious First of June'. The London stage offered much to delight the eye but Georgiana doesn't record her response to events in her diary.

We can image that Keate also took his daughter to hear the prologues and epilogues he written for both professional and amateur actors like Mrs Frances Abington, who gave Keate's epilogue for the *Dramatic Romance of Cymon*. Her opening line was 'Is the stage clear? – bless me!' Sir Joshua Reynolds painted the actress in one of her most famous roles, 'Miss Prue' in *Love for Love*. Possibly the actress was a distant cousin of Georgiana's father for Keate commissioned Sir Joshua Reynolds to paint a portrait of the actress in a red dress, and this painting remained in the family until 1902, when Georgiana's grandson sold it at auction.

Keate regularly wrote epilogues for the pupils, including the sons of earls and dukes, at Newcome's school in Hackney. Georgiana would have attended these annual productions as they were an important part of London's social calendar. She obviously was friends with the founder, Henry Newcome and his family, as she writes that she gave him some of her etchings as a present.

We can see that, from a very young age, the theatre was part of Georgiana's life and that, through her father, she met many of the key players. However, she was only eight years old when the great actor/manager, and family friend, David Garrick died in 1779.

20 Still speaks of your rapturous kisses

During a visit to Bath in the spring of 1766, perhaps to seek solace in the renowned curative properties of the water dispensed at the spa, Georgiana's father met the great actor David Garrick, who had come to 'take the waters' to ease a gastric disorder and the effect of what was known as the 'rich man's disease', gout. The two men would share a close friendship that lasted for well over a quarter of a century. Keate praised the actor on his recent portrayal of Hamlet, 'With thee we melt/with thee we freeze/You guide our spirits and our tears/and rule our Passions, as you please'. Garrick wrote to George Colman the elder, that 'our friend Keate...is a very agreeable man', who had comforted him much in the 'strange mixture of mortals at Bath' and, he added, that 'no man starts a laugh better.' Colman responded with an example of their mutual friend's humour. When his young son had expressed surprise at Keate's decision to have his portrait painted for 'his countenance was more grotesquely ugly than the generality of human faces', Georgiana's father, with his rueful 'bald, wooden visage, explained that he had been enjoying a performance at one of the London theatres when someone shouted 'fire'. For safety's sake he had fled the scene and hurried home where he discovered that 'his eyebrows and eyelashes had dropt off through fright' and, he added, 'they have never, as you may perceive Sir, grown again!' Almost doubled up with pain from his struggle to supress a 'vulgar and uproarious horse laugh', Colman replied that he 'had heard of hair standing on end, or even turning gray due to fear but of its causing eye-brows and eye-lashes instantly to vanish, in the side box of a theatre, unless they were false ones and shaken off in the squeeze to get out', he had 'never before or since met an example'.

On seeing his friend's wife, 'Mrs Garrick in a Country Dance' at the Bath Assembly Rooms, Keate penned a poetic trifle, to this former principal dancer at Drury Lane, on how 'each Motion's Ease' she demonstrated with 'Elegance, and Grace'. The Garricks' constant companion was not forgotten. In his ode 'To Biddy at Bath' Keate wrote that their little dog would often sit and listen to her 'Master's sprightly Jokes, view him practise all those Parts which can chill, or melt our Hearts'. Although 'each Dog must have his Day', Keate concluded, when the elderly Biddy is finally called to 'Elysian scenes...[her] cousin CERBERUS, whose three mouths make such a Fuss, shall on your account stop Two, Barking soft to welcome you'. He added that when Biddy arrived she would have 'new Teeth, new Eyes and Feet' and learn once again 'all the puppy Tricks'. Styling himself as 'odd dog' in an accompanying letter, Keate wrote that these 'Dogrell Verses' had been 'composed by One who is Your Wellwisher'. Continuing the canine theme he said he had recently met an old acquaintance, by the name of Nero, who was 'as much of the puppy as ever'. Keate had also gone 'into the Isle of Dogs on purpose' as 'your friend Mopse has had little ones'.

In May 1769 Stratford-upon-Avon's council made Garrick, the foremost Shakespearian actor of the day, an Honorary Burgess and presented him with the freedom of the town in an elaborately carved casket made from the mulberry tree in William Shakespeare's garden. In acknowledgement of 'his very elegant and spirited defence of that first of poets...Voltaire', who did more than any other writer to bring Shakespeare to public notice, the Mayor and Council of Stratford upon Avon, in July 1769, presented Keate with an inkstand made out of the same mulberry-tree. Inside was a letter written 'with a politeness that does no less honour to the corporation, than to the gentleman whom they have enriched with a relic so truly valuable, as it shows their desire to reward literacy as well as scenic merits'. Garrick wrote to the corporation to say that 'your present to Keate...has brought the scribblers upon us, who think their title superior to his –I felt it would be so – when the Gift and the Reason of bestowing it, was so displayed in the Papers...' In a second letter Garrick added that 'Keate's affair has been Unlucky – I forsaw it'. He added, 'what would it have been had you given the freedom too?'

In thanks for the honour awarded to him by the town council Garrick organised a Jubilee to celebrate the birth of Shakespeare. The three-day long event opened on 6th September 1769 with the orchestra, and most of the acting company, from Drury Lane in attendance, together with many of Garrick's friends, including Georgiana's father. Over seven hundred sat down to dinner on the first evening. On the second day a two thousand strong audience watched Garrick deliver the Jubilee Ode, with musical accompaniment by Thomas Arne, that he had specially written for this occasion. Sadly bad weather disrupted the proceedings. The fireworks got wet, the amphitheatre flooded and the grand Shakespeare Pageant, planned for the third day, had to be cancelled. James Boswell wrote that his 'bosom glowed with joy' when he saw the 'numerous and brilliant company of nobility and gentry, the rich, the brave, the witty and the fair, assembled' at this celebration organised by 'Mr Garrick...who has done so much to make our nation acquainted with...so illustrious a dramatic author with such amazing variety and wonderful excellence as Shakespeare'. Boswell added that 'Garrick may be called the colourist of Shakespeare's soul'. Garrick's natural style of acting, based on sharply observed characterisation and interpretation of the long forgotten works of the Bard, saw London society flocking to see him perform. It was said that he 'drew a dozen dukes a night' and that he 'never had his equal as an actor, and he will never have a rival'.

In 1771 Garrick wrote to the Revd John Hoadley with news of Georgiana's birth. 'Our friend Keate is very proud of his Manhood & struts before Me, as a Game Cock before a Capon! I lower my flag to him & though I cannot hate him for his fecundity I do Envy him a little', he said. Although childless themselves the couple loved children and Georgiana would often accompany her parents when they went to call. Perhaps Garrick, who had grown fond of Keate's daughter, put on a little performance for her in the temple he he had erected to Shakespeare in the grounds of his riverside villa at Hampton. In a letter to Garrick, written in 1776, Keate reports that his five year old daughter, the 'Infanta grows apace, talks almost everything, and still speaks of your rapturous kisses'. Three years later, Georgiana heard the sad news that her friend had died. It took more than an hour for the funeral procession to travel from his name in the Adelphi to Westminster Abbey, and upwards of fifty coaches followed the coffin. The pallbearers were all aristocrats, all friends. Garrick, the first actor to be granted the honour of being buried in the Abbey, was laid to rest in Poet's Corner next to the monument to his great hero, William Shakespeare.

At eight years old Georgiana may have been too young to go to the funeral but her father would certainly have attended the service. Georgiana remained great friends with Garrick's widow. In later years Georgiana and the children visited Mrs Garrick, either at the

Adelphi or at the villa by the river at Hampton. Although no diaries or letters have come to light recording these meetings we can imagine that their conversations turned to memories of the great actor.

21 Everything she touches turns to gold

Through this friendship Georgiana became close to a number of Garrick's actresses including Jane Pope, who first trod the boards in 1756 when she was just twelve years old. Three years later she was a full member of Garrick's company and, except for one season, she remained at Drury Lane until her retirement nearly fifty years later. Her comic timing made her a great success. The poet Samuel Whyte said that 'everything she touches turns to gold' and King George III commanded her to perform her best-known role, Mrs Heidelberg in Garrick's play *The Clandestine Marriage* for his pleasure.

A surviving letter, dated 29th April 1793, provides us with a glimpse of their ease with each other. Georgiana wrote that when Jane's letter arrived they were all out so the maid had placed it on top of the pianoforte to await their return. Unfortunately, she continued, it had lain, forgotten, until it was found between 'the leaves of a Music Book' five days later. When her father opened the letter Georgiana saw 'marks of surprise on his Countenance', as perplexed, he 'looked at the direction, then the Envelope, and read it over three or four times, and as many times articulated in a low voice Isaac Wilkins, Isaac Wilkins'. Then, Georgiana told Jane, her father passed the letter to her and said, 'there Georgiana see what you can make out of that...if he was in a Wood I was in a Wilderness, Georgiana continued, Well Papa?', she replied. Is 'that all you can say. Why Girl, I never felt myself more awkward in my life'. The source of all this confusion, a thank you note for a poetical tribute recently received by the forty-nine-year old actress. Although signed by another name, Jane believed this had been composed by her old friend George Keate and sent to her under a pseudonym. Georgiana continued her account. Her father, who as 'a follower of the Muses' and an admirer of long standing, felt that he should have 'paid tribute to that Excellence', which Jane 'in so high a degree possesses...and now to hear of an Isaac Wilson (what the Deuce is the fellow's name) getting the start of' him had put her father 'out of all patience'. Georgiana joyfully accepted his request to write a reply. She told Jane that he 'most richly deserved...[this] broad hint' of his negligence and, as he 'has gone to the City' to dine and 'will not be home till eight or Nine', Georgiana felt sure that he would not be back in time to read her letter before it was sent, and therefore she felt able to share, with Jane, her father's discomfiture. This 'Comedy of Errors has produced so lively an after piece', Georgiana wrote, that she didn't know whether 'the next performance is to be The Rivals' but she felt sure it would 'terminate with...All Well's that Ends Well'. In conclusion, Georgiana said that she had 'so much the curiosity of a Chamber Maid, or my Grandmother Eve' that she hoped that Jane would indulge her 'with a Sight of these said Verses'. Stung into action Keate immediately wrote his own poetical appreciation of 'the COMIC MUSE' in April 1793 in which he firmly owned 'our POPE infallible'. He also left his old friend thirty guineas, 'as a trivial Remembrance', and his wife honoured his request to leave her a further £100 in her own will. Mrs Keate added her late husband's expensively illustrated edition of the works of Shakespeare, published in 1744, to this bequest.

Another of Garrick's actresses who impressed Georgiana was Mrs Dorothy Jordan. After seeing her performance in Colley Cibber's *She Would or Would Not, or The Kind Imposter* Georgiana went home to paint a portrait of Mrs Jordan in the character of Hippolita 'from recollection'. Sadly this watercolour, which Georgiana exhibited, alongside her painting of Sarah Siddons and John Edwards at the Society of Artists in 1791, is now lost. However, we know how Mrs Jordan, would have appeared in her costume as Hippolita, thanks to a portrait painted by John Hoppner RA. Wearing a high-collared jacket, edged with heavy ornate braiding around the collar, sleeves and cuffs, and a large frothy cravat at her throat, the actress looks out at her audience. A turban, adorned with overlarge ostrich feathers, sits on her tumbling curls. She holds a pair of spectacles in her right hand whilst the hilt of a sword can be seen resting on her left hip.

Mrs Jordan had a number of affairs and four illegitimate children before she began her liasion with the Duke of Clarence in 1791, the same year that Georgiana painted her portrait. It may have been her beauty, wit and intelligence which captured his heart, or perhaps it was her legs, described as the most beautiful ever seen on the London stage, that first caught his eye. The couple lived happily together at Bushy House in Teddington. She was 'a very good creature, very domestic and careful' of the ten children they had together, the Duke told a friend. Their affair lasted for twenty years. Mrs Jordan had no doubt as to the reason for the break-up, 'Money, money', she wrote, 'has made HIM at this moment the most wretched of men'. Popular opinion turned against the Duke and the public press advised him to 'return to Mistress J....n's arms...be wise and play the fool no more'. However, he required a wealthy heiress in order to pay his debts. He eventually married Princess Adelaide, who welcomed his sons into their life, while his daughters stayed with their mother. In 1815 Mrs Jordan, who had returned to the stage, fled to France to avoid her creditors and three years later died just outside Paris.

22 Rage for music

Like many others Georgiana appears to have been caught up in the unprecedented fervour for music that gripped London around the 1790s. One commentator reported that:

> All the Modish World appear
> Fond of Nothing Else my dear
> Folks of Fashion eager seek
> Sixteen Concerts in a week

Georgiana was a frequent concertgoer. We know from her diary that she attended a benefit at Freemason's Hall, Great Queen Street on 24th March 1794, held for the forty-five-year old German soprano Gertrud Elisabeth Mara. The programme included a performance by her English counterpart, Nancy Storace. During her time in Vienna, when she sang at the City Opera, Nancy had so captured Mozart's attention that he created the role of Susanna for her in *The Marriage of Figaro*, and also wrote a duet, 'Ch'io mi scordi de te' (That I forget you), for her farewell concert in 1787. Gertrud, on the other hand, failed to impress Mozart, either musically or personally, although she received high praise from many others for her part in the Handel commemoration at Westminster Abbey, and her role as Cleopatra in his opera *Julius Cesear*.

The following month Georgiana attended a concert to hear new works by 'the inexhaustible, the wonderful, the sublime Haydn!', which had been organised by his friend and impresario, composer and violinist, Johann Peter Salomon. During the course of his visit Haydn performed eleven new compositions that became widely known as his 'London' symphonies. Critics had thought that with 'every new Overture...he can only repeat himself', but they were 'every time mistaken'. Perhaps Georgiana agreed with the comment about the 'Clock' symphony, that 'nothing can be more original than the subject of the first movement; and having found a happy subject, no man knows like Haydn how to produce incessant variety, without once departing from it', but again her diary tells us nothing about her response to the music.

As a daughter of upper class parents Georgiana was expected to be both artistically and musically accomplished. We don't know about her early education but in 1794 her father employed Charles Frederick Horn to improve his daughter's proficiency on the pianoforte. German-born Horn had come to London in the mid-1780s. Destitute, and at first unable to speak English, Horn found employment as music master for the daughters of the 1st Marquess of Stafford. He fell in love and married their French tutor Diana Dupont, and on completion of his contract the couple moved to London where, on the recommendation of the Marquess and Salomon, the twenty-three-year old Horn became music tutor to Queen Charlotte and the Royal Princesses. When Georgiana met Horn he had just become a father for the sixth time and, no doubt, needed to take on extra pupils to help with the expenses of a growing family. Nearly every Friday from 31st January to 18th July 1794 Horn visited Charlotte Street to instruct Georgiana on her technique. However, instead of making their way to the music room on the 21st February Horn took Georgiana to hear 'a German lady play the harmonica'. Although blind from the age of four, Marianne Kirchgessner had achieved fame for her technical mastery and exceptionally delicate playing of this instrument, the design of which had been improved thirty years earlier by the great statesman Benjamin Franklin. He had fixed a spindle through the centre of the base of a series of graduated glass bowls and placed this in a trough of water to keep them permanently damp. Using a foot pedal to turn the glass armonica Marianne rubbed her wet finger along the edge of these bowls to coax out all the subtle details of the music. It was said that the sound she produced was 'like the voice of a nightingale'. Mozart dedicated his 'Adagio' for the glass harmonica to Marianne and Salomon wrote a sonata especially for her London visit. Georgiana doesn't tell us what she played but perhaps as she sat down to supper after the concert she was tempted to wet her finger and run it around the rim of her glass to see if she could make a pleasant sound.

Georgiana appears to have taken her music making very seriously as a fortnight after her first lesson with Horn she received additional instruction from Dr Thomas Sanders Dupuis, Organist to the Chapel Royal, who came to Charlotte Street every Wednesday from 12th February. Her last lesson took place on 15th August 1794 a month before the family left for their holiday in Dover. Although Dupuis's own compositions were thought to be unremarkable he did have a good reputation as a performer. Haydn was ecstatic in his praise of Dupuis. It was said that 'his finger was lively and he knew his instrument well'. That Keate was able to employ two musicians from the Royal court could only have enhanced his reputation.

Georgiana also received instruction in the art of dancing from Simon Slingsby, who had recently returned from the Paris Opera, after a career as principal dancer on the English stage. Considered by his contemporaries as one of those 'fine made men' who was 'perfectly well made...his arms graceful, his knees turned outwardly, his shoulders not elevated or round, his features striking, his eyes expressive', he was such a success that Slingsby's Reel was named in his honour in 1773. After her last lesson on 15th July Slingsby returned to Charlotte Street at 3pm to join the family and their guests at dinner. Henderson and Mr French arrived later in the afternoon and, after tea and toast, everyone adjourned to the music room to hear Slingsby perform on the Jew's harp. After he had returned this instrument to his pocket he proceeded to accompany himself on the harpsichord while he sang. Georgiana records that Horn's sister then entertained them before it was her turn. She encouraged Horn and the explorer John Meares to join her in singing some of the glees, or part songs, which were popular at the time. They had such fun that they did not 'leave off twelve o'clock', she wrote in her diary. Georgiana appears to have had a good voice as she records on several occasions that her friends 'made me sing'.

23. 'The good news of Mr de Sade'

As she took her seat for Salomon's benefit night Georgiana, like many of the audience, expected to hear a cheerful allegro follow the opening slow movement of Haydn's Symphony no.100, in the manner his London audiences had come to expect. Instead Haydn suddenly unleashed a barrage of percussion instruments which proceeded to cast a dark shadow over the rest of the movement. These discordant sounds, which, one critic wrote, perfectly evoked the 'hellish roar of war', struck a chord with Haydn's audience, for many of them had escaped the horrors of the French Revolution, and gave the piece the popular title of the 'Military Symphony'.

By 1794 London had become home to many French émigrés who had fled Paris to escape 'Madame Guillotine', under whose blade over 16,000 people eventually died. It was only when this tool of execution also claimed the heads of Louis XVI and his Queen, Marie Antoinette that Count La Tour left France for the safety of England's capital where he met the Keate family. Accompanying the twenty-three-year-old Georgiana on her regular walks in nearby Gower Street the pair would have naturally discussed the events which had taken place in France following the uprising and the storming of the Bastille in 1789. La Tour also gave some account of his life before these disturbing events. In particular he told her about the incarceration of the Marquis de Sade who, following his arrest in nearby Italy, had been sent to the fortress of Miolans, located in a remote part of the Duchy of Savoy in Chambery, where La Tour acted as Governor.

The French aristocrat, philosopher and writer De Sade found himself imprisoned on a number of occasions over the years on various charges relating to his blasphemy and libertine lifestyle. However, in 1772 his abuse of prostitutes came to a head when he accidentally poisoned several of them with the aphrodisiac Spanish fly during an orgy at Marseilles. He was also found guilty of sodomy with his manservant but managed to escape before the mandatory death sentence could be carried out. His luck was not to last and a few months later he was captured and imprisoned under the authority of La Tour. De Sade wrote frequently to the Governor protesting his innocence, complaining about his treatment at the hands of the warder, and asking for permission for his wife to visit him. She too wrote to La Tour telling him that her thirty-two-year old 'husband is not to be classed with rogues of whom the universe should be purged', and that his crime was, at most, a misdemeanour, a 'youthful folly that endangered no life nor honour nor the reputation of any citizen'.

De Sade turned on the charm offensive. And it worked. Impressed by the prisoner's new gentleness and sweet nature La Tour finally agreed to De Sade's request to be allowed to take his evening meal, in company with a fellow prisoner, in one of the more pleasant upper rooms of the fortress. While they enjoyed their food and wine over the following weeks, and lulled the Count into a false sense of security, the two men were actually plotting their escape. On 30 April 1773 they succeeded with their plan. Charming to the last De Sade left behind a letter addressed to La Tour in which he apologised for the unceremonious manner of his leaving and he hoped the Count would not be made to suffer.

Georgiana records with pleasure calling on the Count on 21 January 1794 with 'the good news about Mr de Sade'. Her family had learnt that the month before police commissioner Marotte and police officer Jouenne had discovered de Sade's address and arrested him on charges of counter-revolutionary activities. With the overthrow of Robespierre and the end of the Reign of Terror de Sade once again escaped the death sentence which had been imposed on him. When Napoleon came to power a few years later a now penniless de Sade was once again imprisoned, before being moved to an asylum, where he died many years later.

Georgiana also met a great hero of the French royalist cause, the Bishop of Pol St Leon. Since his arrival in London in 1791 the Bishop had, on his own initiative, acted as a one-man committee of assistance for the destitute émigrés. When her father announced that he was about to set out to see the 'Bishop's picture' by the French émigré artist, Henri-Pierre Danloux, Georgiana said that she would go with him to see the painting. Georgiana was so impressed by this portrait that she revisited Greenwoods Auction Rooms in Leicester Square a few months later to show the painting to John Henderson, Charles

Fox and Captain Hanforth. The artist has shown the Bishop sitting in a modest room in his lodgings in Queen Street, Bloomsbury. Protected from the heat of the fire by a small screen decorated with a landscape, the Bishop has taken up his quill pen to add a name to the list on his lap, highlighting his important charity work. The nearby table is overflowing with more lists, candles and sealing wax, while the floor is littered with letters from émigrés and supporters.

Georgiana also took an interest in another French émigré, Charles-Alexandre de Calonne, the former Controller General of Finance to Louis XVI. Dismissed from the French court in 1787 for failing to push through reforms to restore the country's economy, de Calonne decided to retire to London. He bought a large house in Piccadilly on the corner of Hyde Park, where he entertained the upper classes of London society, as well as his fellow French men and women. One particular guest captured his heart, another Georgiana, the Duchess of Devonshire, to whom he lent large sums of money to help pay her debts. As he had left Paris before the revolutionary army had taken control he had been able to bring with him his extensive collection of artworks. Georgiana and her father paid a visit to his home one afternoon to view his 'noble & superlatively capital assemblage of valuable pictures, drawings, miniatures and prints'. She saw paintings by Tintoretto, Velsaquez, Rubens and Van Dyck as well as Sir Joshua Reynolds portrait of *Mrs Siddons as the Tragic Muse* for which de Calonne had paid 800 guineas. Prominently on display was the portrait he commissioned shortly after he became Controller General. For this work he chose a French artist who had earned a reputation for stylish portrayals of royalty and aristocratic society throughout Europe. In his formal black dress with lace-edged kerchief and cuffs, and wearing his 'fiscal' wig, Elizabeth Vigee Le Brun has painted the sitter at his desk. The blue silk ribbon and star of the Order of Saint Esprit, together with a letter inscribed *Au Roi* which he holds in his left hand, demonstrate his close relationship with Louis XVI. This fine painting found its way into the collection of George IV and now forms part of the Royal collection.

Nine months after her visit de Calonne sold the bulk of this collection to provide funds for the destitute French aristocracy, who were daily arriving in London.

24 Pure and salubrious air

With travel abroad curtailed, due to the uprising in France, Georgiana and her parents visited some of the favoured seaside resorts situated on the Kent coast. From a surviving engraving of one of Georgiana's watercolours we know that she went to Margate with her parents.

Setting out from Greenwich their coach would have passed many sights, like the remains of a nunnery at Deptford that had been converted into a royal mansion for Queen Elizabeth I. They would also have seen numerous mills, littering the banks of the river, hard at work producing paper and silk for the home and overseas markets, and Georgiana was presented with a fine view of the Thames meandering through the valley below when their coach crested the chalk hill at Northfleet. Their journey continued through many towns whose names are familiar to us today, such as Gravesend, Chatham and Sittingbourne. No doubt Georgiana and her mother were glad of the opportunity to get out of the coach to stretch their legs and take some refreshment at the numerous inns along their route, each time their horses were replaced with fresh animals. After fifty miles of travelling they arrived at the foot of Boughton Hill, where the coachman asked his passengers to get out and walk, in order to lighten the load for the horses as they pulled the heavy coach up this steep incline. 'It will stretch our legs, and give us a fine prospect', Keate told his daughter, and indeed when they reached the top they could see the Isle of Sheppey to their left, the opening of the channel at Faversham, 'which was covered as far as the sight could stretch with innumerable sails' and the towers of the cathedral at Canterbury, their next stop. Georgiana and her parents may have taken time out to visit the shrine of Thomas A'Becket before rejoining the coach for the last seventeen miles of their journey.

After they had settled into their accommodation Georgiana and her parents could walk along the esplanade to enjoy some of the 'pure and salubrious air', for which Margate was famous. They may have visited the commodious bathing rooms on the High Street to see the machines. Margate's flat sandy shore extended for several miles and offered ideal conditions for sea bathing. Georgiana would have known what to expect as her father had painted the scene in one of his watercolours. His painting shows bathing machines lining up outside the steps on the seaward side of the bathing rooms, while other carriages are already making their way down the beach and out to sea. The awning at the back, invented by local glove and beeches maker, the Quaker Benjamin Beale, has been lowered to the level of the water to ensure the bather's privacy, as well as protect delicate skin from the sun. The health benefits of bathing had received the royal seal of approval from George III and Jane Austen, a frequent seaside visitor, who considered that 'sea air and sea bathing together were nearly infallible...being a match for every Disorder'. Did Georgiana make use of the bathing machine, or did she just drink a glass of sea water in one of the bathing rooms. The view from the window included the ruined church at Reculver, with its twin towers, about ten miles distant. Her father knew this structure and wrote to Sir Joseph Banks on 20th April 1780 about the 'Roman Earthenware found in the Sea on the Kentish Coast between Whitstable and Reculver', this would later be published in the sixth volume of *Archaeologia*.

Another familiar sight, and subject of her father's paintbrush, was the Custom House on the corner of the bay. In Keate's painting the Union Jack, on the flag post next to the building, is straining against the strong onshore wind that is whipping up the waves. One gentleman, in order to steady his telescope as he looks out to sea, is resting his elbows on a canon bearing the initials of the King, G.R., while his dog sits patiently at his heel, waiting for his master to continue their walk. On the far side of the bay we can see a figure at the top of the steps that lead to the nearby Fort. Georgiana also visited Margate's famous grotto. She made her way down a chalk stairway to see the profusion of patterns and symbols, created from cockle, whelk, mussel and oyster shells, that decorated over seventy feet of winding underground passages. We can also imagine that she travelled to nearby St Peter's to enjoy the delights of another attraction her father captured in a watercolour - the Pleasure Gardens. He has painted a pleasant scene of visitors dancing by the covered bandstand, while a fashionable couple sit on a bench to watch their child and others promenade in the shade of the trees. The proprietors had thoughtfully added a covered walkway to ensure that visitors could still enjoy a stroll around the gardens when the weather was inclement. In the evening Georgiana and her parents could attend a concert at

Margate's spacious and elegant assembly room in Cecil Square. Said to be the largest in the country at eighty-seven feet long and forty-three feet wide, with magnificent Venetian windows commanding an extensive prospect of the sea, Georgiana would hear London vocalists who had come down for the season, or music played by the local military band. After the Theatre Royal opened in 1786 Georgiana and her parents had the opportunity to indulge their love for performance.

We know from a surviving engraving of one of her watercolours that Georgiana made use of another of Margate's attractions, Hall's subscription library located in Hawley Square. She has captured the magnificent interior of an imposing square room with a screen of columns separating one half of the space that was being used as a toy shop. In the foreground reading room we see visitors perusing the newspapers or selecting a title from the shelves, but this is also a social space. We see other people promenading or engaged in conversation, while their children and dogs play nearby. Busts of the great poets sit on top of the book cases and elegant chandeliers hang from the lofty ceiling to light the room on a dull day. The figure with the peg leg may be family friend, Brook Watson, who later became Lord Mayor of London. If she has painted one acquaintance perhaps others from her circle are also portrayed. It is tempting to think that the family group at the centre of the painting depicts Georgiana and her parents. The young girl has tumbling dark curls, like Georgiana, but the man and woman look younger than her own parents who were both in their late 50s at this time, but perhaps Georgiana used artistic licence. When Joseph Hall, the owner of the library, saw her painting he asked permission to reproduce it in 1789 and sell the coloured engravings as souvenirs. Georgiana granted his request. Thanks to this engraving we not only have a rare opportunity to see the interior of a subscription library but we can also see that Georgiana was a skilful amateur artist.

25 Whose high and bending head

After a breakfast of bread, eggs and meat on Saturday 13th September 1794, Georgiana and her mother said farewell to their next-door neighbour Mrs Carr, and then boarded the coach for another of her father's favourite seaside resorts. They set out along the familiar route to Kent and, although the fees from the turnpikes had led to an improvement in the roads, the coaches could still only manage eight miles an hour and so it was with some relief that they enjoyed the hospitality of the coaching inn when they reached Dartford while fresh horses were put between the shafts of their coach. With evening fast approaching the family decided to stay overnight at their next stop, the cathedral city of Rochester on the banks of the river Medway. Although it was said that the innkeepers along this route were civil enough they were also known to be eager to get all they could from their visitors, so it was with a lighter purse that the Keate family began the next stage of their journey. Eleven miles later they arrived in the small town of Sittingbourne, and went to one of the inns, most probably 'The Rose', described by one traveller as the best in England, and sat down to a three-course meal. As their second day of travelling drew to a close Georgiana and her parents arrived in Canterbury and stopped off at 'The Fountain', said to be the oldest hostlery in England, for tea. They were delighted to see an old friend, Robert Le Geyt, with his son Philip and daughter Maria, who had walked over from their home in the nearby Archbishop's Palace to see them. The next morning, refreshed from a good night's sleep, the family set out on the last leg of their journey. At least the tedium must have been eased by glimpses of the sea as their coach crested the hills, until eventually Dover Castle came into view and they knew, after nearly three days of travelling, that they were almost at journey's end. Georgiana and her parents finally arrived at around 2pm. The Payne family were waiting to greet them as they stepped down from their coach, and took them back to their lodgings for dinner. After they had finished their meal Georgiana and her father stretched their legs with a walk down to the pier, while Mrs Keate organised their accommodation at one of the many genteel furnished houses advertising their availability.

The landscape was very familiar to Georgiana as her father had painted a number of views during earlier visits to the resort. The Dover coastline was William Shakespeare's inspiration for Act 4 Scene 1 of *King Lear* when the blinded Earl of Gloucester instructs Edgar to take him to a cliff whose 'high and bending head/Looks fearfully in the confined deep'. Gloucester tells his son to 'bring me to the very brim of it/And I'll repair the misery thou dost bear'. When Georgiana saw Shakespeare's Cliff in 1794 it had lost some of the majesty that had inspired the bard for there had been a major landslip – a sight painted by Georgiana's father in 1771. On the reverse of his watercolour Keate pasted a label stating that the loss had been 'so considerable that the Ruin of it covered a quarter of an acre of the beach at the foot of it'. A second label said that by a measurement taken two years later 'its perpendicular height was found to be 300 feet.'

Georgiana quickly established her regime of daily walks. Nearly every morning at 7.00am Georgiana and her father would walk along the beach to the home of milk-seller Old Ma Burville, who lived in a converted cave at the foot of the cliffs, beneath Dover Castle. After buying their daily supply they would either retrace their steps along the beach or take the longer route, via the pier or the cross wall, to their lodgings. Following breakfast with her parents Georgiana would often go for a walk along the front with friends from London, who had also come to Dover to partake of the bracing sea air. When the seasonal bad weather caught them out Georgiana would seek shelter with the fruit woman or in the herring house. The nearby Orange Walk, named after the Prince of Orange who had anchored his fleet offshore in 1688, gave Georgiana an opportunity to promenade and on several occasions she walked here, either alone or with Lady Boothby or 'little Penaydo'. Georgiana appears to have been particular fond of the daughter of Captain J.C. and Sarah Catherine Penaydo. On a very wet day in October, when they could not go out for a walk, Georgiana tells us that she made a doll's work basket for little Abigaile, but we have no idea what she used, how it looked, or whether this friendship continued beyond their holiday in Dover in 1794.

Dover, like Margate, offered holidaymakers access to the benefits of the sea. Bathing machines could be hired to take bathers out for their dip, or they could make use of the Bathing Rooms on Marine Parade, where they could enjoy hot salt water baths at a cost of three shillings, or the cold version for one shilling. We don't know if Georgiana partook of this facility but we know from her diary that she enjoyed the musical entertainment they put on for the visitors to the town. She also called on Mr. G. Ledger, the local bookseller and stationer, to subscribe to the Albion Circulating Library which he had established at 86 Snargate Street a decade earlier. Here she could peruse the latest papers, reviews and magazines in a handsome room fitted up for this purpose or borrow books to pass away the hours when the weather was too inclement for her to take walks or go on excursions. She also had errands to run. As well as trips to the fish market, the pig woman and the washer woman, to ensure they had fresh linen during their stay, John Plott had charged his twenty-three-old goddaughter to find him some nankeen cloth as he wanted to have pair of trousers made out of this pale yellowish cotton material. Georgiana also attended Sunday service at St James's, the 11th century Norman church at the foot of Castle Hill.

On the evening of 22nd September 1794 Georgiana joined the crowds on the beach to see a great bonfire lit to commemorate the anniversary of the accession of King George III to the English throne in 1761. A violent storm the following month provided holidaymakers with the opportunity to see a ship driven onshore by the ensuing rough seas. Georgiana doesn't provide the name of this cutter but she and her father went to look at it on several occasions and, no doubt to Georgiana's delight, they found Henderson had also come to see the beached boat. He then joined them on their walk.

Dover had plenty to entertain Georgiana, in November she went to see a puppet show and, on another evening, paid a visit to the circus. Of particular interest, however, was Dover's annual fair. Not only did Georgiana go to see it being set up on Friday 21st November but then visited it nearly every day for a week. Four years earlier a company of gentlemen supported the opening of a theatre in Snargate Street and Georgiana attended a number of performances. She saw the comedies *Everyone has his Fault* by Mrs Inchbald and *A School for Greybears* by Mrs Cowley, as well as two farces; *The Liar* and the *Deaf Lover.*

During Georgiana's stay Dover became a hive of activity as the military were busy building barracks and strengthening the town's defences against the threat of a French invasion. She and her father joined the forty-eight-year old military engineer, Sir Thomas Hyde Page, on his inspection of the works at the battery, and at Archcliffe Fort. He had been responsible for refurbishing Dover's defences some twenty years earlier so could provide his companions with an accurate account of the fortifications. Around ten o'clock on the morning of Saturday 18th October Georgiana and her parents travelled five miles to the small hamlet of Ewell Minnis, just outside Dover. From the comfort of their carriage they watched a review of the newly formed volunteer corps of cavalry and infantrymen, the Cinque Port Fencibles. Dressed in their uniform of blue coats with red facings and brass buttons, worn over a white shirt, waistcoat and breeches, a bicorne or 'cocked' hat completed the ensemble, the men demonstrated their readiness to fight the enemy. Hopefully this show, and the improved fortifications, allayed any fears the visitors may have held regarding the rumours of the French invasion, certainly Georgiana does not express any concerns in her diary.

Back in Dover Georgiana and her father struck up a friendship with Captain South, who they met on one of their walks, and he invited them into 'the Mess Room and made the band play' for them. A month later the military put on a concert and ball for the townspeople and visitors, which Georgiana must have found very enjoyable as she records arriving at 'half past eight', meeting lots of friends and did not come away until 'about a quarter before twelve'.

On Thursday 4th December Georgiana and her parents said their farewells and left Dover at two o'clock in the afternoon, stayed over at Canterbury and Rochester and finally arrived back home at 5pm on Sunday.

26 H:K:M:

Dover had one other attraction to offer Georgiana, the presence of John Henderson. From her arrival in the town on 15th September 1794 to the date of his departure, 2nd December, Georgiana records his name in her diary practically every day, and sometimes two or three times a day. Henderson would often join her when she went for walks along the beach or the pier, and they also met up at the Bathing Rooms when they went to hear the singing. She noted that 'Mr Shafto', thought to be the subject of the popular song 'Bobby Shafto', was in the audience. A couple of weeks later Georgiana spent most of the day with Henderson and then saw him again at the military concert and ball in the evening. Perhaps the event lost some of its appeal when she saw Henderson leave. Georgiana records in her diary that 'we came away about a quarter before twelve...Henderson left it just before us'. Earlier that year Georgiana recorded that Henderson called at her parents' home in Charlotte Street but as 'Papa was out, [and] Mama dressing', she was alone with him. Intriguingly she concludes this entry with the initial letters 'H.K.M'. Was this her shorthand for 'Henderson Kissed Me' and did her heart beat a little faster when she saw him on horseback in Dover. He visited their lodgings ostensibly to draw a view of the harbour from their window, but perhaps he sought this opportunity to spend more time with Georgiana. She was certainly proud of his skill and showed these sketches to friends who called, and copied some of them herself.

After spending a happy two months enjoying the sea air, the busy harbour with view across the straits to France, and the entertainments on offer Henderson called on Georgiana and her parents to say his farewells. Two days later Georgiana wrote: 'Saw H from battery window leave Dover at a little after 10'. A week later she too returned to London but curiously Georgiana only records seeing Henderson twice in December.

What do we know about this man who appears to have captured Georgiana's heart? Born in 1764, he was named John after his paternal uncle. Nothing has been discovered about his early life and education, although he appears to have been an only child, like Georgiana. His father was a well-respected London bookseller and publisher and sent John to study at Queen's College, Oxford. In 1789, at the age of 25 Henderson graduated as a Bachelor of Civil Law and returned to the family home in Robert Street, Adelphi. Several months later his father, known as 'a gentleman [who] by amiable complacency endeared all who knew him' died. Christopher Henderson nominated his wife and son as joint executors of his will. He stipulated that his 'dear wife Olive' should receive 'the sum of One hundred and fifty pounds per annum during her natural life'. He added that, if his wife and son 'should think it proper to live separately from each other' she could take any of the household goods she required, and the rest of his estate, which included three houses in Brentford, Middx, should be sold for the benefit of his son. Six years earlier Henderson's uncle had died and bequeathed over 100 acres of land and property at Highwood Hill, Barnet, together with any monies, after payment of bequests totalling £18,000, to his brother Christopher, which thereby bolstered John Henderson's inheritance.

This influx of wealth meant that Henderson could move to the more fashionable main block of the Adelphi estate, designed by the Adam brothers which now stood on a former derelict stretch of land between the Strand and the River Thames. The twenty-two private houses stood on top of vaulting, which provided warehousing space with direct access to the Thames riverside. Although this project strained their finances the houses had such splendid interiors that, as the brothers believed, they were snapped up by tenants like Henderson who took a lease on no 4, situated in the 'centre of that noble pile of buildings' known as the Royal Terrace. The 'stately and highly ornamented pilasters, which run up the front distinguishing this, and the other two centre houses', coupled with a 'light, airy, healthful' interior and commanding a beautiful prospect had earlier caught the eye of the quack doctor James, who decided that this would an excellent location for his 'Temple of Health'. The 'doctor' used electricity to 'cure' the sick and the lame. He boasted that the hall of no.4 was littered with 'walking sticks, ear trumpets, visual glasses, crutches, etc., left and here placed as the most honourable trophies, by deaf, weak, paralytic and emaciated persons, cripples, etc., who being cured had no longer need of their assistance'. Ever the showman Graham ensured that his electrical apparatus would impress his clientele. The metallic globes, a flying dragon, 'its eyes ablaze with electrical fire', and a curious machine brought from America, would have fascinated visitors. Skimpily dressed young girls were employed to dance in his temple, including Emma, the future Lady Hamilton and Lord Nelson's love interest, provided an additional lure for his wealthy clients. However, his greatest attraction was his 'Celestial Bed'. Designed to encourage conception, the bed, measuring 12 by 9 feet, and carrying the message 'Be fruitful, multiply and replenish the earth', was canopied by a dome covered in musical automata, fresh flowers and a pair of live turtle doves. The bed's inner frame would tilt and, as the air around them crackled with electricity, the couple's movements caused organ pipes to breath out 'celestial sounds', which increased in intensity with the ardour of the bed's occupants. In spite of this attraction, which cost £100 a session, Graham found his expenses exceeded his income and he had to vacate no.4 Royal Terrace, and by the time Henderson took on the lease there was nothing to suggest that this had once been a temple to health.

Henderson's new wealth also meant that he could indulge his passion for painting and collecting. Like Georgiana's father he had gone on a Grand Tour of the continent and, subsequently produced an album of watercolour drawings of this journey, which can now be seen in the British Museum. When Dr Thomas Monro moved into no.8 Royal Terrace and set up his Academy for young artists Henderson was only too pleased to lend works for Monro's students, Thomas Girtin and Joseph Mallord William Turner, to copy. Such was Henderson's skill as an artist that, until recent times, his views of shipping at Dover were misattributed as the work of the young Turner.

Financially secure and with a fine house the thirty-year-old Henderson turned his mind to finding a wife. Judging from the almost constant appearance of his name in her diary for 1794, and the two entries 'H.K.M.', it would appear that the twenty-three-year old Georgiana saw Henderson as a potential husband.

27. Never having a child

From Georgiana's diary for 1794 we know that her father enjoyed Henderson's company at the dinner table and on holiday, and had even supported his election to the Society of Antiquaries, but Keate appears to have been unaware of Georgiana's growing feelings for the man. On their return to London Henderson called on Keate at Charlotte Street and asked for his daughter's hand in marriage. Georgiana's father gave his formal consent but then refused to leave the couple alone together and, according to reports, both Mr & Mrs Keate behaved in a very inconsistent manner. Georgiana later wrote to her godfather and asked him not to complain of her 'hurried writing – for it is hard to be obliged to write in Joke and appear in good spirits with a Heart aching as mine does – Yet so I must appear'. She explained that 'mentioning the least affair of consequence with my Mother is more distant...than ever and to speak to my father impossible', but as she only wanted her parents to be happy she had decided to wait, she told him, to see if the passage of time would make them more amenable to the idea.

Thursday 9th June 1796 was a momentous day. There had been no change over the past year in her parents' attitude and, unable to wait any longer, Georgiana got up, carefully chose her outfit, to which she added one of the bonnets she had bought from Mrs Gould, the hatter in Bond Street. At ten o'clock she sent for her father's coach, closed the front door behind her and set out for the church at the top of St Martin's Lane. The route was a familiar one. She regularly went shopping in Cockspur Street which was in the same direction. Today, however, her mind was on other things. We can imagine that her heart beat a little faster as the steeple of St Martin's-in-the-Fields came into view, as it was here that she had arranged to meet Henderson. Without further ado she climbed the flight of steps, passed through the Corinthian columns, supporting a commanding Portland stone portico, and into the cool interior of this church designed by James Gibbs. This was not the time to admire the rich plasterwork of the barrel-vaulted ceiling, the fine woodwork of the pews, or the monuments that lined the walls. As she crossed the chequered floor Georgiana only had eyes for the man she saw standing patiently by the altar in the shadow of the three-deck pulpit

– John Henderson. To ensure that her parents had no opportunity to upset their plans Henderson most probably purchased a special marriage licence, removing the need for the banns to be read on three consecutive Sundays prior to the ceremony. Georgiana must have had mixed feelings. Yes, she was marrying the man she loved, but there were no family members or friends to witness the event. The couple returned to Henderson's home in the Adelphi. Georgiana gave the coachman a letter and instructed him to return to Charlotte Street and place it in the hands of her father.

At 12 pm after an enjoyable breakfast where they could choose: 'Chocolate, Coffee and Tea, Plumb Cake, Pound Cake, Hot Rolls, Cold Rolls, Bread and Butter, and dry toast', Keate read his daughter's letter and his world changed for ever. Both Georgiana's mother and father declared 'themselves, as never having a child'.

Joseph Farington was told, when he came to call at the Adelphi on 10th June 1796 about the upcoming Westminster Election, that Henderson had already voted as 'he had run away with a lady, and did not think proper to deny himself as He did not know who of her friends might call'. The lady in question, Henderson added, was 'Miss Keate'. In light of her parent's reaction to his proposal Henderson most probably decided it would be better to lie low until Keate's anger had cooled. Dr Carmichael Smyth, and other friends, were unable to effect a reconciliation and Georgiana's parents packed up their daughter's 'cloaths, even including Dolls & childish playthings', and had them sent to her new home in the Adelphi. Keate became the subject of gossip as he continued to 'go about describing Henderson and his daughter's conduct in the most unfavourable manner'. Georgiana's mother was equally incensed; William Bryne, the engraver, was told 'not to mention the name of Mrs Henderson before Mrs Keate' when he visited Charlotte Street. Bryne had encouraged Georgiana's father to consider that his daughter might have 'married a man of indifferent character and of no property', after all 'such a thing might have been'. Henderson was a respectable man with about £1600 a year, had settled £500 a year on her, and had told Georgiana's father that he 'desired no settlement on Miss Keate during Mr Keate's life, having sufficient to support her, but that... after his death allow his fortune to go to Miss Keate and Her Heirs'.

Bryne was 'of the opinion that were Mrs Keate out to the Question he would soften' as he thought Keate was 'struck with some part of their conversation', but in the end he was unsuccessful in his attempt at a rapprochement.

Two months after the wedding Georgiana's father asked Richard Duppa, who had come to breakfast at Charlotte Street, 'to carry a message to Plott, which was that Mr Keate never desired to see him within his doors again, or to see his face'. A fortnight later Keate's servant called and told him that he had been charged 'never to admit Plott should he come to the House' as he had known about the couple's plans and had done nothing to stop them. Mutual friends were put in a difficult position. When a 'Lady from the Country called she was told her that 'she could not see Mrs Keate unless she would promise not to call on Mrs Henderson'. Six copies by Plott of the miniature portrait he had painted of the recently deceased David Alves Rebello, were returned to him by the family. He asked them if the 'Keates had seen and being answered Yes, he said he then understood the matter'. That August Georgiana's father wrote to apologise to his old friend, the naturalist Thomas Pennant, for the tardiness of his reply but Pennant's letters had arrived 'at a time when an only child...in whom so many hopes were placed, and whose talents, whose education, whose expectations, might have entitled her to fill any station enounced [sic] her parental ties and clandestinely threw herself into the arms of one of the last men' he 'could have wished to have seen her united with'. The *True Briton* reported in January 1797 that, 'Mr George Keate so well known in the literary world, is at present employed on the subject of parental duty, which he intends to submit to the world quite in a new light. The rancour continued. Georgiana's mother 'endeavoured to prevent a nurse from attending Mrs H[enderson]' when she was six months pregnant. By March 1797 the newspapers began 'to hint at the conduct of Mr & Mrs Keate' and Henderson expressed concern to Farington 'as it can do no good'. He added that he will so 'conduct himself that His Children shall have no cause to say He was in the way of their interest'.

On 14th April 1797 Georgiana gave birth to her first child, apparently without any difficulties. She hoped that this news would heal the rift with her parents, particularly as Henderson had written to her father to ask him to name their first child, but as they received no reply the Hendersons named their son, John. At the end of June Georgiana heard that her father had 'expired suddenly at breakfast'. With this news she lost any chance of a reconciliation with her parents, as her mother blamed Georgiana for his death.

28 Rent asunder every tie

The poet Hannah More wrote to her friend Mrs Garrick on 6th September 1797 that 'poor Keate I see by the papers is dead'. She hoped that he had 'first reconciled to his daughter' as they had been 'for some weeks made all the talk of Bristol. War and taxes, they say have been a while forgotten'. However, this reunion never took place and Keate and Georgiana continued to be the subject of gossip.

There isn't a record of the funeral but it is unlikely that Mrs Keate welcomed her daughter to the event. On reading Keate's will we find that Georgiana's name does not appear until the bottom of page two. Firstly, he dealt with bequests to his friends, and servants still in his employ. Secondly, he then instructed his wife to 'fix up with proper permission…as near as convenient to the place of my internment a Monument of Marble with such English inscription thereon as she shall approve'. He added that this was to be erected within fifteen months of his death, and to be 'sufficiently large as to admit of such Memorial as some surviving friend of my dear wife may be disposed to pay to her dignified character'. Mrs Keate fulfilled his request and erected a fine monument on the wall of All Saints, Isleworth – the church in which her late husband had been baptised sixty-eight years earlier. Under a medallion likeness, sculptured by her husband's friend and Royal Academician Joseph Nollekens, the text described Keate in glowing terms, as an 'elegant Historian of pure and simple Manners' whose 'literary Compositions both in Verse and Prose give Evidence of his Genius.' This 'author of Works of Fancy, Gay Sentimental, Tender; his imagination in its freest sallies paid respect to these decorums the sense of which was ever so conspicuous in his private life', the memorial continued. It was destroyed in 1943, along with the church, by a fire set by two boys.

Finally, Keate mentions his daughter, 'Georgiana Jane Keate the wife of John Henderson now living in the Adelphi'. In spite of proving to be 'a thankless child [who had] fled disgracefully from her parental roof to give her hand to a man whose principles and whose manners she well knew I abhorred, and whose unfeeling gratitude to the most affectionate of mothers had rent asunder every tie between us', she should receive an annuity from his estate. He instructed his Trustees to 'keep in their hands...a sum of Money' to provide an annual payment of 'one hundred pounds, payable quarterly'. This was a testimony of his forgiveness, and in hope that the goodness of providence 'may one day bring back her heart to the sentiments of truth and virtue' in which she was raised 'with such unremitting attention'. Philip Le Geyt had always 'appeared to pay to his worthy parents the filial duty and affection', that was their due which led Keate to instruct his executors to bequeath the residue of his personal estate to this son of his old friends Robert and Jane Le Geyt. Georgiana's father hoped that this symbol of excellence would not 'suffer the bad examples of the world to lessen [his affection] but Cherish it as the Guardian of his own happiness and the most likely means of calling down the blessing of God on his future life'. As this benefaction would only come to Philip after Mrs Keate's death he was to receive £50, and his parents £1100 each, in the meantime. We can imagine Georgiana's father would have been equally generous to Maria Le Geyt, the 'most amiable accomplished and only daughter' of his old friends, if she had not died at the age of nineteen, a year after their meeting at Canterbury in 1794. Family friends were saddened at this example of Keate's continuing admonishment of his daughter.

Keate also wrote that in thanks for 'her unbounded affection to me and in grateful Remembrance of those endearing virtues which have so much graced and adorned her own life', he wife would have full power to dispose of any of his 'pictures, books, jewels, medals or curiosities', as she wished.

Just over a year after her father's death, and eighteen months after the birth of her son, Georgiana had her second child, a daughter this time. Aware that cases of typhoid and TB were rising in the city, and maybe also to get away from the gossip, Henderson decided, in 1799, to leave the Adelphi and take his wife, who was pregnant again, and young family to Hadley, near Barnet. Although only eleven miles from London this Georgian resort offered fresh country air and a more conducive atmosphere in which to raise his children. The Henderson family moved into 'White Lodge', a fine house that still stands opposite the parish church of St Mary the Virgin. As she entered through the front door Georgiana may have noticed the frowning face of a moustachioed man incorporated into the elaborately carved door case. This conceit of the 18th century craftsman belied the welcome of the house. Although not as fine as the Adam interiors she had previously enjoyed White Lodge was elegant, as well as homely. When they sat down to dinner they could see the adze marks, left by workmen, in the heavy cross beams supporting the ceiling. Hay packed tightly under the floorboards of the upper rooms and a large open fireplace ensured that the family were warm and cosy during the long, cold winter months. A large informal garden ran alongside the stables behind the house and provided a pleasant area for Georgiana to continue her daily walks.

On 29th November 1799 Georgiana gave birth to her second daughter and, perhaps in an effort to build bridges, she named the child Jane Catherine, after her mother.

29 Any other husband

Georgiana's mother did not respond to this attempt at a reconciliation and a few months later she died. Two of Keate's 'most valued' friends, Martin Fonnereau and William Pitt, also acted as executors for Mrs Keate. She honoured her late husband's directives to leave Philip Le Geyt the sum of £2,000 and to remember their two loyal servants, if they were still in her employ. The coachman James Barlow received £10 and £12 went to the footman William Grills. Mrs Boyer, who had nursed the young Georgiana, was left £10 'for the care she had taken'. The executors were instructed to put the money in Mrs Boyer's hands - it was not, she stipulated, on any account to be given to her husband. It is likely that Mrs Boyer had been employed as a wet nurse as upper class women did not breastfeed at this time. Although she was not talking to her daughter it would appear that Jane Keate was aware of the daily comings and goings in the Henderson household for she noted in her will that Mrs Boyer was, or had lately been, living with her daughter.

Georgiana's mother instructed her executors to sell whatever land and property was needed to meet the nearly £16,000 cost of the bequests and annuities she had made. The accumulation of rents from the remaining property on the Fossan estate at Spitalfields was to be paid to her daughter, for 'sole, separate and peculiar use and benefit' but, she added, if Georgiana didn't accept the condition that her husband had no control over this money, then the executors were to place the income into a trust for Georgiana's children by 'any other husband than her present'. The executors had to arrange for 'An act...to sell the...tenements...for investing the...purchase monies...and also for authorizing the granting of Building and Repairing leases, until Sale', passed in 1805, to fulfil this instruction. In her own will Georgiana expressed her sense of injustice at the exclusion of her husband and children from the inheritance of the northern and eastern parts of Spitalfields which had been in the Keate family since 1676. It had originally been acquired by her paternal grandfather although the houses, were of the poorest quality. In fact, these 17th century buildings were in such an appalling condition that Georgiana's father had to arrange for their reconstruction. However, he did nothing to improve the quality of the structures and they gradually fell into decline and, over time, it became an area of disrepute.

Georgiana's mother identified the three married daughters of Keate's mentor, the former agent for the Duke of Bedford, Robert Palmer, as particular beneficiaries in her will. Mrs George Beauchamp was left the portraits of Georgiana's mother and father, painted by John Russell R.A,. together with a blue and white Worcester dessert service. The breakfast set of Frankfurtan china, with a glass cover, which had been sent to Georgiana's father from Charles Theodore, late Elector of Palatine, as an example of his manufactory, went to Mrs Holland Edwards, together with the little inlaid table on which it stood. She also received a set of Dorset agate handles for knives and forks and a miniature of her late father, while the Arabesque breakfast service, from the late Queen Marie Antoinette's Sevres porcelain factory, went to Lady Beauchamp Proctor. Their brother, Richard Palmer, was not forgotten. Georgiana's mother left him a bronze of two centaurs, based on an original in Rome.

Her executors were also rewarded. As well as a sum of £1200, William Pitt received a small miniature of the young George Keate, an ivory vase carved with the figures of Silverius and Famio; two white marble ewers featuring a satyr and a water nymph; and Jane Keate's (now lost) portrait by her old friend Angelica Kauffmann. His wife, Mary was given an oval papier-mâché snuff box set in gold. Martin Fonnereau received £1200, plus a wax medallion by Isaac Gosset, the painting of the *Monument in Arcady* by Angelica Kauffman; two paintings by John Russell RA including one described as a 'child and dog' – perhaps this was a portrait of the young Georgiana, and the finely bound volume of Keate's Grand Tour drawings. However, as Georgiana's eldest son left this volume to the British Museum it would appear that Fonnereau declined this part of the bequest. He may have felt that Georgiana had been treated unfairly and that these drawings should not go out of the family. Fonnereau's wife, Charlotte, was left an agate cup on a silver gilt stand. Both executors were also invited to take 'such of the drawings of George Keate' as they wished, but we have no idea how many and the subject matter of those they may have selected.

It would appear that the family lawyer, Richard White shared Keate's passion for Shakespeare. Together with the last edition of Shakespeare's works edited by George Steevens he received the inkstand from Shakespeare's Mulberry tree, with the earnest hope, she wrote, that 'he will preserve it in remembrance' of her dear husband. In addition, she also left him a small enamelled picture of her father-in-law, the lava table from the back parlour, drawings and pictures by Antonio Zucchi, the bust of the young Bacchus by Joseph Nollekens, and all the books and pamphlets on law and politics. Other old friends remembered in the will were the 56 year-old actress Jane Pope, who received the fine edition of Shakespeare edited by Sir Thomas Hanmer, and her sister Susan Pope was also included, with a bequest of £20.

Georgiana's mother made the largest bequests to Dr Carmichael Smyth and his family. Although the Keates had fallen out with John Plott following Georgiana's marriage, they had kept the portrait miniatures he had painted of them. This were left to Mrs Smyth, together with a memorandum book with agate cover set in gold with a gold pencil, and her choice of any of her jewels, trinkets, china, fur, etc. The eldest daughter, Maria, received a gold filigree smelling bottle; a small cornelian egg set in gold, a silver inkstand, and an enamelled watch with the chain and trinkets belonging to it, which, Jane Keate wrote, had been a present from her late husband, and which Georgiana may have expected to inherit. The second daughter, Georgiana Smyth, was given two little blue and gold glass bottles with gold tops in a shagreen case, an amber bonbon box and a gold repeating watch, £5,000, together with the interest from a further £5,000 to be invested by the executors was left to Dr Smyth and as a further slight to Georgiana, the interest from this investment would then go to Maria, who had always behaved in a dutiful and loving manner. Maria would have to marry with her parents' consent to qualify but if she remained unmarried, or died, then this income would be paid into a trust for the benefit of the remaining Smyth children to claim on their twenty-first birthdays.

Georgiana must have been heartbroken. Instead of passing on personal portraits and items to her daughter they were sent out of the family. Both her parents had emphasised the filial duty and respect paid by their friend's children, unlike their own 'thankless child'.

30 Rather a brilliance of talents

After Mrs Smyth had made her choice, as directed in Mrs Keate's will, the executors put the house with the remaining contents up for sale. Skinner & Dyke, issued tickets to potential buyers to look over the property before the auction, which took place at Garraway's Coffee House in Cornhill on Friday 13th June 1800. The accompanying catalogue highlighted the 'costly Marble Chimney Pieces, ornamented and painted Cielings [sic], Mahogany Doors', and informed the reader that the whole building had been 'improved and enlarged by the late Proprietor at a very considerable Expence'. The rent from numbers 38 to 43 Wimpole Street, Cavendish Square, with their respective offices, back courts, coach houses and stabling, totalling £120 p.a., which Georgiana's father had leased from the Duke of Portland, were included in the sale. The lease on the Charlotte Street house still had 71 years to run.

With the building sold the auctioneers turned their attention to the contents. The first day saw the sale of the seventeen books of prints, which included *The Tudor Family* after the pictures by Holbein...*The Views of Venice* by Canaletto, and Hogarth's *Works,* together with a large collection of drawings, maps and miniatures. The sale moved into the drawing-room to sell the paintings on the wall, including pictures by Thomas Gainsborough and Paul Sandby, together with architectural drawings by Robert Adam. The majority of these works were sold for between £2 and £20 but 'a very highly finished and capital picture of Flowers' by the 17th century female Dutch artist, Rachel Ruysch, fetched £66.3s and Zoffany's painting of *Mr Garrick and Mrs Pritchard, in a scene from Macbeth*, went for £23.12s.

The next day the buyers were back to bid on the remaining china, plate, linen, bronzes, carvings and many scarce antique objects, although the library and natural history collections were excluded from this general sale. As well as the 'handsome chimney glass...ornamented with paintings', located in the museum room, the auctioneers took bids on 'a blue silk parasol'. We can imagine the young Georgiana making use of this accessory to protect her delicate skin from the bright sunlight on her walks along Gower Street. On the third, and last, day the auctioneers went from room to room selling the bedsteads and mattresses, stoves and tables, mirrors and commodes, carpets and curtains. The 'Butler's Pantry' yielded 'a neat bronzed tea urn', a caddy, sugar canisters, coffee pot and cutlery. Even the kitchen was not immune from this wholesale clear out with the copper boiling pots, fish kettles, baking tins, 'blamonge moulds', chopping boards and storage boxes all put up for sale. The auction finished in the wash house and yard, with bids sought for the ironing board, clothes beater, clothes horse, 'tressels' and wash tubs, while the wine from the cellar was sold at a dozen bottles a time.

A week later, on 23rd June 1800, the bidders once again flocked to Charlotte Street, this time for the auction of 'the Elegant and Valuable Collection of Books of George Keate, Esq...(deceased)'. It took three days for the auctioneer, Mr King of Covent Garden, to dispose of nearly 700 lots ranging from English, French and German grammars to works by Voltaire and various editions of Keate's own published poems. Although the 'elegantly bound' volume of Robert Adam's *Ruins of the Palace of the Emperor Diocletian at Spalatro* appears in the sale catalogue we know that Georgiana's son would later present this book to the British Museum, so it would appear that either Henderson brought it for his wife or perhaps Georgiana had asked for it to be removed from the auction. At the beginning of 1801 there was a further auction. This time it was held at Sothebys in Covent Garden, and the lots were composed of the Greek, Roman, English and Foreign Coins and Medals that Georgiana's father had collected during his lifetime. The sale raised over £400 (around £13,000 today).

It was most probably the death of her parents that saw Georgiana's return to London at the end of 1801. As no.4 Adelphi Terrace was now the home of their friends, Sir Brook and Lady Watson, Henderson looked elsewhere and found a house for them in Devonshire Street, just off the grandest road in 18th century London – Portland Place. We know from her surviving diary for 1802 that, although heavily pregnant with her fourth child, Georgiana took an active part in preparing her late father's natural history collection for auction. She records going to Beaufort Buildings, just off the Strand, where the collection had been put in storage after the sale of her parental home in Charlotte Street, 'to take off the names of the donors from the shells'. Georgiana doesn't say why this was necessary but perhaps it was to prevent embarrassment, or any problems of ownership, when these items came under the hammer. She spent many hours cleaning, organising and labelling the objects but still made time for her children. She also fitted in social calls and shopping trips, buying shoes for her young son, a small writing box for herself, and on a visit to Wedgwoods' showroom in St James's Square, she purchased a small water basin. Many happy evenings were passed making 'patty pans', little scalloped shaped cakes, for her family and friends.

Georgiana regularly returned to Beaufort Buildings to get everything ready for the auction. She sought advice on the best method of cleaning the insect displays and sent her maid to dust the cases. Her intimate knowledge of the shells, marbles, jewels and curiosities that had once been displayed in her late father's museum made her the best person to write up the lots for the sale catalogue. Mr King commissioned four copies to be printed on fine paper. He kept two for his own use, a third copy went to an old friend of Georgiana's father, the physician Sir George Baker, who had attended King George III during his periods of madness, and the last copy was presented to Henderson, 'who married the only daughter of George Keate'.

Even though she felt unwell Georgiana was determined to see this work through, even though she knew that her parents had not bequeathed any of the proceeds for her use. Henderson, concerned about her condition, arranged for their bed to be moved into the drawing room so that she did not have to climb the stairs. The obstetrician, Dr John Clarke, attended Georgiana during this last stage of her pregnancy. Described as energetic and efficient, Clarke also possessed 'an acuteness of perception superior to most of his competitors, and rather a brilliance of talents'. Taught by the great Dr John Hunter, Clarke would enliven his own lectures with colourful anecdotes, like the story of one private company that would sometimes bury two women in one coffin to conceal the high death rate, when puerperal fever swept through the lying-in hospitals. At half past six on the morning of Friday 19th March 1802 Georgiana sent for Clarke, and four hours later she gave birth to her third daughter. Her other children were allowed to visit 'for a few minutes to see their little sister'. With his wife confined to bed Henderson would spend his evenings in her room, although Georgiana doesn't tell us what he read to her during this time. Dr Clarke called every day and by Friday she was able to get up and 'lay on the side of the bed', and gradually Georgiana got back into her normal routine, and was able to go out ten days after giving birth. She bought lamps to decorate their house in celebration of the signing of the Treaty of Amiens, which temporarily ended hostilities between Great Britain and France. On the morning of Tuesday 30th March Georgiana went to the auction rooms 'to put out things for the sale' but she discovered that Mr King was holding a sale of books, so she had to return in the afternoon to carry out this task and she didn't arrive home until 9pm, when she had a flounder for her dinner. She discovered that the children had already been to see the Illuminations in Portland Place and instructed that their own lamps should be lit. As she was still recovering from her recent confinement Georgiana asked Henderson to go to King's to ensure everything was ready for the public viewing. Prices ranged widely for the 1224 lots originating from exotic locations such as Barbados, South America, the Galapagos Islands, New Zealand, Australia, India, China and the South Seas, as well as the United Kingdom. One very rare shell fetched £5 2s 6d, while specimens purchased by Georgiana's father from the sale of the Duchess of Portland's cabinet were sold for nine guineas. Although the lots mainly featured shells there were also curiosities that the bidders could acquire, such as the nest of a humming bird or a hornet, asbestos from Scotland, sea urchins from the Bahamas, 'elegant Chinese feathered fans', and the rattle of a rattlesnake. The complete skeleton of the blue porgy fish from Bermuda reached £8 but the most expensive item was the egg of the emu, or cassowary, which sold for £15 6s. Among the gems and other curious articles offered were crystal models of three large and famous diamonds, including one that had once belonged to the late Empress of Russia, Catherine the Great. The last day saw the sale of the cabinets which Robert Adam had specially designed to house Keate's collections. Even though she had been excluded from her parents' wills Georgiana appears to have gone to great efforts to ensure that this auction went well.

One particular item in the catalogue provides an insight into her father's friendships before his daughter was born. 'A land tarapoin, with 2 of its eggs laid while in Mr Keate's possession', which fetched six shillings, was most probably a gift from Mrs Eliza Pinckney. He had met the American agricultural innovator and her husband after they came to England in 1753. This may have been during the season in Bath, which they both frequented, or in London, but wherever it was they quickly became firm friends. Shortly after her return to South Carolina, Eliza wrote to Keate to apologise for her long silence which had been 'occasioned by the heaviest stroak [sic] of affliction that could be supported by a poor mortal'. She was referring to the death of her husband Charles and, she asked Keate, 'if you upon a 5 years acquaintance loved and lament him, what must I do that knew him long and intimately!' She extolled his virtues, his 'sweetness of temper and his good sense added to his partiality and uncommon tenderness and affection…a harmony…which never was interrupted by the least domestick Jarr [sic], or one word in anger the whole time (for more than 14 year)'. She had been 'his happy wife'. She thanked Keate for his 'most humane and friendly letters'. 'They confirmed', she said, 'that the tenderness and condolence of friendship soften and alleviate, tho' nothing…can heal the wound'. It had given her comfort to hear of his kindness to her 'poor dear boys', who were at boarding school in England. 'Tis Generous and kind in you, Sir', she continued, 'to countenance those dear remains of your deceased friend, young, inexperienced, fatherless, and in a strange Country as they are'.

Although it is possible that the two friends never met again they continued to write to each other throughout the years until Eliza's death in 1793. Indeed, the last known letter from her pen was addressed to her 'much valued friend Mr Keate'. She could hear his voice as she read the poems in the 'elegant edition' he had sent her and, she added, it brought to mind the many happy hours they had spent together with her 'ever dear Mr Pinckney'. She sent him a 'thousand, thousand thanks' for his 'goodness to my dear Daniel' and her children sent him and Mrs Keate 'their affectionate respect'. However, 'compliments is too cold a word', she added and asked him instead to give her 'love to Mrs Keate'. As it was common practice for people in the colonies to send live turtles (American term for tortoises) to their friends in England, it is very likely that the 'tarapoin', described in the sale catalogue, was a gift from Eliza. We don't know when it arrived in Keate's collection but Georgiana would have known the story behind this gift, and may even have seen it when it was still alive. Georgiana's father, no doubt, encouraged his daughter to take note of the excellence qualities possessed by Eliza and apply them to her own life.

Over one thousand pounds (around £50,000 today) was raised from the sale, which ran over twelve days.

31 Retiring into the country

Georgiana must have had mixed emotions as she prepared the lots for the auction. From a very young age her father would have told her stories about these objects that she saw, and most probably, handled as she grew up at Charlotte Street. However, these happy childhood memories had been soured by her parents' reaction to her marriage. The sale confirmed that the opportunity of a reconciliation with them was now lost for ever. We can imagine that she must have been emotionally drained and it is unlikely that she attended the sale but perhaps she sent Henderson along to report on proceedings. Mourning the loss of her parents, dealing with the arrangements for the auction and recovering from the birth of her fourth child, Georgiana had to oversee the preparations for another move away from the polluted air and oppressive fogs of London. It was no place to raise a young family and Georgiana, like many other parents, would have agreed with the philosopher, Jean Jacques Rousseau, that it was better for children to live in close harmony with nature. Henderson found a suitable home for them in the town of Chertsey, where several of their friends already had properties. They dispatched their maid, Molly, to get the house ready Georgiana sent 'Snuggs to Chertsey'. Joseph Snuggs, a silk mercer based in Chandos Street, Covent Garden, renowned for presenting customers with a cup of chocolate on cold winter days, was probably commissioned by Georgiana to provide the curtains and soft furnishings, ready for their arrival.

Before they left London she helped Henderson select nearly 100 items from his art collection to send to auction. Maybe there wouldn't be enough room in their new home or he may have wanted to increase his funds to support his growing family. The sale of 'a valuable and choice collection of Modern Pictures and...Drawings, the property of a Gentleman retiring into the country...' took place at Christie's Great Room, Pall Mall, at 12pm on Saturday 17th April 1802. As well as forty or more of his own paintings and drawings, the items on offer featured works by J.M.W. Turner and Thomas Girtin, who he had met at his neighbour's house in the Adelphi before his marriage to Georgiana, and a view of *The Royal Terrace from the River Thames* by William Marlow. Prices ranged from five shillings to just over six pounds, with the exception of George Morland's 'spirited picture' of dogs which made £9 9s and a now lost painting by Wright of Derby, *Inside an Italian Stable*, described as in his best style, which fetched over £13.

A month later they were finally ready to move. With the help of the nanny Georgiana spent the morning of Sunday 16th May packing. The following day they left Devonshire Street at half past twelve. Georgiana was in one chaise with her three older children, while the new baby, together with the nurse and cook travelled in another. Three hours later Abbey House came into view. They passed through a pair of large iron gates onto the circular gravel road that encased the front lawn, and led their carriages to the front door of this hundred-year-old building. While the servants dealt with the luggage Georgiana and her children climbed the broad flight of stone steps and entered a large hall, with a black and white marble chequerboard floor and a grand staircase to one side. Opposite the entrance another set of doors led to an inner hall with a library on the right and a parlour on the left. Ahead was a glazed door that opened onto another broad flight of stone steps that led down to the garden. To help the children settle Georgiana decided to sleep in the nursery that evening.

After breakfast the following morning she took the children into the garden, with its large central lawn bordered by leafy walks, and when Henderson arrived that afternoon they extended their walk to investigate the groves which framed the pleasing vista of open countryside beyond the terraced wall which separated their formal garden from the natural landscape. Thanks to an earlier occupant, the poet Thomas Love Peacock who spent his childhood here, we know the delights that the grounds at Abbey House offered Georgiana and her family. The pleasant grove on the right hand side had sloping banks covered with flowery turf, whereas the one on the left was known as the 'dark grove' because the trees were so tightly packed their canopies prevented the grass growing underneath. Peacock recalled that on one summer evening, when the air was full of the scent of the jasmine that covered the back wall of the house, he saw 'something like the white head dress of a tall figure advance from...the dark grove...and after a brief interval recede from view. Presently it appeared again, and again vanished'. He ran into the parlour and told all there that there was a ghost. Everyone came out to see this apparition and conjectured what it could be until 'at last, the master of the house leading the way', they 'marched in a body to the spot and unravelled the mystery'. The 'ghost' was a large bunch of flowers, on the top of a tall lily, at the edge of the grove waving in the wind and disappearing at intervals behind the trunk of a tree. No record survives to let us know if Georgiana and her children saw this 'ghost', but it is unlikely that anyone felt the need to wander in the 'dark grove' at night.

At six o'clock on Tuesday evening the carts with the rest of their belongings finally arrived. Henderson, with the help of the land agent Bowyer and their servant William unloaded all the boxes and packages and put them in the hall ready for Georgiana to begin unpacking the following day.

32 Breathing tranquillity

Georgiana unpacked the luggage and boxes that had been left in the hall, helped by her housemaid she gave the glassware into the care of her footman William and the Yellowware bowls and jugs were sent down to the cook for use in the kitchen. The following day she spent arranging everything in all the different rooms before taking the children out for their walk. On her return Georgiana 'made some loose sleeves to fix to gowns', perhaps to protect her dress before starting work on the lumber and store rooms. Finally, she unpacked her own clothes and put them away before gathering together all the bed linen, curtains and covers for a 'Great Wash'.

Nearly two weeks later Georgiana felt ready to welcome visitors to her new home. Twenty-two-year old Benjamin Lewis Vulliamy arrived on a very wet day at the end of May and after showing him around Abbey House Georgiana, with her husband and guest, dined for the first time in their dining parlour. As a partner in the family firm, and son, of the King's clockmaker Vulliamy would often stay with the family when he had to attend to the clocks at Windsor Castle. They obviously all got on well together because Vulliamy dallied over his breakfast on Monday 28th June and missed his coach back to London. The following morning Georgiana got up before six o'clock to make Vulliamy's meal so that he wouldn't miss the stage again. He repaid this kindness by bringing sugar plums for her children and he also made a hobby or 'galloping horse' for Georgiana's son on his next visit. Vulliamy developed a considerable reputation as a clockmaker and, as a result, the architect Sir Charles Barry invited him to submit a design for the clock tower for the new Palace of Westminster. However, the Astronomer Royal, Sir George Airy put the task out to tender and gave the contract to make what would be the largest clock in the world, and known to us today as 'Big Ben', to Edward Dent and his firm.

Another early house guest was Georgiana's friend Annabella Norford. Whereas Georgiana was an only child, Anabella's father, a medical doctor practising in Bury St Edmunds, had at least 12 children from two marriages, although other records suggest that the number is nearer 26. When their father died in 1793 Annabella and her sister Marianne, erected a memorial expressing 'the united testimony of their love and veneration' for their recently deceased father. This tablet also records the deaths of three of their brothers, all 'prematurely cut off' in their mid 20s and that of a fourth killed in action in the East Indies.

We don't know the circumstances of their first meeting as there is no mention of Annabella in Georgiana's diary for 1794, however, they must have met soon after this date as a print, signed in Georgiana's married name, of *A Devonshire Bull in the possession of Charles Thomas Hudson Esq of Wanlip, Leicestershire* carries the statement that the original had been painted by Annabella in 1800. Georgiana's engraving appeared as an illustration in *History of Leicester* by John Nichols. With their family connection Georgiana may have encouraged her cousin Charles Thomas Hudson (changed his surname to Palmer when he married) to 'sit' for her friend as the figure standing beside the bull is more finely dressed than a common herdsman. This image does suggest that the two women were friends although Georgiana's entry in her diary for Friday 4th January 1802 is quite formal, 'Miss Norford breakfasted with us'. Later in the year Georgiana uses her friend's Christian name to record her arrival in Chertsey by the morning stage on 4th June. She had come to stay with the Henderson family for a couple of weeks and Georgiana took great delight in showing her around the house and gardens. Henderson joined them on their regular walks down to Chertsey Bridge and along the riverside for a mile or so until they reached the ferry at Laleham, or over the meadows to Weybridge. They also travelled by post chaise to Hampton with the intention of calling on Mrs Garrick but, as she was not at home, they had to content themselves with showing Annabella the house and grounds, with which they were quite familiar.

Georgiana also took her friend to another favourite place, St Ann's Hill about a mile west of Abbey House. Once they had negotiated the lower wooded slopes they came to an almost level walk, terminating in two venerable elms, at the top of this 250ft eminence. The prospect has been described as 'wonderfully extensive' and the Thames showed itself to great advantage, 'making a bold sweep to approach Chertsey Bridge, and intersecting the plain with its various meanders. The counties of Surrey, Middlesex, Buckingham and Berkshire were laid out before them and on a clear day they would see not only Windsor Castle but also the dome of St Paul's Cathedral in the city of London.

St Ann's Hill belonged to the former courtesan and mistress of the Prince of Wales, Elizabeth Armistead. She shared a platonic friendship with the gambler, womaniser and politician Charles James Fox for nearly a decade before the pair became lovers. It was obvious that Fox was smitten. He wrote: 'I have examined myself and know that I can better abandon friends, country, everything than live without Liz'. She sold her London houses and annuities to help relieve his debts and the couple retired to her modest villa on St Ann's Hill where she introduced Fox to the joys of domestic life. He wrote to his nephew: 'I think my affection for her increases every day. She is a comfort to me in every misfortune and makes me enjoy doubly every pleasant circumstance of life. There is to me a charm and delight in her society which time does not in the least wear off, and for real goodness of heart if she ever had an equal she certainly never had a superior'. They secretly married in 1795 and Fox increasingly spent more and more time away from Parliament to be with his wife. Their days were filled with reading, gardening and exploring the nearby countryside. This was the place, wrote the poet Samuel Rogers, where Fox 'most loved to be. In his own fields – breathing tranquility'.

Georgiana and Henderson must have shared this sentiment as they often took their friends to see the grounds, the greenhouse filled with scented flowers and plants, and the dairy with its white tiles edged in green. They most probably strolled with Annabella through the romantic avenue of trees at the bottom of the garden to show her the grotto, with its Gothic arches and chinoiserie, or Chinese style, staircase leading to the upper floor, before moving on to the Temple of Friendship and the teahouse. Statues were scattered around the grounds to provide a classical air to the whole scene. On the extreme western side of the hill stood an old beech tree where Fox had erected a bench around its trunk. This was his favourite spot. He would visit it nearly every day to take the morning air and, on occasion, he would bathe in the waters of the nearby river Bourne.

Annabella was, like Georgiana, a gifted amateur artist. During the course of her visit, when Georgiana was busy with the children, she went out on her own to paint the local scenery. She took a view of Chertsey Green as well as the nearby farmyard belonging to Benjamin Elcock. We know from Georgiana's diary that Annabella also drew a [now lost] picture of five-year old John. When it was time for Annabella to leave Georgiana and Henderson joined her in the coach for London. After they said their goodbyes Georgiana went shopping and then to Southampton Street to spend the night at her mother-in-law's house. The following morning, she walked to Bond Street to buy a gown and some books for the children and then called at Barkers for sponge cake and raspberry vinegar. After dinner the couple were accompanied by Henderson's mother, who was keen to see their new home, for their journey to Chertsey.

With its fresh air and countryside, yet close enough to London to visit when necessary, Chertsey certainly appears to have been the perfect place for Georgiana to raise her young family.

33 I am related to Kings

With Henderson searching for a suitable home in Chertsey for his family Georgiana took the opportunity to reply to a letter from her cousin James Smithson. He may have been enquiring about the forthcoming natural history sale as he had shared an interest in mineralogy. She would have welcomed him when he called at Charlotte Street to see her father's museum and they would have discussed the exhibits and exchange specimens. Unlike Georgiana's father he had no desire to pursue knowledge in the tradition of the gentleman amateur, he was seriously committed to a scientific life amd at the age of twenty-two, he had been elected a Fellow of the prestigious Royal Society of London. His letter may also have referred to his research into zinc ores and his recent discovery of a new mineral – later named Smithsonite in honour of its finder. Georgiana responded positively and invited him to call at their lodgings in Portland Place.

A couple of weeks later he visited again. He took his tea, with Georgiana and Henderson, in her room so that he could look over the Hungerford papers in her possession. Like Georgiana and her father, he had also been the subject of public gossip because his widowed mother, Elizabeth Hungerford Keate Macie, had enjoyed a long affair with the aristocrat Hugh Smithson. When she discovered she was pregnant, she fled to Paris and early in 1764 James Macie was born who became a naturalised British citizen when he and his mother returned to London. Following Elizabeth's death in 1800 James sought, and gained, permission from the Crown to formally change his surname to that of his biological father, who had subsequently married into an aristocratic family and been created the 1st Duke of Northumberland.

Smithson claimed 'the best blood of England flows in my veins; on my father's side I am a Northumberland, on my mother's I am related to Kings'. He visited Georgiana again and, together with Henderson, they spent over three hours deciphering the various documents, to establish their connection to the royal throne. Georgiana and James claimed kinship through the marriage of Sir George Hungerford to Frances Seymour (great grandmother of James and Georgiana's father) and it is through the Seymour line that they could trace their lineage back to Lady Katherine Grey, sister of Lady Jane Grey, Queen of England for nine days. Elizabeth I, had contemplated making Katherine heir to the English throne until news reached her of Katherine's clandestine marriage to Edward Seymour.

Georgiana's father had written about Katherine's sister, the 'sad Victim of relentless power', in his *Epistle from Lady Jane Gray to Lord Guilford* – supposed to have been written in the Tower, a few days before they suffered. Such had been Keate's pride in this connection that he commissioned his old friend John Plott to paint a portrait of the young Queen to illustrate the second volume of his Poetical Works.

It would appear from Georgiana's diary that Smithson didn't visit them at their new home in Chertsey. The recent signing of the Treaty of Amiens, and the resultant cessation of the revolutionary wars in France meant that Smithson could resume his continental travels in search of new minerals and so had no time to see his cousin. His journey took him via Paris through France to Frankfurt. The peace failed after a year but Smithson was able to avoid warring factions until his arrival in Denmark shortly before the Danes declared war on Britain. Seized as a suspected spy and imprisoned in squalid conditions Smithson wrote to Sir Joseph Banks for help in gaining his freedom. Banks responded to his appeal and eighteen months later Napoleon gave formal approval for Smithson's release and his return to London.

We don't know if Georgiana and her cousin corresponded after 1802, or if they ever saw each other again, but we can imagine that she was sorry to learn of his death in the summer of 1829. Unmarried and childless this 'son to Hugh, first Duke of Northumberland & Elizabeth, heiress of the Hungerfords of Studley & niece to Charles the proud Duke of Somerset', as Smithson described himself, had left his whole estate to 'the United States of America, to found in Washington under the name of the Smithsonian Institution, an establishment for the increase and diffusion of knowledge'. Many questioned, no doubt Georgiana among them, why he left just over the equivalent of £12million to somewhere he had never visited, and a country quite unknown to him. He had earlier expressed the thought that 'if the millions of money and the thousands of individuals which are at present sacrificed to war, should be applied to the promotion of sciences and arts, what may we not expect, even in our time'. The appalling impact of the French revolution on his beloved science with the execution of the Antoine Lavoisier and his own travail as a prisoner of war had most probably led Smithson to consider that only a new country, like America, could support his extraordinary vision.

Although he was denied rank and privilege as an illegitimate son of the Duke of Northumberland, Smithson ensured that his name 'shall live in the memory of man'. Sadly a devastating fire at the Smithsonian Institution in 1865 not only destroyed his 'choice and beautiful' mineral collection, considered one of the 'richest and rarest in the country, but also his archives including any correspondence with Georgiana.

A Hungerford/Seymour family tree, written in an unknown hand, has survived in a small cache of papers which have descended down Georgiana's family line, providing a tantalising glimpse into this relationship to 'kings' that was so important to her father and her cousin, James Smithson.

34. Elixir of Life

As her own mother had caused her such anguish Georgiana must have been grateful for the comfort offered by her mother-in-law. Soon after their arrival at Abbey House she showed the 'old Lady', as she called Mrs Henderson, around the family's new home and garden. A few days later John Plott arrived by the morning stage to spend the summer with them.

Georgiana embraced country life. She could be found in the meadow, during the long sunny days of June, helping Henderson with the haymaking. It's unlikely that she took on the hot and sweaty work of scything the swaying grass. Instead she most probably spent her time spreading out the new mown hay with a rake to ensure that it could dry before being stored in their barn. July saw her busy in the fruit garden gathering strawberries, raspberries and other soft fruits. The crops must have been plentiful as she then spent days bottling currants and making raspberry jam and blackcurrant jelly. The Elcock sisters called at Abbey House to ask Georgiana how she 'did her currants' but she doesn't reveal whether she told them her secret. They had picked so many blackcurrants that year, 1802, that Henderson turned his hand to making currant wine, considered to be the 'elixir of life' because, as a stimulant, it had an energizing effect.

During a visit to Windsor, with her friend Miss Allaway to see the alterations being made by George III to the town's famous castle, Georgiana walked over the bridge to Eton. Here she bought some live chickens to join the four she already had at Abbey House, a present from her friend and neighbour, Richard Clark – a former Lord Mayor of London, to provide the family with fresh eggs.

With autumn approaching Georgiana went in search of barberries to supplement her store cupboard. As they are high in pectin she would have used them to thicken her jams and jellies. She might also have dried some of these little red jewel-like berries as they were known to have medicinal value. They could be used to reduce fever and relieve upset stomachs. To ensure that her daughter would know which berries she could, and more particularly, could not eat safely she took Jane with her to clear poisonous fruits from plants in the garden. All her children would have been given this important lesson. As the season progressed Georgiana preserved apricots and, with the help of John Plott who was visiting, made cherry brandy. The whole family were engaged with collecting fallen apples in the orchard during the month of September. Henderson no doubt took the fruit to his brew house to turn these windfalls into cider. At the end of the month Georgiana writes in her diary that she dressed a haunch of venison, we don't know if Henderson had been out shooting, or if she was preparing it for an important guest, but it was certainly a meat that denoted her social status.

Georgiana managed to find time away from harvesting and bottling to spend some time with her young family. In the warm summer sunshine of a late June afternoon Georgiana took five year old John, four year old Georgiana and three year old Jane, for a walk along the nearby riverbank to see the dragonflies dancing over the placid, flowing water. They had such a pleasant time that she took them aboard the Laleham ferry, 'the first time the children were ever on the water', she wrote in her diary. They appeared to have enjoyed the experience as a few weeks later Henderson took his wife and children for a trip along the Abbey river in his punt. This appears to have been a favourite mode of transport as Georgiana records Henderson taking her, and their friends who came to call, out in the punt on several occasions. On one occasion he took them to see the favourite bathing place, at the bottom of St Anne's Hill, of their friend Charles James Fox, and on another he punted for over a mile in the opposite direction until they had reached the mouth of the River Thames. Henderson's mother, together with Plott, went out in the punt on a fishing expedition. We don't know if they were successful and brought something back for the dinner table. However, Georgiana does recall one amusing incidence when her husband failed to balance the punt as she stepped onto land at Laleham and, she writes, he 'nearly fell into the river'.

The garden and meadows at Abbey House offered a delightful environment for Georgiana's regular walks but on a number of occasions she ventured further afield to visit the gardens at the Weybridge home of 'The Grand Old Duke of York', of nursery rhyme fame, and his Duchess. Oatlands had recently been rebuilt in the

Gothic style by the architect Henry Holland. From the top of the slope, on which this little castle stood, visitors could wonder at the glorious panoramic view of the Thames valley laid out before them. The couple then made their way down a gentle slope to see Broadwater lake and the circular temple, loosely based on the one dedicated to Vesta at Tivoli, which had been installed here by the architect William Kent. However, the main attraction, described by the composer Joseph Haydn during a visit in 1791, was 'a most remarkable grotto, which cost £25,000 sterling (equivalent to £2m today), and which was 11 years in the building. It is very large', he said, 'and contains many diversions...actual water flows in from various sides'. Other reports state that it took between five and twelve years to finish and cost nearly £40,000 (equivalent to £3m). Whatever the facts the grotto, at sixty-five feet long and two stories high, was a sight to see. Georgiana took her visitors to see this amazing structure on several occasions. The complicated design gave the impression of great size. The first chamber, described as 'terrifying', with its man-made stalactites covered with little teeth of feltspar hanging from the ceiling and the walls decorated with clams, led on to a short passage made of quartz with constantly changing star patterns laid out in satin spar. This opened out into the Gaming Room. Here stalactites, thickly encrusted with shells, hung from the ceiling while tight patterns of spar decorated the walls. This room also boasted a fireplace, a chandelier and 'Chinese' style chairs made from bamboo. Georgiana saw another passageway beckoning. She entered its looping coils and eventually found herself in a chamber covered in shells. A strange greenish light illuminated the large tiled bath, and the copy of a second century Roman statue of 'Venus de Medici', that occupied this room. Finding that she had completed a circuit of the ground floor spaces Georgiana then climbed the stairs to the upper chamber. By contrast this space had been designed to be light and airy. This was the Duchess of York's favourite room and it was here that she liked to take her meals as well as play with her dogs and monkeys. She loved these animals so much that when they died she arranged for them to be buried just outside the walls of the grotto. It was this Upper Chamber that the Duke of York chose to hold an important celebration supper for the victors of the Battle of Waterloo with the Emperor of Russia as guest of honour. The room must have appeared quite magical with the candlelight reflecting in the mirrors, supported by encrustations of pink and white shells, and bouncing off the white spar stalactites and sconces of crystal which hung under branches of red coral.

Georgiana maintained her social status with visits and dinner invitations. She did not neglect her musical interests and would often play for her guests after they had enjoyed tea or dinner at Abbey House. She even brought a fiddle for her eldest child, John but doesn't record his progress on the instrument. A loving mother, Georgiana continued to take the children for walks either around the garden or meadow or down to the river to watch their father fishing. Young John was given a kite, which he flew with the help of his father, once his grandmother had made a tail for it, while the girls had their dolls and carts to play with. In thanks for their help in looking after her young family Georgiana presented Nurse with a shawl and gave a silk handkerchief to the nanny. John Plott, considered an excellent miniaturist at the time, painted the portraits of Georgiana's son and daughter during his stay at Abbey House. Both children sat at least four times during the summer, and John had additional sittings later in the year. Plott may also have painted portraits of Georgiana and Henderson, but sadly all these paintings are now 'lost'.

As the evenings closed in and a chill entered the air, Georgiana took to indoor pursuits, mending and other jobs around the house, as well as attending to her correspondence. Her diary is full of such matters until Sunday 17th October 1802 when she writes that she did not go to church as she was too busy packing for a trip to Southampton.

35 One of the finest

On the following morning Georgiana left her children in the care of the nanny and, with her husband and the 'wonder of a man to be so fat', John Plott, she boarded the post chaise at 7.00am to travel to Southampton.

As the sun rose Georgiana enjoyed the views as they travelled through the local countryside bathed in early morning light. Their first stop for fresh horses was ten miles out, at the busy staging post of Bagshot. Further changes were made at Murrell Green near Hook in Hampshire and Popham Lane, Basingstoke, where the Wheatsheaf Inn also acted as a postal receiving house. The young Jane Austen frequently walked to this Inn from her family home at Steventon in order to collect their mail. As Georgiana had travelled this route with her father it is tempting to think that the two women may have met on an earlier occasion, but there is no evidence to suggest that they knew each other. After some light refreshment the travellers resumed their seats in the carriage for the next leg of the journey. Four and a half hours after leaving Chertsey they arrived in Winchester, the home of her dear godfather. Plott's sister, Mrs Lydia Lucas, had prepared dinner for them before Georgiana and Henderson set out for Southampton, but their journey was delayed as the coachman couldn't 'get horses for a long time'.

The couple finally arrived in Southampton at 8.00pm. They were surprised to find their eighty-year old host 'Mr Sadlier alone' as he loved entertaining. His gentle and unoffending manner, inexhaustible supply of anecdotes, coupled with his sincere desire to diffuse happiness around him endeared him to a large circle of friends. They delighted in listening to Sadlier express his thoughts – light or serious – in elegant and classical verse. As local and borough magistrate, he was seen as just and candid, without being rigorous or severe, liberal yet free from ostentation, pious though untainted by enthusiasm. Sadlier does not appear to have supported his old friend's disapproval of Georgiana's choice of husband and welcomed the couple into his home. We can imagine that over dinner their conversation turned to memories of earlier times when Georgiana had accompanied her father to Sadlier's home, but it is unlikely she would have welcomed any mention of her parents now. The following morning she walked with Henderson along Southampton's 'long fine street of a quarter mile in length' but they only got as far as the ferry when heavy rain 'obliged' them to turn around. The weather improved over the next few days making it possible for Georgiana to go shopping on what had been described as 'one of the finest high streets in Britain'. She also walked to the market and brought fresh fish which she then sent, as a gift, to Plott who had remained with his sister at Winchester. The better conditions meant that she could walk, with Henderson, the three miles to the village of Redbridge, where they saw the barges plying their trade along the Andover Canal. Another time they walked to Northam on the west bank of the River Itchen, twenty minutes from their host's home. Like the elegant couple in her father's watercolour of 1760, which he later exhibited at the Royal Academy, Georgiana and Henderson most probably took the same path through the wheat field to the gate that led to the riverside, although the ground would have been bare unlike the painting where we see labourers busy stacking the mown grass oblivious to the walkers nearby.

On her return from Redbridge they met one of her former neighbours from Hadley. Miss Hester Mulso who, with her aunt Hester Chapone, the author of conduct books, had moved to the Barnet village around the same time as Georgiana and her family. The two women had maintained their friendship over the years and no doubt they took this opportunity to share memories of the village and of Mrs Chapone, a well-regarded member of the Bluestockings, who had died the previous Christmas at the age of 74.

During their stay Georgiana took Henderson to see the ruins of a medieval Cistercian monastery located about five miles from Southampton. This was another place that had strong links with her father as he had published *The Ruins of Netley Abbey* in 1764. His poem, which pleaded for the preservation of the remains of this Gothic structure, led to visits from dramatists, poets and artists, such as J.M.W. Turner, who filled his sketchbook with drawings. Another artist, Francis Towne captured the luxurious ivy that bent 'its winding Foliage through the cloistered Space'. Did Georgiana recall her father's atmospheric description as she stood beside Henderson in this ancient place:

> While the Breeze whistles through the shattered pile
> Or wave light – dashing murmurs on the Shore
> No other noise in this calm Scene is heard
> No other Sounds these tranquil Vaults molest
> Save the Complainings of some mournful Bird
> That ever loves Solitude to rest

As they left the ruins for the walk home the heavens opened. In spite of the weatherproof qualities of a warm plaid cloak, a present from her husband, it was no match for the October storm and by the time they reached Sadlier's house they were both soaked to the skin.

The following Saturday Henderson decided to take his wife fishing. They sailed to Calshot Castle, at the entrance of Southampton Water where, in sight of the Tudor fort, Georgiana caught two whiting to Henderson's one before returning for dinner at a quarter before five – she doesn't record if their catch formed part of the meal.

Although it could still attract stars of the calibre of Sarah Siddons the local theatre had become so dowdy and run down that fashionable people did not care to attend performances, which may be why no mention is made of it in Georgiana's diary. She would have known it in its heyday as her father was a close friend of John Hoadley, Rector of St Mary's Church Southampton. Known for his loyalty, good humour and personal modesty, Hoadley would encourage acquaintances to take part in amateur dramatics at every opportunity and so it is not surprising to find that he supported the establishment of a theatre in the town. He also encouraged Georgiana's father to write a prologue for the grand opening ceremony in 1766:

> Children ready to be strangled
> Couples fit in love to be entangled
> Traitors that on the Rack never think of Pain
> Virgins oft ravished, that quite chaste remain
> Women, who tho' they are murdered still survive
> And men who bear a stabbing every night

This close connection with her father may also have dampened Georgiana's interest in any dramatic productions that were on at the time of her visit. However, their host made sure that he invited a number of his friends to dinner to provide his visitors with amusing and entertaining company. On Sunday morning Georgiana and Henderson set out for the ancient village of Wickham, about eleven miles away, in response to an invitation from one of her uncle's relations, an Elizabeth Woodcock. Georgiana was delighted to find that the Lee family had also been invited to dinner. During the course of their conversation she learnt from Mrs Lee that their second son had been 'breeched' that day. Now that John was six Georgiana realised, it was time for her to make an appointment with the tailor to measure her son for trousers - no more would he have to wear a dress like his sisters. After an enjoyable meal the couple said their goodbyes and made their way back to Sadlier's home.

They awoke the next day to very wet weather but after breakfast, when 'it had cleared a little', Georgiana took a last walk around the town with Henderson. They made their way down to the West Quay to visit the 'Long Rooms' where the baths were designed to fill and empty with the flow of the tide. Here Georgiana strolled along the indoor promenade with its views over the water, before returning to the house to pack. Sadlier had invited George Pitt, who succeeded his father the following year, as Baron Rivers, to join them for dinner. Pitt would later sell Stratfield Saye House and estate so that it could be given as a gift to the Duke of Wellington from a grateful nation, following the defeat of Napoleon at the Battle of Waterloo. Georgiana and Henderson took their leave of Sadlier after supper as they had to be up early in the morning to catch the coach. 'Set off a quarter before 7, got to Winchester at nine', Georgiana wrote in her diary. As they sat down for breakfast at The George inn on the north side of the High Street, they were joined by John Plott for the return journey to Chertsey. When they stopped at Murrell Green to change horses Georgiana took the opportunity to buy a fresh turkey. In spite of a violent rainstorm they arrived at Abbey House at a quarter before four no doubt glad to be home again.

36 A most useful lesson to youth

The following morning the children helped Georgiana unpack. With everything safely stowed away she joined her husband and godfather to go fishing on the Abbey river. It would appear that the fish weren't biting as she makes no record of their catch. Henderson was a keen angler and Georgiana appears to have shared his passion. She wrote in her diary that, on occasion, they dined early to give them more time on the river. No doubt we would have found a copy of Izaak Walton's *The Compleat Angler* in Henderson's library, and perhaps he also shared the author's preference for a fine, fir-wood tapering pole. These 'light' rods measuring between 15 and 18 feet long, with an 8ft fishing line made of braided horsehair, were usually painted a pale warm gray or greenish tint to blend in with the sky.

It wasn't long before the two of them were on their travels again but this time it was to go shopping in London. They set off on the morning of Wednesday 3rd November 1802. Henderson gave his wife £20 in a banker's draft to settle her bills with several retailers. She also purchased wax candles, dried cherries and a patent silk hat. The couple stayed overnight with Henderson's mother at Southampton Street and the following morning they made their way to Georgiana's first marital home, no.4 Adelphi Terrace, now occupied by their friend, sixty-seven-year-old Sir Brook Watson. As they joined their host for breakfast Georgiana would have seen the large dramatic painting by the American-born artist John Singleton Copley. On a canvas, measuring 6ft x 7½ft the artist has dramatically captured the moment when Watson lost his leg to a shark.

This event occurred in 1749 when Watson was fourteen years old. With his ship sitting at anchor in the bay of Cuba he decided to go for a swim. Nearby some of his fellow crewmen saw a shark heading straight for the cabin boy. Unable to warn him in time they watched in horror as they saw Watson dragged under the water. Before they could reach the boy they saw the shark strike a second time and it was only prevented from making a third attempt when one of the sailors drove it off with a boat hook. To their surprise the boy was still alive although, from the calf down all the flesh had been stripped to the bone from his right leg and his foot had been bitten off. Watson included an image of this severed limb in his coat of arms and he would eventually bequeath the painting to Christ's Hospital school in the hope that it would prove 'a most useful lesson to youth'.

Thanks to the skill of the surgeon at the hospital in Havana, who had to amputate the leg a little below the knee, and his own good health, within three months Watson had made a full recovery. The loss of his leg does not appear to have held him back. On his return to Canada he began trading with local tribes of native Indians and developed a number of lucrative business partnerships with people who had commercial interests in Nova Scotia and Quebec. He also supplied provisions to the British army based nearby and soon came to the notice of the colonial administrator Robert Monckton and General James Wolfe, who charged him with a number of tasks and appointed him their 'wooden-legged commissary' for the 1758 Siege of Louisbourg. Watson then settled in London to further his career as a merchant. The following year, at the age of 25, he married Helen Campbell, the daughter of an Edinburgh goldsmith. Not unnaturally, Watson, to protect his commercial activities, took a great interest in the politics of the day. Growing unrest in America had a direct effect on him as he had been a guarantor for the tea which had been unceremoniously dumped in the harbour by rebels in 1773 – an event which became known as the Boston Tea Party. Elected Member of Parliament for London in 1784 Watson gained a reputation for frequently intervening in debates, often contradicting himself and, even when he could speak from experience, he would resort to platitudes. Five years later he was appointed chairman of the House of Commons Committee charged with drawing up plans for a Regency but, thanks to the pioneering work of Dr Francis Willis, the King recovered from his bout of madness before the Bill could be approved by the House of Lords. As a consequence of his management of the King's mental health Dr Willis, a friend of Georgiana's father, became something of a celebrity.

When Watson, as the newly elected Lord Mayor of London, attended the Royal Court of Justice in 1796, we can imagine that Georgiana and Henderson were of the party that saw their friend swear his allegiance to the Crown. Watson's flowing red velvet robe, edged with ermine and decorated with gold thread, kept his finely turned peg leg, which would not look out of place on a Chippendale table, hidden from view. Although he had achieved the distinction of being the first one-legged Lord Mayor many mocked his intellectual ability for the role, and one wit wrote in *The Rolliad*:

> That leg, in which such wondrous art is shown
> It almost seems to serve him like his own
> Oh! Had the monster, who for breakfast ate
> That luckless limb, his nobler noddle met
> The best of workmen, nor the best of wood
> Had scarce supplied him with a head so good.

But others championed him. Lord Liverpool described Watson as 'one of the most honourable men ever known'. Georgiana's father was certainly a close friend as in reply to an invitation he wrote that he was already, 'under an engagement with my family to pass a week at the house of my friend Mr Brook Watson at Sheen'. It was Watson who first introduced Georgiana and her parents to Prince Lee Boo, and he also wrote the moving inscription on the South Sea islander's tomb at St Mary's Rotherhithe, following the Prince's early death from smallpox.

After her marriage Georgiana remained friends with the Watsons and their names appear in all three of her surviving diaries. Perhaps it was this friendship that led Henderson to sell his home in the Adelphi to Watson, who was looking for somewhere in easy reach of the city. As Georgiana sat down to eat she could once again take pleasure in Robert Adam's decorative scheme but she tells us nothing about her feelings on revisiting her first home as a married woman.

37 The sailors came for our luggage

After breakfast with Watson and his nephew Georgiana called on a number of friends as well as her uncle, Charles Grave Hudson, and then returned to Chertsey in time for dinner. Life returned to its social round. As a result of the damp November weather Georgiana caught a bad cold and did not go out although she was able to start packing for their planned trip to the Isle of Wight. Ten days later Georgiana was again in London. This time she had come to collect a trunk she had lent to her godfather and to order greatcoats for the children. The journey home was not without incidence. On the road between Shepperton and Chertsey she came to the rescue of Mrs Wilson whose coachman was blind drunk and incapable. Georgiana instructed the boy to take the distressed woman home while she waited in the lane for his return. Not surprisingly Georgiana's cold worsened and, as she now had a sore throat too, Henderson wrote to their friend Steers on Thursday to ask him to put off his visit. Steers didn't get the message and turned up the following day.

Georgiana spent the weekend finishing off the packing and at 7.30am on Monday 22nd November they set out for Southampton. Henderson and Steers were in one chaise. Georgiana travelled in a second carriage with her maid Molly and her two eldest children. Baby Harriet and three-year-old Jane were left behind in Chertsey in the care of a nurse. 'It was a very fine day' which meant they could enjoy the views along this familiar route and when the children were hungry and, as she didn't want to extend their journey time with more stops than was necessary, she gave them cold chicken to eat. After nine hours they reached their destination, the Dolphin Inn in Southampton, at half past four. Their cook, who had travelled by the stagecoach, arrived two and half hours later. While they waited for their ship Henderson arranged rooms for them at the inn. Behind its handsome Georgian façade, with magnificent bow windows believed to the biggest in England, this coaching house still retained remnants of the original timbers and stone vaulting from its medieval past. Jane Austen attended the winter assemblies held in this fashionable social space during her stay in Southampton and wrote that she regretted 'so many young women were without partners and each of them with two ugly naked shoulders'.

The following morning, before their ship was due to sail, Georgiana and Henderson took the children to meet their friend, Mr Sadlier. It then rained so much that they could not cross to the Isle of Wight and instead had to spend a further day in Southampton. However, about three o'clock in the afternoon the weather cleared a little providing the family with the opportunity to go for a walk and Georgiana also visited the shops to buy a long fur tippet, no doubt to help protect her throat from the cold biting November wind. Sea conditions improved overnight and at ten o'clock the following morning, she tells us, 'the sailors came for our luggage'. It took an hour and a half to make the crossing and although the cook and her daughter succumbed to seasickness Georgiana did not fall ill. They landed at the Fountain Inn at Cowes and while the children had something to eat Henderson and Steers secured suitable lodgings nearby. The maid and the cook were then sent to 'get the Beds aired and ready' while Georgiana, her husband and Steers dined at the Fountain. At 6pm Molly returned to say that all was ready and Georgiana left with the children. The two men, however, remained behind at the Dolphin for another couple of hours to enjoy the hospitality on offer.

On one of their morning walks Georgiana took her children to see Cowes Castle, at the top of the High Street. Originally built as part of Henry VIII's chain of coastal forts the castle was once again serving a defensive role. Heavily garrisoned and boasting three tiers of nine pounder guns the castle showed Napoleon that the island was ready to repel his invasion. This display of strength might have persuaded Georgiana that it would be safe to join her husband for a sailing trip to Portsmouth Harbour and Spithead. It would appear that the trip was uneventful as all she records is that they returned about half past three. During their stay on the island Georgiana kept busy. With Henderson and Steers she walked to East Cowes to see Mr Ward's cottage and the progress being made on nearby Norris Castle, which was being built for her uncle Lord Henry Seymour by the architect James Wyatt. The weather was so fine that Georgiana decided to repeat this walk, with her son and daughter, the following day. However, they only went as far as the cottage and then caught the ferry from the rope walk for the return journey. The air was so clear on this December night that Georgiana went out again to walk with her husband by the brilliant moonlight for over an hour in the evening. She writes that she didn't go out the next day as she 'was poorly with a bowel complaint'. Perhaps she had caught a chill or it might have been morning sickness as she was pregnant again. She recovered quickly and was well enough to accept Dr Cooper's invitation to dinner. Cooper provided such convivial company that Georgiana and her husband also stayed on for tea and supper. They spent the evening playing cards and did not return to their lodgings till it had gone midnight.

On the second weekend of their stay news arrived of a wreck thirteen miles to the south-east. Leaving the children in the care of her maid Georgiana, Henderson and Steers set off for the village of Shanklin. The carriage could only take them as far as the barracks and they then had to get out and walk along the beach towards the Chine. This area, regularly used by smugglers, saw many ships wrecked on its rocky shoreline. After they had looked over the scene of devastation as the waves dashed the ship to pieces, they called on Mrs Williams, whose cottage stood nearby. She provided them with shelter from the cold blustery wind and a meal of hot lobsters.

One of Henderson's favourite artists George Morland regularly stayed with Mrs Williams in order to paint the broiling seas and wild coastline which featured in many of his works. His 1791 oil painting *The Wreckers* presents us with dramatic black storm clouds filling the sky and creating an onshore wind which has pushed one ship onto the rocks, while another vainly tries to avoid the same plight. Local men are busy gathering the ship's cargo, dumped by the huge waves onto the shore, and load it onto their horses nearby. One of their number is helping a half-drowned sailor escape from the tide that is threatening to pull him under. Nearly two years later Mrs Williams provided rooms for the poet John Keats when he visited the area. Keats wrote to his sister Fanny that the 'window looks...onto the sea' and 'when the ships sail past the cottage chimneys you may take them for weathercocks'.

Georgiana, Henderson and Steers said farewell to Mrs Williams and made their way back to where the horses were waiting and, on a 'very fine moonlight night', returned to Cowes in time for a seven o'clock dinner.

38 High walk towards Egypt

After nearly three weeks in their company Steers had to leave his friends to return to London. Georgiana and her husband decided to make the crossing with him. At 11.00am on the morning of Tuesday 7th December the three of them set sail for Southampton on the packet boat Medina. They landed at a quarter before two and first went to see Sadlier to pass the time until the stage coach was ready to leave. After they had seen Steers off Georgiana and Henderson went for a walk about the town before returning to Sadlier's home where they dined and slept overnight. After breakfast with their host the following morning they boarded the packet boat which should have left at ten am. Instead they had to wait for nearly an hour for the other eight passengers to arrive before the captain finally weighed anchor. The wet and squally weather meant that Georgiana rather than stay on deck had to join the others in the cabin. Stuck below for the two-hour crossing Georgiana sat beside a girl travelling on her own. During the course of their conversation she discovered the young woman was about to start work as a servant and that once they landed she would be travelling further inland. Georgiana couldn't bear to think of her sitting in the cold and rain for the next three hours for her coach and she invited the young girl to accompany her back to her lodgings to sit by the kitchen fire to wait until the Newport stage was ready to leave.

This cold and wet December weather didn't put Georgiana off her daily walks and she appears to have particularly enjoyed the crisp clear moonlit nights when, as she records in her diary, she would stroll with her husband along the quay. One Sunday morning she writes that the family took the 'high walk towards Egypt'. This curiously named location is on the northernmost part of the Isle of Wight, between Cowes and the small village of Gurnard. Some believe that it acquired this name after a ship called 'Egypt' was lured on to the rocks by false lights, or it was wrecked during one of the worst storms of the nineteenth century. Others said it referred to the peace treaty negotiated with Napoleon when he was in Egypt, but the most likely explanation is that it relates to the gypsy colony that occupied the point from the 17th century. It was believed that gypsies came from Egypt and were therefore known as Egyptians. Whatever the source of its name this appears to have been a favourite area for Georgiana and other walkers, including the future Queen Victoria.

The island was on high alert. Georgiana watched from the window at her lodgings as three hundred soldiers disembarked from a transport ship and then marched in close order to their barracks at Newport. Six days later more troops arrived to defend the island. Thankfully invasion fears were ungrounded as Napoleon never made it to the English coast. The sight of the castle her uncle was building no doubt helped provide Georgiana with a feeling of security unlike the neighbouring East Cowes Castle designed by John Nash. This architect, who was behind much of the layout of Regency London and Brighton Pavilion, which he remodelled for the Prince of Wales, had built this fairy tale fantasy with complex castellation, gothic-style turrets and towers for his own use. Georgiana's uncle, who had a reputation for eccentricity and benevolence, had chosen Nash's rival, James Wyatt to design his seaside home nearby. Using locally mined stone Wyatt created a castle of stern simplicity in the medieval style. It sat in a stunning position on top of the most northern hill on the island. Access was via the gatehouse, which because of its three-storey high tower and parapet, a slightly taller turret, and pointed casement windows led to it being named Fort Norris. Even the farm and stables presented a fortified front as they were encased in castellated walls, and visitors thought that they had already arrived at their destination, but Norris Castle was still further along the road that meandered through a 225 acre landscape designed by Humphry Repton. The massive structure designed by Wyatt, with its amazing views of the Solent, was certainly impressive and over tea with her uncle in the 30ft diameter circular drawing room Georgiana could wonder at the Norman grandeur and Georgian elegance that had cost him over £200,000 (equivalent to £8m today) to create.

If only we had access to Georgiana's missing diaries we could find out if she was a guest when the Prince Regent came to the island in 1819. Although he was not known for high living, her uncle hosted the entertainment for the visiting royal and we are told that he attended the event with 'unusual conviviality'. No doubt Georgiana's children enjoyed exploring the many towers, turrets, nooks and crannies of Norris Castle before venturing down to the private beach.

When her unmarried uncle died in 1830 Georgiana's cousin Sir George Seymour inherited Norris Castle and he immediately made it available for the use of the twelve year old Princess Victoria for her holiday. The future Queen of England fell in love with the place. Two years later she returned, with her mother the Duchess of Kent, and spent an idyllic summer there. Visiting German cousins joined the young Victoria on the mile long beach to search for shells, and other curiosities left by the tide, which the Princess would then turn into pictures. Victoria was a regular visitor and after her marriage she wrote in her diary that 'Albert and I talked of buying a place of our own, which would be so nice; perhaps Norris Castle might be something to think of'. However, Albert thought the asking price was too high and instead the royal couple bought the neighbouring estate, Osborne.

39 A Plan for living

When Georgiana was not out visiting friends and relatives, or taking walks she liked to go sailing. Joined by her husband, five-year-old John and Mrs Neate, Georgiana boarded Captain Wassell's boat and set out at 1pm on Monday 13th December 1802. They went as far as Lymington, on the Hampshire coast, before turning back and arrived at Cowes three and a half hours later. Georgiana records in her diary that her son was sick on the return voyage, no doubt due to the heavy swell that was common in the Solent at this time of year. By the end of the week the weather was so bad that the packet boat carrying the mail was unable to sail.

Two days later Mrs Powell called and asked Georgiana if she 'would take half a pig' as she didn't want the whole animal. In return she invited Mrs Powell to join her other guests, Mr & Mrs Chapman, Dr Cooper and Mrs Neate for supper that same evening but we don't know if pork was on the menu. After what appears to have been a satisfying meal Georgiana fetched the playing cards and while four of them paired up to play whist the others continued their conversation, and they all enjoyed each other's convivial company until one o'clock in the morning.

Perhaps it was this combination of late nights and exposure to the elements that led Henderson to develop a sore throat. In spite of feeling poorly he went to see Mrs Powell, who had asked for his opinion about iron rails for her garden, but by the time he returned his throat was so bad that their friend Dr Cooper ordered him to gargle. The following day he was worse and Georgiana had to cancel their dinner engagement. To make sure her husband took the prescribed medicine Georgiana stayed up until one o'clock in the morning to administer it, and then after four hours sleep she returned to continue the treatment. The doctor called two or three times a day to check on his patient and after three days Georgiana was able to write that Henderson was better. News of his illness had spread around their circle of friends and many came to call to ask after his condition, and some sat with him for a short time. Shortly after appearing to rally Henderson had a relapse and the doctor sent Georgiana to the local apothecary to get a purge for her husband. The following day, which happened to be Christmas Eve, Georgiana had to get up twice in the night to see to Henderson. Christmas Day was a bitterly cold day and neither Georgiana or the children ventured out. Henderson was still very poorly and unable to eat the plate of cod Mrs Powell had sent him from her own meal. He felt so ill on Boxing Day that he went back to bed before dinner. Another friend, Miss Powney, bought him a jar of calves foot jelly. Perhaps he felt able to stomach this combination of gelatin, wine, lemon juice and spices as he appears to have rallied a little but by the next day he was worse again. Georgiana also bought a woodcock and some snipes at a cost of three and a half guineas to tempt her husband's appetite and ordered beer from Newport to aid his recovery. Over the next couple of nights Georgiana sat with him into the early hours of the morning and on occasions she did not get to her own bed until 5.30am. By the end of the year a weary Georgiana was able to record that her husband was better and by New Year's Day he felt well enough to go for a carriage ride. However, Dr Cooper, who had visited the patient every day, was still concerned about his friend's slow improvement and applied a mustard plaster to Henderson's side to draw out the infection. This created a blister which had to be drained the following day and Cooper instructed Georgiana to apply a poultice to the area to provide some pain relief. The skin continued to blister and require attention from both Cooper and Georgiana over the coming weeks. Cooper also wrote out 'a plan for living' to help Henderson recover and prevent further episodes of ill health. This document has not survived so we are unable to determine the quality of Cooper's advice to his patient.

Dedicated to her husband's care Georgiana did not neglect her children. Except when the weather was particularly bad she took them for a walk each day, or deputed her maid to take them out if she was unable to leave Henderson's side. With the paths becoming difficult to traverse in the wet winter weather and after she had to carry her daughter over the dirt to the leeward side of the castle, where the ground was 'dry and fine', Georgiana went shopping and bought her son leather gaiters to protect his leggings, while she and Georgy slipped their feet into metal frames on two inch wooden bases. These patents, which kept their shoes out of the muddy conditions. Georgiana acquired a small magic lantern to amuse the children when it proved to be too wet to venture outside. By the flickering candlelight they watched in wonder as beautifully coloured images were projected onto the wall of their room. She was so taken with this invention that she bought a smaller version for her younger daughter Jane, who had been left behind at Abbey House.

The family had planned to leave Cowes on 15th January but Cooper successfully encouraged Henderson to postpone their journey for a week in light of his delicate health and the stormy weather. Georgiana took advantage of this extra time to catch up on her correspondence and settling her debts. She also thanked Mrs Craw for letting them use 'her great chair', although she doesn't tell us why they had borrowed it, and of course she had to see to the packing. Perhaps her son John used the trunk his parents had given him for Christmas. His sister's present was a Tunbridge coffee pot – a curious gift for a four-year-old girl. Seven days later, the sea was so calm that the morning mail had been ferried over in a row boat and at 4pm on that same day Georgiana and her family left Cowes aboard Captain Wassel's ship on the first stage of their journey home.

40 In testimony of my forgiveness

After an uneventful crossing the family disembarked at Southampton and made their way to the Dolphin Inn where they spent the night. Once they had breakfasted the following morning Georgiana's daughter, cook and the maid set off for Chertsey in a hired Hackney carriage. However, Georgiana would be travelling in style. General Sir John Doyle had asked the landlord of the Dolphin to arrange for his chariot to be returned to London as he had to sail to Guernsey. The King had appointed this veteran of the American War of Independence as well as the French Revolutionary Wars in which he had been wounded seven times, Lieutenant Governor of Guernsey in recognition of the zeal in which he had carried out his military duties.

As they were about to set out for the city Henderson was happy to oblige and he, Georgiana and their son John settled back into the well upholstered seats for their journey home. Light, airy and well sprung this vehicle provided a much more comfortable ride than their usual coach, and no doubt turned many heads as they travelled through the towns along their route. Nine hours after setting out they finally arrived at Abbey House at 6.15pm, in time for dinner. Georgiana took every opportunity to make use of the chariot while it was in their care. As well as visiting friends in the area she travelled to nearby Walton to enquire after a laundry maid. She also took great delight in showing it off to Miss Mulso, the niece of one of their neighbours Miss Hester Chapone at their old home in Hadley, who had come to stay with them for the night. After their guest had gone Georgiana spent the rest of the morning catching up with her correspondence and bottling elderflower wine, to take with them as a gift for her mother-in-law. They arrived in London in good time and after leaving their luggage with Henderson's mother at Southampton Street they made their way to the West End. While her husband took the chariot to the coach maker in fulfilment of the General's request Georgiana made her way to Mrs Clarke's in Burlington Street in order to interview a cook. Then she went shopping. Her first stop was at Barto Valle's Italian warehouse in the Haymarket where she may have bought some of the herbal concoctions they sold to cure various illnesses and ailments. She then went to Wedgwood's showroom, near St James's Square, to buy a ceramic mortar bowl for Henderson, before returning to Southampton Street to join her husband for dinner. John Plott then called on them giving Georgiana the opportunity to pay him ten guineas for cases for the miniature portraits he had painted of the family.

The next day, Saturday, was equally busy. After breakfast Georgiana called on Miss Savage in Weymouth Street to ask after the character of a cook. We don't know if this was the same person she had interviewed the day before but after conversing with her hostess Georgiana decided that she 'did not do' for the position. Then she was off to the shops again, buying gloves for the children, linen from Cappers and finishing at her favourite Bond Street milliner, Mrs Davis, where she bought a hat for her oldest daughter Georgy. She also found time to pay her creditors before calling on her friends, Sir Brook and Lady Watson, at their home in the Adelphi. After a leisurely Sunday morning Georgiana and Henderson set out for Chertsey bearing gifts for the children: a ship for her son and a tea set for the girls.

A day and a half later Georgiana tripped on the cellar stairs and badly sprained her ankle. To add to her discomfort the cook left and, as she was incapacitated, she had to accept a replacement who had been interviewed by Mrs Woodcock on her behalf. As she was in desperate need Georgiana agreed to pay the cook's coach fare and she also gave her a guinea to ensure her service. Then the maid Betty gave notice that she was leaving. There is no explanation for these sudden changes but as the Nurse had been with the family for six years it doesn't suggest that Georgiana had a bad relationship with her staff. Frustrated by her limited mobility Georgiana had to ask her husband to travel over to Farnham to ask Miss Richardson if Elizabeth Berry would make a suitable laundry maid for them. She must have received a good reference as Georgiana took her on and paid her £10 9s per annum. She also hired an Elizabeth Gammon as housemaid at nine guineas, but Sally the kitchen maid only received four guineas over the same period.

Her ankle took a long time to heal. Ten days after the initial injury Georgiana was still housebound and so must have been delighted when Captain Wilson and his son Harry travelled out from London to visit the family, and they brought gifts with them. China for Georgiana, dried oranges and a jar of sugar candy for the children and Chinese crackers for young John. It rained so hard that day that everyone had to stay indoors. Henderson showed their visitors his drawings and Georgiana made a present of the print she had made of her cousin's prize bull to Harry Wilson.

Not long after their friends had returned to London Georgiana became concerned about her husband's health. He complained of a sore throat and had a bad cold. Georgiana wrote to her cousin, Harriet Hudson, to postpone their planned visit by a week as she didn't think he would be well enough to travel. Thankfully his health improved and the couple spent his recuperation sorting out a bookcase and playing backgammon. After three weeks of hobbling around Georgiana was finally able to leave the house. The couple travelled to London for their delayed dinner engagement with Harriet. They stayed, as usual, with Henderson's mother in Southampton Street, although Mrs Henderson was 'very poorly' and could not go out with Georgiana on a shopping trip.

Georgiana took this opportunity to call at her lawyer's office to collect an annuity that had come due in January. This money came from her late father who in his will had instructed his executors to 'appropriate a sum of Money that may enable them to pay Georgiana...an annuity of one hundred pounds, payable quarterly'. 'Although she has proved to be in the highest degree a thankless child', Keate added, he had made this bequest 'in testimony of his forgiveness'. Georgiana makes no further mention of this slight. She returned to her mother-in-law's home to change her dress before setting out for the Hudson family house in Arundel Street, about half a mile away. She arrived at four o'clock and Henderson joined her there an hour later. With the other guests, Mrs Biggs and Mrs Sarah Dashwood, they sat down to dinner with John Hudson and his sister Harriet. It appears to have been a very enjoyable occasion and they did not leave until 9 o'clock that evening. Before setting out for Chertsey the next day Georgiana went shopping again, this time to buy tin ware for the kitchen before calling in at the consulting room of French émigré dentist, Nicholas Dubois de Chemant, in Frith Street near Soho Square. She may have ordered a pair of the patented porcelain dentures which had made him famous but we don't know the reason as she only records the visit.

The couple then returned home and arrived at Chertsey in time for a six o'clock dinner and to news that 'Nanny was bought to bed of a girl.'

41 Prior to going to Bath

Who was the father? Was the Nanny married – perhaps her husband was away fighting against the French. Georgiana doesn't provide any answers to these tantalising questions but she didn't dismiss the Nanny who remained in their employ for at least the rest of 1803.

A neighbour Mrs Bridges, although busy with preparations for her imminent move to London, took time out to call on Georgiana and the two women spent a happy hour in each other's company. Georgiana returned the visit and wished her friend well. She asked after one of the servants and in response Mrs Bridges arranged for the father of young George Roberts to call on Georgiana to discuss terms. After some discussion it was agreed that she would pay his son 79s to come and work for her as a footboy and, if 'he stayed a twelvemonth', he would receive an additional ten shillings a year. That very evening young Roberts started work as Georgiana's page.

Georgiana certainly needed the extra staff as she was expecting guests. A longstanding family friend, Captain Shepherd failed to turn up that weekend, or the following two weekends. Perhaps naval matters had detained him. However, Charles Marshall and his wife did arrive, as arranged, on Tuesday 1st March. As was their custom Georgiana and Henderson took their guests for walks around their garden as well as the local area, which included a trip up nearby St Anne's Hill to see the home of Charles James Fox, and to admire the view. Georgiana also arranged for the dressmaker, Mrs Goring, to call at Abbey House to make a gown for her friend but Mrs Marshall had little opportunity to wear it as her husband became 'unwell with the gout' and wished to return to their home in Hampshire.

Realising that the lightweight two wheeled carriage that had bought the Marshalls to Chertsey would not provide adequate protection from the weather, Henderson arranged for a more spacious and comfortable post-chaise for their journey. Several days later a servant arrived at Abbey House to reclaim his master's gig from the stables and drove it back to Hampshire.

Now that Georgiana had got the children settled in their new home and her guests had left she had time to indulge in her new hobby – woodturning. Dominick Jean, who had helped her sort out her late father's cabinets of insects for the auction which had been held the previous Spring, came down from London to help with setting up the lathe which the couple had acquired the previous summer. Georgiana appears to have been a quick learner. She took great pleasure in creating presents for her family. For her husband she made a handle for an awl he used for wood carving, she turned a bottle and barrel for her son John, a saucepan for her eldest daughter Georgy and another bottle for young Jane. She even tried her hand at a silk winder, which she gave to the nurse. By the middle of March Georgiana had to set the lathe aside to prepare for another trip to London.

Henderson had business to attend to in the city and Georgiana needed to go shopping for bed furniture for the nursery, and toys for the children, 'prior to going to Bath'. It was all a bit of a rush but they managed to do everything they needed to do and take their leave of Henderson's mother to arrive back at Abbey House in time for dinner at seven o'clock. However, they both had a terrible night and resorted to laudanum in order to get to sleep. The blister on Henderson's side was still causing him a lot of discomfort and Georgiana continued to apply poultices to reduce the inflammation. Pregnant again, Georgiana felt so poorly she wondered if she should postpone her planned trip to Bath. She wrote to a man she respected, Dr John Clarke, for his advice. As a man-midwife Clarke had recognised that puerperal fever could be spread via the attendants' clothing. As soon as he had realised this he destroyed his entire wardrobe and no further cases of fever appeared among the mothers he treated. While Georgiana waited on his reply she entertained several old friends who had come to call, including Mrs Bridges, who had returned to Chertsey to 'give up her house', and had brought a hen and a brace of chickens for Georgiana.

Although Dr Clarke replied that he saw no objection to travelling Georgiana felt so unwell she took to her bed and stayed there all day. Henderson wrote to Dr Cooper at Bath to let him know that they would be arriving four days later than originally planned. The bed rest appears to have done Georgiana good as she wrote that she felt 'rather better' and was able to attend to packing for the trip. She took time out on Saturday to celebrate her daughter Harriet's first birthday and comforted her young son, John after his father had drawn a tooth, 'the first he has shed', she wrote. After spending an hour playing with the children in the nursery on Sunday morning Georgiana sent instructions, and no doubt payment, to the wet nurse to come and feed baby Jane. The nurse received £10, the cook £4 and Molly the maid £2 to secure their service at Abbey House while Georgiana and Henderson were away.

42 Took possession of their lodgings

Georgiana and Henderson, with their maid Bailies, climbed into the post chaise at 11.30am on Monday 21st March 1803 and set out for Bath to take part in the social season before it finished in June, and to imbibe the mineral rich spring waters, for which the city had become famous. After three and a half hours their carriage rumbled into the yard at the Crown Inn at Reading for a change of horses and a chance to stretch their legs. Georgiana took this opportunity to call on her friend, Fanny Bisley, who lived nearby while Henderson saw a 'Mr Austwick'. Ninety minutes later they set off for the Pelican Inn near Newbury, where they had arranged to spend the night. Georgiana makes no mention of her stay at this hostelry but an Irish actor penned this amusing epigram:

> The famous inn at Speenhamland
> That stands below the hill
> May well be called the Pelican
> From its enormous bill.

After breakfast the following morning they continued their journey. They had to stop twice for a fresh change of horses: first at The Lamb located in the heart of Marlborough and next at the Artichoke in Devizes. At 5 pm they arrived at the village of Batheaston, just two miles outside Bath, where they had planned to call on an old friend. However, they 'found a girl waiting in the lane' with a message for them. It said that Dr Cooper was too ill to receive visitors so Georgiana and Henderson continued their journey and their carriage finally decanted them at the White Lion Inn beside the Guildhall, on the corner of Bridge Street and Market Place. They left their maid to sort out the room and went for a walk. Their path took them pass the Abbey with its large windows and sculptures of angels climbing to heaven on stone ladders and then along the North Parade towards the river Avon. The wide paved avenues and elegant buildings designed by the city's architect, John Wood and his son, no doubt provided a pleasant environment for their walk. As their route took them along Pierrepoint Street the couple decided to call at the home of Dr Davies and ask after Cooper's health. Seemingly satisfied with his response to their enquiries Georgiana and Henderson returned to the inn for their dinner and a good night's rest.

As they planned to stay for around six weeks Georgiana sought advice from her friend Mr Lee, who had already established his family in one of the lodging houses that had sprung up to cater for the influx of tourists during the season, about suitable accommodation for the duration of their visit. He directed them to the home of Mrs Vesey in Argyle Street, just across the river. Terms were agreed and the following morning Georgiana and Henderson 'took possession of their lodgings'.

Bath offered visitors the opportunity to promenade and admire the fashions of the day, to see and be seen. Leaving their maid to unpack the couple went for a stroll. Before long they came across their friends, Captain Francis Fayerman and his wife. No doubt Georgiana congratulated Fayerman on his recent promotion to the 3rd rate 74 gun *HMS Terrible* following his years of service on the 5th rate *Beaulieu*, in which he had taken part in the battle of Camperdown off the Dutch coast. Fayerman would rise to the rank of Rear Admiral of the Red by the time of his death, eleven years later.

When it proved too wet to venture out of doors Georgiana took the opportunity to catch up with her correspondence. She sent a note to Captain Henry Wilson, and his son Harry, 'to wish them a good voyage'. No doubt the news that they were about to set sail for China aboard the East Indiaman Warley bought back memories of a similar voyage nearly twenty years earlier when Wilson's ship had been wrecked. Her late father had recalled the whole story of Wilson's survival and subsequent homecoming in his *Account of the Pellew Islands*. Georgiana also wrote home to enquire after her children's health and well-being. In spite of the inclement weather Georgiana received a visit from Thomas Leir, who had travelled over from the family home at Weston and most probably spoke of his relief that the constant legal wrangling with Elizabeth Macie, mother of Georgiana's cousin James Smithson, over her management of their estate was finally at an end, following her death in 1800.

Within a few days of their arrival Georgiana awoke to the news that her maid was poorly and unable to carry out her duties. No symptoms are recorded but Georgiana felt it necessary, even though it was a Sunday, to send for the local apothecary, Thomas Horton. Georgiana's concern appears to have been justified as Horton attended their lodgings over the next three days and successfully treated Bailies' illness.

As many of her friends were also in Bath for the season Georgiana was kept busy with entertaining visitors, or making calls of her own. When Henderson went off to negotiate the sale of a post chaise to a nearby coach maker Georgiana ventured out to the market, but in spite of the 'excellent order and abundance' that surpassed anything in London, as one visitor described it, Georgiana makes no reference in her diary to buying anything.

At the beginning of April Georgiana and Henderson undertook a five mile journey through the irregular and picturesque countryside to see Miss Wiltshire. Her home, a fine example of Georgian architecture, stood on a small knoll halfway up a steep hillside, and had been built fifty years earlier thanks to the success of her grandfather, Walter Wiltshire who, with the secret support of the celebrated dandy Beau Nash, ran one of the two lucrative gaming establishments in Bath. The Wiltshire family also established a successful and prosperous business as carriers with their 'flying wagon' service and were key figures in Bath society, with the younger Walter serving as Mayor of the city on three separate occasions. In thanks for conveying his paintings to their destinations, safely and without charge, Thomas Gainsborough had given the Wiltshire family a number of his pictures and these, alongside other fine portraits and landscapes graced the walls of Shockerwick House, which had been designed for domestic comfort rather than formal grandeur.

After a pleasant visit and promises to call again Georgiana and her husband set off for Bath. As they passed through the village of Batheaston Henderson instructed the coachman to stop and, while Georgiana waited for him in the carriage, he went to enquire about their friend's health. He returned within 'two or three minutes' and told her that Cooper was still not well enough to see them. Although it had been a pleasant day Georgiana 'had a very bad night' and she felt quite poorly the next morning. Then her maid took a turn for the worse and Georgiana had to send for the apothecary again. The landlady, Mrs Vesey, was displeased. She complained 'of her maid having too much to do' as a consequence of Bailies' illness. A few days later she returned to tell Georgiana that she needed their bedroom and therefore they would have to find alternative accommodation as soon as possible.

43 Taking the waters

The next day Georgiana and Henderson searched without success for new lodgings. Georgiana also paid a visit to the Post Office. It was her son's seventh birthday and she had not received a message from home regarding the specially printed letter she had sent him but she came away empty-handed. She then went to Stall Street, to the home of 'Mrs Lamb where the mail arrives', but there was nothing for her there either. The next morning bought the news she had been waiting for - a letter from Abbey House telling her that 'all well'. Her joy was short-lived. Mrs Vesey sent word that she was ill and they had to leave. They 'very nearly took lodgings' in nearby Walcot Street, with the miniature painter Lewis Vaslet, but were advised by friends that this 'would not do'. They called on the artist, after dinner on Friday, and told him they had changed their mind. Instead they took rooms in one of the grand town houses located in Milsom Street. After dinner on Saturday they left Mrs Vesey and, no doubt with a lighter heart, moved into no.15, the home of a Miss Cuff. In her novel *Northanger Abbey*, which Jane Austen completed at this time, although it was not published for another fourteen years, the wealthy Tilney family also had lodgings in Milsom Street.

In the midst of all this upset Henderson had started his treatment at the Pump Room. 'Bath-water is better than Bath-wine' said the inscription at the entrance to the 85ft long room. Some may have queried this statement. It was said that the water tasted like that in which eggs had been boiled and smelt sulphurous, although experience had demonstrated that many ailments were eased by drinking this mineral-rich water. The medical profession saw it as a great business opportunity and, by the time of the couple's visit, Bath could boast 18 physicians, 13 surgeons and 25 apothecaries to tend to visitors' medical needs. The servant in charge of the pump handed Henderson the smallest size glass of this water. Four hours later he had another dose. A few days later Henderson moved onto the second size glass. Nearly three weeks after Henderson's first drink Georgiana finally decided to give it a try. She doesn't tell us what she thought about it, although she does continue to record Henderson's treatments in her diary.

By Sunday they had settled into their new lodgings. After church the couple travelled the two miles or so to call on Mr & Mrs Leir at their home in Weston. Later in the day Georgiana walked with Henderson through old Bath towards Beechen Cliff Hill. They climbed the steeply sloping path that led to a flight of steps, known locally as 'Jacob's Ladder'. These led to the top of the 360' high hill, but the panoramic view was worth all the effort. Georgiana wrote in her diary that she had walked between five and six miles that day so it is not surprising that a few days later she had to order a new pair of half boots made from durable nankeen cotton.

Her days were busy with shopping and visiting. When they heard that Dr Cooper was now well enough for visitors Georgiana and Henderson took the post chaise out to Batheaston to see him. While the men discussed the matters of the day she joined Cooper's sister-in-law and Miss Chapman, his niece by marriage, who were old friends, for a stroll around the garden. During the course of their conversation Georgiana accepted Mrs Powell's invitation to a dinner she had organised for Admiral Arthur Phillip. The sixty-five-year old Admiral was something of a celebrity. He had established the first British penal colony at Botany Bay in 1788 and, as the settlement took shape, he was appointed the first Governor General of New South Wales. Poor diet, arthritis and an injury to his shoulder had bought Phillip to Bath 'to take the cure'. He stayed at no. 3 South Parade during the course of his treatment before returning to naval duties. Two years later he retired from the service and returned to Bath where he, and his wife Isabella, took a house in Bennett Street, near the Assembly Rooms. Georgiana adds in her diary that they took Dr Davies with them, and brought him back, and that Mr & Mrs Williams were also of the party, but we learn nothing about the meal or any gossip she may have heard over the dinner table.

Georgiana decided to hire a pianoforte at four shillings a week, with the music one shilling extra, so that she could play for friends when they came calling. The couple do not appear to have taken out a subscription for the twice-weekly balls held at, what was considered, the 'most noble and elegant' of all the assembly rooms but this may have been due to the fact that Georgiana was heavily pregnant at the time. However, they did go to a public breakfast and they set off with

Captain and Mrs Fayerman to the 'newly laid out and very agreeable' Sydney Gardens. Georgiana wore the loose fitting short gown she had specially ordered from Shonbergs together with a new hat and cloak made for her over the weekend by the milliner Miss Hoblyn in King Street. While they drank tea or hot chocolate and enjoyed their meal the 'Harmonick [sic] Society' provided the entertainment. Georgiana's friends, Drs Cooper and Davies, were members of this glee club and they may have joined in with singing catches like 'Come, let us a Maying go' and 'Behold the sweet flowers around'. After their meal they could take a stroll around the sixteen acres of small groves and lawns, intersected with serpentine walks and pleasant vistas that made up Sydney Gardens. Features included a sham castle, bowling green and a moss-covered grotto which, by means of a shell lined underground passage led to the centre of the Labyrinth and a swing designed by John Joseph Merlin, best known for his countless inventions such as musical instruments, watches, automata, roller skates and Bath chairs. His swing would invert the user so that the stresses of the body were relieved from the effect of gravity. No image of this curious machine has survived and Georgiana, in her pregnant state, is unlikely to have tested its beneficial qualities. There were plenty of shady bowers and thatched umbrellas around the grounds under which they could shelter from the weather. One nearby resident, Jane Austen, had jokingly written to her sister that 'there is a public breakfast in Sydney Gardens every morning, so we shall not be wholly starved'.

On another occasion Georgiana paid a visit to Henrietta Maria Hungerford. The two women sat together for over two hours before Georgiana had to leave to get ready for dinner with the Leirs at Weston. After church the following day she went again to Brock Street but this time her cousin was out and so Henderson had to wait until Monday to be introduced to Mrs Hungerford. They stayed about an hour. No doubt they talked about the children, the impending birth of Georgiana's 5th baby and how Henderson had benefitted from 'taking the waters'. The next few days were spent in a whirl of shopping, packing and calling on friends to take their leave. The first stop on their journey home was Batheaston where Henderson joined Dr Cooper in his carriage while Georgiana and her maid rode in the post chaise. They stopped for dinner at the hamlet of Petty France, which Jane Austen would later describe in Northanger Abbey 'as a dull two-hour rest stop...there was nothing to be done but to eat without being hungry, and to loiter about without anything to see'. They then travelled another fifteen miles or so to Rodborough where they spent the night at the Bear coaching inn, which stood on the common beside the Stroud-Cirencester turnpike. After breakfast the next morning the couple paid a visit to two of the ten working cloth-mills that were located in this small but important area, before continuing on their journey. They stopped at Birdlip, the highest village in the Cotswolds, to enjoy the view. She writes in her diary that they 'saw from thence into Wales'. Then it was back into their carriage and by half past three they finally arrived at Cheltenham. They dined in the ground floor room with the large double bow window at Smith's Boarding House. After breakfast the next morning they all made their way to the well where Cooper took a glass of the mineral rich water. Georgiana writes that she only tasted it. She also wrote to Captain Wilson to ask him to get 'Cooper a Chinese boar and sow' if he could before she joined the public table, at which 25 sat down, for dinner. Then it was off to Cooper's lodgings for tea. They left Cheltenham and stopped at the King's Head in the market town of Northleach, to change the horses. Their next stop was the Oxfordshire town of Witney where they may have gone to The Blanket Hall, where the Master and Wardens kept excellent dining facilities, for their meal before visiting one of the many studios or mills in the area to see how the blankets, for which the town was famous, were made. At 5.30pm they climbed back into their carriages and set off for Oxford, their next overnight stop. They left early the next morning and covered fifteen miles before sitting down to breakfast in Wallingford. As arranged, Fanny Bisley and her little girl met the carriage, when it stopped at Reading, so that Georgiana could give her goddaughter a gift – a bonnet from Bath.

Then Georgiana and Henderson were on their way again. After sixteen miles they came to the Dog & Partridge in the village of Yateley, in Hampshire, where they by chance met their friends Mr & Mrs Charles Marshall, who were on their way to visit Mrs Parfait at Eversley, about three miles away. They decided to go with them but only stayed for fifteen minutes as they had to continue their journey. There was one more stop at Blackwater, on the border of Surrey and

Berkshire, for a change of horses until finally, in the late afternoon, they arrived back home in Chertsey.

44 Opened the door out of their bedroom

Weary after her long journey Georgiana left the unpacking until the next day. After dinner she called the children down to give them their presents from Bath. No sooner had she unpacked then she was packing again for a trip to town to collect her mother-in-law. When they arrived at Southampton Street they discovered that she was too poorly and not ready to return with them to Chertsey.

However, Georgiana and her husband had errands to run while they were in London. Firstly, she went to Barto Valle's Italian Warehouse at the Sign of the Orange Tree and Two Oil Jars in Haymarket to settle her bill. Among the many delicacies on sale she could have bought were olive oil, Parma ham, anchovies, macaroni, plums and bottled mangoes. Then she was off to Bond Street to buy a 'new garden hat' for young John and a straw bonnet from her favourite milliner for her daughter Georgy. As well as collecting the £25 quarterly allowance from the office of her late father's executors, she went with her husband to Temple Gate to see Thomas Pitt to sign their accounts before visiting her cousin Harriet Hudson in Arundel Street. They arrived back at Abbey House in time for a six o'clock dinner.

Back home she returned to country life, calling on friends, helping her husband to thin the trees in their orchard to improve the size and quality of the fruit ripening on the branches, as well as bottling their homemade wine. Arrangements were made for the porker they had been fattening, together with four suckling pigs, to be slaughtered and prepared for the table. The next morning their maid clambered aboard the London stage with two of the carcasses which she had been instructed to deliver as presents. One was to go to Georgiana's uncle in Arundel Street and the other to Mrs Woodcock in Lincolns Inn. Molly also had to manage a parcel of gowns that Georgiana wanted her to take to the dressmaker, Mrs Murray, to be altered - perhaps to fit her expanding belly.

Now eight months pregnant Georgiana spent several days putting her affairs in order; sorting her papers and paying outstanding bills, as well as tidying drawers, closets and the storeroom, in preparation for the birth of her fifth child. On Saturday she took young John with her to the Bush Inn at Staines. They had gone to meet her cousin Harriet who was visiting for a few days. The coach had been delayed so Georgiana took her son for a walk around the garden that ran alongside the river. As they enjoyed their stroll she may have told him that the great Lord Nelson, who had successfully defended England from a naval invasion by the French Emperor Napoleon, had stayed at this very tavern some years earlier. After a ninety minute wait the coach finally arrived and after welcoming Harriet the three of them climbed into the chaise for the journey to Abbey House.

Georgiana was able to introduce her cousin to Sir Richard Clark and his wife Margaret when they came to call after Sunday service at St Peter's Church. The Clarkes lived nearby in Porch House, the former home of the 17th century Royalist poet Abraham Cowley. Harriet couldn't admire the picturesque porch, which had given their fine timber home its name as it had been removed in 1786 because it projected ten feet into the public highway and proved hazardous to passers-by. A Chamberlain of the City of London, a successful attorney and former Lord Mayor of London, Clarke delighted in the company of literary men and when he was young he met and became a close friend of the lexicographer Dr Samuel Johnson. Her father would have been a member of this circle too so Georgiana would have known Clarke from her early years. This was obviously a close friendship as the Clarkes gave their son Richard the middle name of Henderson, and they may also have let them know about Abbey House in Chertsey when they were looking for a suitable family home.

Later Georgiana welcomed Harriet's parents, who had been visiting Mrs Barwell in Buckingham. Cook and the servants were kept busy preparing meals and sorting out rooms for these extra visitors. Amazingly Georgiana still had the energy to take her guests for a walk to one of her favourite places, St Anne's Hill. After admiring the view they then took a leisurely stroll around the grounds of the nearby home of Charles James Fox and his wife. The heady scent of the roses and other flowering plants filled the air as they made their way to inspect the grotto and other garden features. This was a short, but we hope, pleasant visit as the next afternoon Georgiana's uncle, aunt and cousin climbed aboard the coach to set out for their London home.

As their carriage disappeared from sight Henderson left Georgiana and joined Richard Clark to inspect land that was up for sale, about three miles away in Laleham. The men repeated the trip the following day to attend the auction but we don't know if they made a bid or were just interested in how much it raised for its owner, Lord Lonsdale. Later over dinner at the Three Horseshoes, the oldest public house in the village, they met James Smithson's lawyer, a Mr Graham. The three men may have discussed what the successful purchaser, Lord Lucan, planned to do with the land.

Three weeks later Henderson 'opened the door out of their bedroom into the back spare bedroom'. He then put up a new bed in the nursery for their eldest child John, who slept in it for the first time on the night of 7th June 1803. His sister Georgy now had his old cot while her bed was given over to the next oldest daughter, Jane. Nothing is said about the sleeping arrangements for fourteen-month old Harriet.

Not long after her seventh wedding anniversary Georgiana began to feel very unwell. Henderson became so concerned that, in spite of the thunder, lightning and rain he asked Vulliamy, who was staying with them at the time, to go to town to arrange for a chaise to fetch a Mr Boone from Sunbury. The man-midwife arrived at midnight and, after seeing his patient he decided there was no urgency and 'went to bed in the spare room'. Meanwhile, Georgiana writes, 'H[enderson] lay down on nurse's bed', while the nurse sat up with her through the night.

45 Slept with Henderson again

Henderson was up at 6am the next morning to see their visitor before he left to catch the stage. Vulliamy took breakfast with the man midwife who had advised Georgiana to get up. She put on a loose gown and went along the corridor to sit in the spare room which had been set aside for the nurse. As his patient felt much better Boone left about 1pm with a promise that he would return later. Georgiana did not go downstairs all day and by the evening she felt 'very bad again' and returned to her bed. On his return around 10pm he checked on Georgiana then went to lay down on the spare bed, while Henderson once again rested on the nurse's bed and the nurse sat up all night with the expectant mother. From her earlier experiences of childbirth Georgiana realised that her contractions had become more frequent and around 1pm she sent for both her husband and the midwife. Their 'little boy was born about twenty minutes before three' on Tuesday 14th June 1803, seemingly without any complications.

Like all mothers, except those from the poorer classes, Georgiana spent the next two weeks in bed, although six days after giving birth she did venture downstairs to sit, wrapped up in a blanket, in the 'Great Chair'. She had the children with her on two or three occasions and Henderson spent most of the afternoons in his wife's company. Friends and neighbours came to call on her during her confinement to see the baby. On one occasion, to help relieve the tedium, Henderson brought a young owl into her room for his wife and the children to see, and on another, to tempt her appetite, he sent her a plate of strawberries from the family's dinner table.

Four days after giving birth Georgiana was alarmed to discover that someone had broken into their garden and destroyed the cucumber and melon islands in the greenhouse, and upset the cask of vinegar most probably used by the gardeners as a weed killer. They believed this was the work of a William Mews, who had been one of their gardeners until he walked out after complaining that his wages had not been paid. He may also have been upset at the news that his employers, on the recommendation of their neighbour Charles Marshall, had engaged an additional worker to join the outdoor staff.

This is not unsurprising as it required many hands and a lot of effort to keep the vegetable beds, fruit orchards, greenhouse, hay fields and formal gardens in good condition. Henderson had discussed the situation with his lawyer, and with Bowyer the agent, but the outcome, it would appear, was not to the liking of their old gardener and so, in the dead of night he had broken into their greenhouse and caused all the damage. Nearly three months later Georgiana woke up news that the 'gardens had been robbed'. Henderson offered twenty guineas reward, nearly double the cook's annual salary, for information about the perpetrator of this act. Six weeks later they heard that Mews, their old gardener and no doubt the culprit, had been arrested for highway robbery but no further information has come to light about the outcome of his trial.

Boone made twice daily visits to check on Georgiana's progress and when he called on Tuesday 28th June and discovered that she was still in some discomfort he ordered her 'to take bark three times a day'. Like its modern counterpart, aspirin, which is made from the same salicylic acid, the willow bark provided pain relief and helped to reduce her temperature. To disguise the bitter taste of the bark he advised her to take it in port wine, and he also advised her to take ale with her dinner and to help build up her strength she drank a caudle every day for a week. This warm, comforting, milky drink, thickened with egg yolks, sweetened with sugar and reinforced with wine or ale, acted as a tonic to promote general health and wellbeing. Towards the end of her second week in bed Georgiana's son John had a nose bleed, and then complained of a sore throat. She kept him with her all day and ordered blackcurrant leaves to be boiled in milk that night for John to drink to help alleviate the soreness. The following morning Dr Summers called to see John. He said that the boy should be given calomel to relieve his symptoms. Although his throat improved John suffered another nose bleed on Saturday morning but then appears to have fully recovered. Summers called on several occasions to check on the general health of the household. On one visit he prescribed columbo and valerian for Georgiana, who he found 'very indifferent' and feeling 'poorly'. These herbs were normally prescribed for an upset stomach, although valerian also had properties to help those suffering with anxiety and insomnia.

Still concerned over his wife's slow progress Henderson called on Dr John Clark, who specialised in obstetrics, to ask for advice and returned with yet another prescription for her, together with a mixture to settle her nerves. He also came back with an expensive treat - milk chocolate. Georgiana also walked in the garden every day and slowly her health improved. To aid her recovery she hired an ass and foal for a week in order to drink the animal's milk which was reputed to have beneficial properties. She also gave some to young John, whose health must still have been giving her cause for concern. After dinner all the family walked down to the field so that the children could take it in turns to ride the ass. At this time Henderson received a quantity of Madeira wine. There was so much Georgiana wrote in her diary that they had to cut through part of a wall to enable them to get it down the stairs and into the cellar.

On Thursday 21st July the baby was moved into the nursery and Georgiana 'slept with H[enderson] again. First time since my confinement' she wrote. In preparation for this event she washed her feet which, as she recorded this in her diary, must have been an unusual event.

46 To be churched

When she felt strong enough Georgina left her baby under the care of the nurse and joined her husband in a row boat to take a trip down the Abbey River, a backwater of the Thames, to visit friends who lived nearby. On their return she took her children for a walk in the field and then down to the canal to see their father, with the help of the gardener James, put trammels in the water but she doesn't say if any fish were caught in these three-layered nets. A couple of days later Henderson helped his wife into their punt, stowed the turkeys she was taking as a present to their friend, and gently poled their craft to visit Mrs La Coste at Abbey Mill.

Early one morning in July Georgiana and Henderson set off early for London. They broke their journey at Turnham Green as Georgiana wished to call in at the home of the journalist and dissenting minister Dr Christopher Lake Moody and his wife, who had recently moved to the village. A respected poet, who often wrote under the pseudonym of 'The Muse of Surbiton', it is not surprising to find that Elizabeth Moody was part of her father's literary circle and Georgiana met her on a number of occasions. The founder of the Monthly Review Ralph Griffiths described Elizabeth as one of the 'ingenious and learned Ladies, who have excelled so much in the more elegant branches of literature'. This devoted couple regularly made contributions to the Morning Review and the St James Chronicle. Christopher was sixteen years his wife's junior and when she died at the age of 77, which although considered a great age - it was said that she 'was young to the last'. Her loving husband followed her to the grave twelve months later.

The Hendersons finally arrived at his mother's house at half past twelve. Georgiana left her husband there as she wished to go to the shops to pay her outstanding bills. She also brought enough nankeen cloth to make a fishing jacket, trousers for Henderson and a straw hat for herself. That evening they took a hackney coach to the home of the obstetrician and friend Dr John Clark and his wife in New Burlington Street, off Savile Row, in the West End. It was said that:

On earth while he lived, by attending men's wives
He increased populations some thousands of lives

In light of his reputation the novelist William Godwin had called on Clark's services five years earlier. Following the birth of Godwin's daughter (the future Mary Shelley) the attending doctors had to remove the placenta to stop the mother haemorrhaging but, as a result of this intervention, she succumbed to an infection. In spite of Clark's best efforts to help Mary Wollstonecraft there was nothing he could do to save her life and she died eleven days after giving birth. This sad outcome was no reflection on Clark's skill and knowledge as he had been called in too late.

It is highly likely that Georgiana's visit was not purely a social occasion as Clark took her into his consulting room to check that she had had fully recovered from the effects of giving birth to her fifth child. With a seemingly clean bill of health they returned to the dining room to join their spouses for a convivial dinner before retiring to bed later that evening. After a leisurely breakfast the following morning they said farewell to their hosts. Henderson put his wife in a hackney carriage and directed it to Southampton Street. He went onto John Bell's pharmacy in Oxford Street to place an order for various medicines before joining his wife and mother an hour later. The couple took the opportunity while they were in town to see London's latest attraction: the Panorama of Rome which had recently been opened by Thomas Barker, in partnership with the artist Ramsay Richard Reinagle, on the Strand. After paying three shillings at the door they made their way along a dark, narrow passageway to a spiral staircase which led them up to the viewing platform. Georgiana doesn't record her response on seeing spread out before her the skilfully painted scene as seen from a window of the second floor of the tower on the Capitoline Hill. This 360 degree view ran from the Temple of Romulus and Remus to the Colosseum, to the ruins of the Palace of the Caesars on the Palatine Hill, to St Peter's, the Vatican and Trajan's Column. Henderson may have spent a further shilling on the guide, which provided a history on the most conspicuous objects on view as well as pointing out the locations of some remarkable buildings that had been sadly destroyed. Although Georgiana may not have seen Rome at first hand, due to travel restrictions in place as a result of the French Revolution, she would have been able to compare the artist's record of the city with her father's paintings made during his Grand Tour nearly fifty years earlier.

Georgiana would probably have visited the first Panorama building in Leicester Square which had been established some ten years earlier by Barker's father, who had also employed Reinagle to paint the scenes. Robert Barker invented the term 'panorama' for these views in the round. His son Thomas had managed the business but over time felt the need to strike out on his own, particularly as he had devised a complex sky lighting system which, he advertised, 'had been constructed...to admit a powerful addition of light in cloudy weather', a problem his father had been unable to solve satisfactorily in the original building.

On their return to Southampton Street they sat down to dinner at 5.30pm before boarding the coach for Chertsey. Henderson's mother had joined them in order to meet her latest grandchild. Three and a half hours later they arrived at Abbey House. Their neighbour Mr Douglas wasted no time in calling on them to find out if they had any further news on an unsuccessful rebellion that had taken five days earlier. It was common knowledge that a group of Irish republicans and nationalists led by Robert Emmet, wanted to secure Ireland's independence from the United Kingdom and, to this end, had attempted to seize Dublin Castle and other strategic positions in the city. A premature explosion at one of his arms depots led Emmet to bring the date of the rising forward before the authorities became suspicious. This, however, led to confusion among the rebels, compounded by bad weather and other setbacks. The rising failed at the cost of the lives of twenty military personnel and fifty rebels. The newspapers reported the capture of Emmet a month later, his trial for treason and his subsequent execution.

Georgiana was able to return to her country life idyll. She helped to gather apples and pears from the orchard and raspberries, gooseberries and currants from the fruit beds. Some of this bounty she turned into jam while her husband made wine with the rest of the crop. Dr & Mrs Clark sent over a basket of apricots and a melon from their greenhouse to add to her bounty. The sun beat down and on the first day of August it proved too hot to go outside, when the thermometer registered 76o. Never one to sit still for very long Georgiana took this opportunity to help her husband 'put things to rights in the closets in the breakfast parlour and the spare room'.

Although her diary suggests that she was not an active church goer Georgiana attended morning prayers at St Peter's on Friday 12th August 'to be churched'. Normally this traditional blessing for mothers would take place forty days after giving birth but in Georgiana's case, perhaps due to ill health, her churching ceremony had to wait until sixty days after the birth of the baby. Perhaps to mark the occasion, or possibly due to the heat and their exertions in the hayfield, in the orchards and in the fruit and vegetable gardens, Georgiana records that she 'prescribed [a] bath' for both Henderson and herself. That she wrote this in her diary suggests that bathing was not a regular event in the Henderson household.

It would appear that the couple took an active role in maintaining the house and grounds. Georgiana wrote that her husband had repaired a fence that had been kicked down by a pig, cleaned the underside of the punt, although he had to call on a carpenter to carry out necessary repairs, and also to fit a locker to store his fishing gear. He then waterproofed the hull with pitch while Georgiana mixed the paint in the workshop ready for him to decorate the craft so that it would be ready to take their visitors out on the water. When all this work had been completed Henderson took his wife and children, together with Mary Croft who was staying with them at the time, for a trip down to Abbey Mills. Georgiana also managed to stow away a drake and two ducks as a present for Mrs La Coste. In spite of the full load the journey appears to have been uneventful.

With its flat bottom and square cut bow the punt provided a useful base from which to cast a line. A keen fisherman Henderson made his own floats to attract the fish but if they didn't bite near Abbey House he would pole the punt down to Nettlebury Hole at Laleham and then out onto the faster flowing Thames in search of a catch. The couple regularly used their punt until the days shortened, autumn turned into winter and the weather turned decidedly colder and wetter.

Henderson finally took the punt out of the water and put it under cover on Christmas Eve.

47 Charles Cooper

It was time to arrange the baby's christening. She wrote to their old friend Dr John Hutton Cooper and asked him to be her son's godfather. He appears to have accepted the invitation and replied that he planned to arrive at Abbey House on Friday evening. He added that as he would have to leave early on Sunday could Henderson make an appointment on his behalf to meet with Clarke the lawyer. This meant that Georgiana only had a week to make the arrangements. She immediately sent for the tailor to order waistcoats for her husband and for Cooper, as well as a new jacket for her son John. When Friday came Georgiana was 'busy in the morning giving directions for the next day'. She also had to deal with the tailor, who had called to carry out a final fitting, but as Cooper had not yet arrived she had to hope that his waistcoat would fit, as there would be no time for it to be altered before the ceremony the next day. It would appear that everything was ok as she makes no further mention of the garment. After dinner, and with the children in bed, the couple retired to the drawing room to wait for their guest. Georgiana entertained her husband by playing some of his favourite pieces on the pianoforte. When it became evident that Cooper had been delayed they went to bed.

What a relief it must have been when he finally made an entrance in time for breakfast on Saturday morning. Georgiana couldn't relax however as Cooper discovered he had left a box of legal papers at the home of Sir William Clayton, where he had spent the night. As these were needed for his meeting with the lawyer an express was immediately arranged to fetch them from Marlow, nearly thirty miles away. The christening party then made their way to St Peter's Church and, at 12.30pm on 27th August 1803 Georgiana's little boy was christened 'Charles Cooper'. He was the only one of her five children to have a name taken from outside the family circle. Georgiana had named her children John after her husband as her parents had failed to respond to the invitation to name their first grandchild, second was Georgiana, third Jane after her mother, even though she was still estranged from her daughter and Catherine after an aunt, fourth was Harriet after a favourite cousin and finally the new baby, Charles after an uncle with Cooper as his middle name after their friend. It may have been that they wished to acknowledge the medical care he had provided when Henderson had been taken seriously ill during a visit to the Isle of Wight the previous winter. He had complained of a sore throat and in spite of the gargle that Cooper ordered Henderson's health worsened. The doctor visited two or three times a day while Georgiana stayed up until one o'clock to give her husband his medicine, and then got up four hours later to give him another dose. He did initially start to feel better but then relapsed and took to his bed. He was so poorly on Christmas Day that he couldn't eat any of the plate of cod that Mrs Powell had sent for him from her own table. Cooper continued to call twice a day to check on Henderson and after three weeks a blister appeared on his patient's side. Cooper cleaned it out and advised Georgiana to dress it with a poultice. Concerned at the rough seas and bad weather the doctor advised Henderson, no doubt to his wife's relief, to delay his proposed return to Abbey House until the weather was a little calmer.

The ceremony over, the christening party returned to Abbey House for a cold collation and, no doubt, a glass of their homemade wine to mark the occasion. After the guests departed Georgiana went for a lie down while Henderson and Cooper decided to take the air. The express returned shortly after they finished dinner and the men collected the box and went to the lawyer's office to settle Cooper's affairs. Aware that their friend had to be away early the following morning Georgiana got up at 7am to ensure that he had a decent breakfast. Cooper then took the older children for a walk around the garden before saying goodbye to his hosts and climbing into his carriage.

Georgiana returned to her usual social round. Towards the end of August after a cold snack by way of dinner, the couple accepted an invitation from Mrs La Coste to see the mill pond being dragged. They then walked to the ponds at the end of the town to see them being cleaned too. The continuing warm weather saw Georgiana join her husband on a fishing trip. They spent most of the day in the punt and dined off cold duck. She doesn't mention their catch but perhaps she was too busy to detail the outing as she had to prepare for another trip to London where they revisited the Panorama of Paris on display at Thomas Barker's building in Leicester Square. Nearly ninety feet in diameter the paintings covered 1,000 square feet of canvas, there was always someone in attendance to act as guide to the experience. They then visited Dr Clarke's consulting rooms before going their separate ways. While her husband visited a Mr Squire Georgiana went to Barto Valles warehouse to place an order on behalf of Dr Cooper, then onto her dressmaker to order gowns for the maid, nurse and her friend Mary Croft, who had recently been widowed. She and Henderson made their way to Spring Gardens Coffee House soup room for a dinner of mock turtle soup and ice. They then took a coach to Hyde Park Corner and walked the two miles to Chelsea to call on a number of friends who lived in the village, including the miniature portraitist Samuel Cotes and his wife. Georgiana certainly kept herself busy. The following morning they returned to Dr Clarke's for breakfast. She then went to John Bell's pharmacy in Oxford Street to buy medicine, then to Whites in St James for chocolate, a nearby toy shop to acquire a sword and bayonet for her son John and finally shoes for her daughters. After dinner they boarded the coach to return to Chertsey.

Georgiana invited a friend from her early married life to come to Chertsey to see her new home. Mrs Garrow thanked her for the invitation but would have to delay her visit as she was 'going to Pegwell' to see the house her husband had bought as a family retreat. This seaside home was much grander than its name 'Pegwell Cottage' suggested. As well as the main house, the grounds boasted ornamental cottages, a pavilion, salt and freshwater baths, stabling, walled gardens and a sweeping view of the bay. Sir William Garrow, who had established a reputation as a formidable barrister at the Old Bailey, where he introduced an adversarial style that led to the idea that a defendant was 'presumed innocent until proven guilty', no doubt appreciated an opportunity to escape his busy calendar to spend time with his family. Garrow had grown up in Hadley, where his father ran a boarding school in the Priory, the largest building in the village, which also served as the family home. As their paths crossed at social gatherings, it may have been Garrow who suggested to Henderson that he set up home at White Lodge when the couple were looking to move out of London. Although the barrister no longer lived in Hadley when they arrived his sister Eleanor did and the intimacy of village life would have provided opportunities for the two women to meet and become lifelong friends.

Mrs Garrow finally arrived at Abbey House on Monday 12th September. Described as particularly elegant she was accompanied by her fourteen-year-old nephew Joseph. Although the Hendersons had 'done dinner' they 'had it again for them' suggesting the friendship was close. They also shared a mutual acquaintance in the Royal Academician and pastel portraitist John Russell. Joseph, the natural son of Sir William's older brother and Sultan, a native of India, had been sent to London to be placed in the care of his uncle. Shortly after his arrival the artist was commissioned to paint the young boy, wearing a light blue knickerbocker suit over a frothy shirt, pointing at a portrait which his eight-year-old cousin Eliza Sophia was unveiling of her father and his uncle. A few years later Russell painted an equally charming portrait of Georgiana. The following day the visitors were taken out in the punt to call on Mrs La Coste and then 'up the river to Fox's bathing place'. Later Henderson took their visitors for a walk to St Ann's Hill before taking them out in the punt on a fishing trip. Towards the end of the week Georgiana welcomed her friend Annabella Norford to Abbey House but she had to wait to meet Mrs Garrow and Joseph as they were spending the day in Egham. That evening they 'had some music' and they spent a pleasant evening around the pianoforte. Joseph may have contributed to the occasion as within a few years of his visit he was recognised as an accomplished violinist. We can only wonder what Georgiana would have thought when she heard the news that the now 23 year old Joseph had married a widow twice his age, and already a mother of two children. No doubt music had brought the couple together as she, Theodosia Fisher, was a singer at London concerts with a voice described as 'the most beautiful contralto ever heard'. It is possible that Joseph wrote to Georgiana with the news that he had become a father. His daughter, named Theodosia after her mother, had inherited his olive complexion, grey eyes and mass of dark hair. Some twenty years later he moved his family to Florence where his daughter was able to renew her friendship with the poet Elizabeth Barrett Browning, who had a villa nearby. Theodosia Garrow became a darling of the literary circles of her day and would later marry the older brother of Anthony Trollope, author of the Barsetshire novels.

After a very pleasant evening around the pianoforte Mrs Garrow and Joseph said their farewells to their hosts and Annabella then as they were leaving very early the following morning, indeed they had departed by 7am. Later in the month, while Annabella was staying with them, the Summer family sent an invitation to tea. They begged Georgiana to 'bring some music and some glees' with her. She may have included one of Charles Dibdin's most popular songs *Tom Bowling* in her repertoire. This piece has maintained its appeal and is generally sung at the *Last Night of the Proms*:

> Here a sheer hulk, lies poor Tom Bowling
> The darling of our crew
> No more he'll hear the tempest howling
> For death has broached him to
> His form was of the manliest beauty
> His heart was kind and soft
> Faithful below, Tom did his duty
> And now he's gone aloft
> And now he's gone aloft

It appears to have been a convivial evening as Georgiana records that they did not leave the Summers' home until 11.00pm.

48 Inoculated Charles for cowpock

Georgiana next welcomed her cousin John Hudson. She eagerly 'showed him all over the house' before they joined the children for a walk around the garden and adjoining field. They then made their way down to the river and went out in the punt with Henderson. The next day Georgiana joined her cousin and Annabella for Sunday service at St Peter's church. Later, while the two men chose to walk the 3½ miles to Oatlands, the two women and young John took the post chaise. They all met at the entrance to the park and the group made its way down to the lake so that they could see the amazing two-storey 65ft long grotto. Georgiana doesn't mention if the 'harmless but eccentric' Duchess of York, 'with an extraordinary fondness for cats and dogs' was there to welcome them but the visitors could not help but be impressed at this folly.

Shortly after their 6pm return to Abbey House Georgiana welcomed 'Mrs Barber, Agnes Douglas, Mrs Davies and Colin' for tea. Once they had left she sat up 'till ½ past twelve' chatting with her cousin. Henderson had gone to bed early as he was 'not very well'. He appears to have recovered by the next morning as, although it was raining solidly, he and John Hudson were determined that the bad weather would not stop their fishing expedition. Not surprisingly they were wet through when they returned for dinner. The women had spent the day indoors painting whiskers on the children. They also dressed up eighteenth month old Harriet as a Dutchman and were so pleased with their efforts that they took the children into the kitchen to show them to the servants. Later that evening, while Georgiana and her cousin played a number of patriotic sea songs composed by Charles Dibden, Henderson and Annabella looked at each other's drawings.

They awoke to another very wet morning and, recalling their soaking the previous day, the men wisely decided to stay indoors. Hudson read to them for a while then the children came down to be entertained by the adults. Georgiana got out her treasured 'Tunisian' doll which had been a gift from her uncle, and Hudson's father, many years earlier. She was up early the next morning to prepare breakfast for her cousin before he boarded the early stage coach. The wet weather continued and again the two women were forced to stay indoors. However, Mrs Catherine Swale braved the rain to travel the twenty miles from Hartfordbridge in Hampshire, where she had been staying, for her dinner engagement with the family. She was an old friend who had first met Georgiana when they both lived in Charlotte Street. Thankfully, the weather finally cleared and they all went out in the punt and they had a very pleasant time as Henderson took them along the Abbey River and out onto the Thames. The following day, 'Mrs Green who had been on a visit to Oatlands, came for Mrs Swale' and the two women returned to Hampshire.

With the September weather continuing fair Georgiana, Henderson and Annabella decided to visit Hampton Court some nine miles away. On arrival 'they got a sandwich' before Henderson paid the shilling entrance fee to see the State Apartments, the 'Cumberland Suite' designed by William Kent for George II and many other fine rooms before going outside to look at the grounds, where there was much to delight the eyes. Although the head gardener had earned a reputation as a 'destroyer' of gardens Lancelot 'Capability' Brown declined to remake the palace's 17th century formal gardens with their parterres and avenues 'out of respect to himself and his profession', he said. Instead he took care to maintain the historic layouts and gravel paths. He did, however, stop the practice of clipping the topiary yew trees. After they had admired this visual feast they could have tried their hand at negotiating the many twists, turns and dead ends of the one-hundred-year old hornbeam, yew, holly and privet hedge maze, as well as visiting the glasshouse to see the grape vine which had been planted by Brown thirty years earlier, and which is still going strong today. Georgiana certainly kept busy entertaining her friends and neighbours. Sadly, when on another occasion she took Annabella to meet Mrs Wightwick at nearby Sandgate they discovered that 'one of the young ladies' had just died. They expressed their condolences and left.

Life at Abbey House appears to have suited the Hendersons. Her husband appreciated the opportunities for fishing, often accompanied by his wife except when she had guests to entertain. No doubt the beaver bonnet, that she bought on her last trip to London, helped protect her from the inclement weather. On one of their outings they caught 70 roach and a 'jack' or small pike. The haul was far too much for their own use so they gave Mr Collins, who had joined them on this occasion, most of the roach. Curiously she records taking the older children into the kitchen to see the fish.

Annabella's last evening at Abbey House coincided with the feast day for St Michael and All Angels on 29th September and she joined the family for the traditional meal of a Michaelmas goose fattened on stubble from the hayfield, which it was believed would protect the family against financial need for the year ahead. The next morning they joined Annabella in the London bound coach. They accompanied her to the home of her sister Marianne, the wife of the actor, stage and theatre manager, George Walthen, who lived in Park Row, Knightsbridge. Then, as usual, Georgiana spent the day shopping before joining her husband for a trip to Covent Garden, where they managed to get 'in the upper boxes', and then Drury Lane theatre. They saw part of *John Bull* and the French play *Paul and Virginia* but she doesn't tell us what she thought about the performances.

On their return to Abbey House they heard that their neighbour 'poor Mr Douglas' had died 'at Maidenhead on the road from Bath'. Henderson attended the funeral which was held at St Mary's Walton on the morning of 8th October 1803. Georgiana had stayed at home to await the arrival of their friend Vulliamy. As he was wet through she sorted out some of her husband's clothes for him to wear while his own dried in front of the fire. She also provided him with a warming drink of elder wine, while he waited for Henderson's return.

At the end of October the couple arranged for Dr Summers to inoculate baby 'Charles for cowpock'. However, it didn't take as his arm didn't become inflamed and they had to go through the process again. Summers returned with a boy from whom he took infected matter and injected it into her five-month old baby's arm. This time it was successful. Georgiana gave the boy's mother five shillings (around a month of a housemaid's salary). The doctor received a set of Henderson's and her own engravings, as well as his usual fee. She also responded positively to Summers' request to bring two children with him so that he could inoculate them from Charles.

49 The Defence and Security of the Realm

It was at this time that Georgiana received news that her much loved godfather 'poor Plott was dangerously ill'. She immediately wrote to his sister, who was looking after him, but her letter crossed in the post with a message from Lydia telling Georgiana that he had died. As her son had only recently been inoculated she may have felt that she couldn't leave him to attend the funeral, which was held just over a week later at the parish church of St Maurice near Winchester Cathedral. However, on her next trip to London Georgiana did visit his old lodgings to find out what had been 'done with his effects'.

Back in Chertsey she was kept busy with domestic matters. She had to reorganise their cellars for the pipe of port that her husband had purchased from Thomas Swayne, the landlord of the White Hart Inn. In order to make enough space for the 720 bottles they decanted from the cask they had to move their currant wine into the ale cellar. The servants helped with the labelling before 'laying down' the port to allow it to mature. As this process took a long period of time Henderson most probably saw this as an investment for his son's future inheritance. The couple then fortified their homemade wine with brandy and unpacked three hampers of port and one of sherry for their own use. Once she had finished in the cellar Georgiana made her way to the garret where, with the help of her maid Molly, she 'looked out drawing boards and portfolios...and brought them down'. When the weather was too wet to venture outside Henderson used these to mount his pictures and Georgiana drew lines around the borders to create attractive frames for his paintings. She then spent her evenings putting their drawing desk, portfolios and engraving box to rights. Henderson spent some of his time painting his wife's portrait (now lost) while she read him Shakespeare's history plays, in particular *Richard the Third*, *Henry VI* and *King Lear*.

Whenever the weather allowed the couple would go out for walks. As well as their usual round of local friends they also made their way to Weybridge to stroll through the Arcadian landscape adjoining the terrace of Sir John Aubyn's home, Woburn Farm. On another occasion they walked to Foster House in Egham to call on a Miss Merry. Although the weather was 'indifferent' they were still able to mark the anniversary of the Gunpowder Plot on 5th November. Henderson first 'let off squibs', parchment tubes, or perhaps shafts of feathers, filled with black powder to make them explode. Then the night sky was lit up by the blue flares which Captain Wilson had left for the children. These 'Bengal Lights' were really meant to be used for signalling but no doubt provided great amusement

The couple had planned to attend the review of volunteers on Ashford Common the following week but this had been postponed as the recent wet weather had made the ground too boggy for the event. Henderson had been unable to attend the first meeting, organised by his friend John Wightwick, to set up a local reserve as his mother, who had been staying with the family, insisted that he take her back to her home in Southampton Street in London, on the same day. He did, however, send five guineas towards the establishment of the Chertsey and Thorpe Volunteers. Chertsey, like the rest of the county, responded to a call for 'every inhabitant, capable of bearing ARMS, to manifest his Zeal...by enrolling his NAME as a VOLUNTEER...to enable his Majesty more effectually to provide for the Defence and Security of the Realm during the present War' with France. The threat of invasion was very real and the locals responded with a force made up of a Captain, two Lieutenants, an Ensign, 14 Sergeants, 10 Corporals, 255 men and a band of three drummers, three fifers, two buglers and two clarinettists. The family and friends would direct their walks to the nearby burway to see the volunteers exercising on this water meadow which lay between the Abbey River and the Thames. In mid-October Georgiana's eldest son and daughter told their mother that 'the Duke of York' had 'gone with the volunteers in the burway', but it turned out that 'it was only Mrs Chawner in her carriage'. In November Henderson took his wife, son John and daughter Jane in the post chaise to see the Duke of Clarence (the future King William IV) and Colonel George Dalrymple inspect the volunteers on parade on Ashford Common. The Duke had brought his seven children by his mistress, the actress Dorothy Jordan, with him to watch the proceedings. After the men had gone through their paces the Duke said he was delighted to have 'the Honour and Happiness of commanding such Officers and Volunteers and with such a Corps the Duke would not only feel a pride, but a confidence, in being ordered to March against the Enemy, if he should attempt these Realms'. Another review was held on 4th December in the presence of the Duke's brother. Due to very bad colds neither Georgiana or Henderson were able to attend. Newspapers reported that at the end of the exercise the Prince of Wales addressed the Royal Spelthorne Legion. He told them that the colours he had presented to them would be a reminder for the common cause in which they were all engaged. 'For your King, your Country, your religion, your laws, liberty and property, your children and your wives; nay in short for everything dear to Englishmen'. He then commended the men to 'accept this pledge, this sacred pledge, which you will take care to defend with your last drop of blood, and only resign with your lives'.

Georgiana could forget about the preparations for war for a brief period in order to celebrate the fifth birthday of her eldest daughter. The following month it was 'Little Jane's birthday – four years old'. Although she records giving the younger child a harlequin doll which had been her own when she was the same age, nothing is said about what young Georgiana received as her birthday gift. Further good news arrived. Her cousin Harriet Hudson wrote to tell them that she was getting married. Her future husband John Richardson had recently been called to the Bar and would go on to be a judge and subsequently knighted by the Prince Regent at Carlton House in 1819, thereby making his wife, Harriet, a Lady. These relationships emphasis Georgiana's place in the upper levels of society.

50 Quit Chertsey

The summer months had been idyllic. When she wasn't walking through the Surrey countryside with her husband, children and friends Georgiana was helping with the harvest or collecting soft fruits from her own garden. When the weather was too wet to go outside she spent her time making jam and fruit wines for their cellar. All this activity however didn't mean that she didn't regularly leave the children in the care of the nurse and nanny to take the coach to London to go on shopping expeditions, visit the theatres to see the latest plays and to call on friends and family members. Unlike the previous winter which they spent on the Isle of Wight, where there was much to entertain the family they had no travel plans for the same period in 1803. On the rare occasions when the rain eased and they were able to venture out for a walk their boots, shoes and clothes quickly became caked in mud. Georgiana came down with a very bad head cold, suffered the agonies of toothache and, to make matters worse, she had to apply leeches to the leg of her maid who had injured it in some way. As the days shortened and the weather worsened it would appear that country life lost its appeal. There had been the attack on her garden and the damage perpetuated by their former gardener William Mews, who had subsequently been 'taken up for highway robbery'. The threat of invasion would have been another cause of concern. Although she had watched the local volunteer force practise their drill in preparation for repelling French soldiers that made their way onto English soil it may not have been enough for her to feel secure and so she decided to let the house and 'quit Chertsey'. To this end she travelled over to Egham to ask the Merry family to let it be known that Abbey House would shortly be available to rent. On her return she called on her neighbour Mrs Douglas who said she would ask William Dickson, the Bishop of Down, if he would be interested as she knew he was 'wanting a home' in the area. Before Georgiana and Henderson left for a planned trip to Hampshire she told the maid and her cook of the family's plans to leave in the near future. The continuing atrocious weather meant it took them three and a half hours to cover the twenty-one miles to the Marshall family farm at Yateley but they managed to arrive in time to 'dress for dinner'. In spite of frequent heavy showers during their two day stay they appear to have had an enjoyable time. On their last evening, she dressed the Marshall's 'little girl like a Turk and played tricks to amuse her'. We don't know how this was achieved but we can imagine scarves were used to create a loose costume with a sash tied around her waist. Perhaps Mrs Marshall gave her daughter one of her turbans to wear, or they may have wrapped another scarf around her head, to which they added a feather and perhaps a diamond or pearl to create the fashionable headdress. Georgiana would have been familiar with oriental attire as she had hosted a dinner, some seven years earlier, for Mahmoud Effendi, a nephew of London's first Turkish Ambassador. Perhaps seeing Marshall's little girl parading as a Turk bought back memories of this guest with his large bushy beard. He couldn't speak a word of English, even though he had been in the country for nearly three years. His interpreter on the other hand had such a facility for learning that within six months of his arrival he was able to speak English with a copious choice of expression and great fluency. Persani, as he was named, was 'a very intelligent man of liberal and extensive notions' wrote another of Georgiana's guests, the artist Joseph Farington. He also noted with interest that both men had several glasses of wine. Over dinner the interpreter told the diners that Constantinople, including Pera, contained about a million inhabitants and was not as large as London and he thought the Prince of Wales was too familiar in his manner and this would make it difficult for him to preserve dignity and insure the respect due to someone of his rank. We must hope that the guests had finished their meal before he described the effects of the plague that had raged through his homeland. After breakfast, with Mrs Marshall and their child, Georgiana and Henderson boarded the chaise that had come for them at eleven o'clock. They were unable to say farewell to their host as he had left the house early to go hunting.

The persistent wet weather meant that on her return to Abbey House, Georgiana had to stay indoors. It even prevented the family from attending the Christmas service at St Peter's Church. Henderson made a bowl of punch for the children to drink in the nursery and gave the servants two bottles of wine for their festivities. He also took the opportunity, during a break in the weather, to go down to the river and take the punt out of the water for the winter. As the storm had broken on Boxing Day morning Georgiana walked to the home of the Douglas family to see if they had heard from the Bishop but no one was home. On their return they met their friend John Wightwight, a Mr Cunningham and naval hero Sir Richard Onslow, who had played a distinguished role at the Battle of Camperdown. This sea battle led directly to the surrender of the Dutch navy. In appreciation of the part he had played Onslow was created a Baronet, presented with the Freedom of the City of London, a 100 guinea sword with an enamelled hilt and had his portrait painted by John Russell RA. The year after Georgiana met him on her walk he retired from active service and took up residence at 'Fangate', a small lodge on the edge of Chertsey Heath. When he died fifteen years later he left instructions that no more than £20 was to be spent 'to prevent any unnecessary ostentation' for the 'funeral of an honest sailor costs a much less sum', he wrote.

A few days later Georgiana called the servants together and told them that the family would be leaving Abbey House and Chertsey for good as soon as they had found new accommodation. Cook agreed to stay with them 'until they went to town in the winter' and before they left she arranged for Summers to come and draw a tooth for the nurse, to relieve her pain.

The couple set out for London on another wet day. On their arrival, while Henderson went off to deal with business matters, Georgiana took a hackney cab to call on her old friends, Mrs Clarke and Mrs Royal. She took them a present of a pig each, this would have been a carcase rather than a 'live' animal. She then called on Nurse Beaver to 'beg her to enquire about servants' on her behalf. The next morning they went to no.4 Royal Terrace in the Adelphi to have breakfast with Sir Brook and Lady Watson, and to collect the rent owed to Henderson on his former home. Georgiana then went on another shopping trip. She ordered shoes, bought a spelling book for her son John, visited Miss Kerr and Miss French to pay her outstanding bills, as well as calling on several friends. When she returned to her mother-in-law's house in Southampton Street she discovered that Mary Croft had called and left a twelfth night cake for the children. This rich crumbly fruit cake with sumptuous icing and decoration was an important element of the feast of the Epiphany held on 6th January. The Georgians would bake this cake with a dried bean in one half to be sliced for the men and a dried pea in the other side for the women. The discoverer of the bean would be King of the Revels for the night while the pea identified the Queen.

The weather remained wet during her stay in London. On New Year's Eve she took a hackney carriage to Wigley's Auction Room in Spring Gardens to buy a doll for her daughter. She then went on to Mrs Nichols to buy shawls as thank you gifts for the nurse, cook and Molly the maid. She visited other establishments to acquire a gown for a Mrs MacDonald and then to Binks to ask his advice about 'getting a stain out of a habit and greatcoat', before joining her husband for dinner with a neighbour from their Adelphi days, Dr Thomas Monro. Sadly his wife was unwell and she did not come down to join them for the meal.

This is the last entry in Georgiana's surviving diaries but other sources have allowed me to continue her story.

51 An excellent one

The couple left Chertsey as planned and moved into one of the fine houses in Montagu Street, a terrace built by James Burton, one of the most significant builders of Georgian London who had worked with John Nash on the development of Regent's Park. The large sash windows provided a light and airy feel to the rooms in this four-storey townhouse, the basement kitchen and utility area. Burton had encased the ground floor exterior brickwork with large rectangular blocks of smooth white stone to add weight to the building. A delicate iron balcony graced the first floor. They took up residence in their new home sometime in 1804 and the house appears to have suited them. It was large enough for the family of five, their servants and the various objects and pictures they brought with them from Abbey House.

No doubt Georgiana delighted in showing visitors around although Fanny Chapman wrote in her diary that when she and her aunts 'called on Mrs Henderson in Montagu Street' and added 'fortunately she was out'. However, Fanny had to admit that Georgiana's home was 'an excellent one' after being invited there to dinner. She and her aunts were given a tour. Firstly, they were taken into the study to see the paintings by J.M.W. Turner, Thomas Girtin and other artists, including works by her husband. The Peace of Amiens, signed in March 1802, temporarily ended ten years of hostilities between Britain and France and English tourists could once travel again on the continent. Early one morning Henderson caught the coach from Charing Cross to Dover where he joined the ferry for the eight-hour Channel crossing and then took a coach to Paris. The through ticket cost him £4.13s (over £200 today). The couple's former neighbours from Chertsey, Charles James Fox and his wife toured Belgium and the Netherlands before arriving in the French capital where they may have seen Henderson painting views of the Tuileries, Pont St Michel and the Louvre. Turner also took the opportunity to travel and filled a whole sketchbook with his impressions of the city. Madame Tussaud decided to travel in the opposite direction to set up an exhibition of her waxworks in London.

Georgiana then continued the tour of the house and took Fanny and her aunts into the drawing room to see an impressive display of early Dutch and Italian masterpieces, including work by Canaletto, together with the portraits of her parents by Angelica Kauffman and John Russell, miniatures of the family by John Plott and a commissioned portrait of the 18th century actress Mrs Frances Abington 'in the costume of a page' by the pre-eminent artist Sir Joshua Reynolds. They would also have seen examples of 15th century majolica from her late father's collection displayed on the furniture. The dining room featured a collection of Dutch paintings of fruit and fowl and genre pictures such as the 17th century *Couple at Breakfast* by Hendrick Sorgh.

We don't know when the Chapmans and the Hendersons first met but it was most likely at one of the spa towns, Bath or Cheltenham, where we know they both went 'to take the waters'. By the time Georgiana writes about meeting them on the Isle of Wight in 1802 it is obvious that they were already friends and moved in the same social circles. In spite of her apparent dislike of Georgiana due to their shared close friendship with Dr John Hutton Cooper, Fanny wrote that after dinner 'Mr H came home to tea and we had a pleasanter evening than…expected'.

Georgiana quickly settled back to life in the metropolis. The various attractions were in easy reach, either on foot or by hackney carriage, and the shops beckoned with the latest fashions, the theatres offered entertainment and of course there were plenty of dinner invitations. She most probably took the children to the British Museum just around the corner from Montagu Street. Perhaps she reminisced with them about the times she visited the museum gardens when she was a young girl but she may not have mentioned her expulsion. There was also the newly laid out Russell Square where the children could explore the fashionable landscape designed by the last great English garden designer of the 18th century, Humphry Repton.

Three years after leaving Chertsey she heard that a former neighbour, Charles James Fox had died at the age of fifty-seven from a dropsical complaint, from which he had suffered for many months. The post mortem revealed no fewer than thirty-five gallstones lodged in his gall bladder and seven pints of transparent fluid in his abdomen. Although his funeral was not a state affair it was nonetheless attended by the great and the good and it is highly likely that Georgiana and Henderson were among the mourners at the ceremony in Westminster Abbey.

Wherever she was the following year Georgiana would have witnessed a natural wonder. Visible to the naked eye, its brilliant nucleus 'bordering on a gold colour, and its train a bright gold colour near the comet, fading to a silvery brightness, and terminating in the thinnest white flume'. This comet was so large that it could be seen equally well in Bath and London. A Mr Capel of Troston near Bury wrote that it was 'much the finest of any observable in England for 38 years'. After being declared the marvel of the century an even grander comet appeared in the sky four years later, which was visible to the naked eye for around nine months. The astronomer William Herschel and his sister Caroline, who were monitoring the night sky, described its brightness as equalling that of the Milky Way. Napoleon took this comet as a good omen and moved forward with his plans to invade Russia, but this proved to be a disastrous campaign. Winemakers erroneously believed that it provided ideal conditions for their grape harvest. The most famous of the comet vintages, an 1811 white Chateau d'Yquem sold for £75,000 two centuries after it had been bottled and was still drinkable in the 21st century.

Another rare natural event entertained the family. Heavy falls of snow, a continuous hard frost and an intensely cold northerly wind brought misery to the country in 1813. Skaters flocked to the frozen Serpentine in Hyde Park and ice floes were seen floating in the Thames. It was the fourth coldest winter ever recorded. An impromptu fair was set up on the frozen stretch of water between London Bridge and Blackfriars. Wrapped up warm against the freezing temperature Georgiana took her family to join the thousands of people who had ventured out. The last time this natural phenomenon occurred had been the year before she married Henderson, so its possible that he may have taken her in 1795 to see the frozen river, or she may have gone with her parents. Georgiana would have paid two or three pence to take her children onto the ice.

There was plenty to amuse them as they surveyed the temporary stalls set up by tradesmen on 'The City Road' as it was called. They could buy trinkets, books, toys and souvenirs. Anything labelled 'bought on the Thames' found an easy market, even at silly prices. Enterprising George Davis set up a press on the ice to print the title page for his edition of *Frostiana, or a History of the River Thames in a Frozen State*. Henderson may have bought a copy for his own library. Alcoholic refreshments were also available in the bars or 'fuddling tents' fashioned out of sailcloth and oars, which littered the ice. Hawkers sold tea, coffee chocolate, hot apples and mince pies, while gingerbread vendors also sold cups of gin. Spectators paid six pence to watch a small sheep being roasted on an open fire. An additional shilling secured a slice of this 'Lapland mutton'. Sledging, skittles and donkey rides as well as gambling tables were all on offer, as well as the sight of an elephant being taken for a walk across the ice near Blackfriars Bridge. After four or five days a thaw set in and the ice started to break up. Soon the river began to flow along its whole length again. What a pity we don't have Georgiana's diaries or letters to hear first hand her impressions of the Frost Fair, particularly as it was the largest ever held. It also turned out to be the last one due to the demolition of the medieval London Bridge a few years later, which changed the force of the water meaning the river never froze again.

52 Much grown and improved

A heatwave hit the county in 1808. Luke Howard, 'the father of meteorology', took a reading of 90° in east London while in Newnham it reached 96° in the shade. In Yorkshire honey melted and drowned most of the bees as it flowed out of the hives and onto the ground. Elsewhere birds fell out of the sky, people and livestock dropped down dead. Georgiana and the family were therefore grateful for the cooling sea breezes as they were holidaying in Weymouth at the time. This resort became fashionable after King George III visited the town in 1789 on the recommendation of his doctors who thought that sea bathing would help alleviate his many ailments. His first dip from an early bathing machine was witnessed by the novelist Fanny Burney, who was in attendance as the Queen's Keeper of the Robes. She wrote that a second machine was used to take musicians to the dipping spot so that they could play 'God Save the King' when George III emerged from the water. The experience proved to be a great success. Queen Charlotte declared that her husband was 'much better and stronger for the sea bathing' and the Royal family continued to visit the resort over a number of years to take advantage of the health-giving properties it offered.

As a result of this royal stamp of approval fine new houses were built along the promenade to provide lodgings for the influx of tourists who came to Weymouth in the summer months. As well as the benefits of salt water there was plenty to amuse and entertain visitors. The Theatre Royal located on the seafront, one of the first purpose-built theatres outside London, had a capacity of around 300-400 people. Fanny Burney wrote, 'Tis a pretty theatre' but she was not impressed by the entertainment on offer. The Assembly Rooms were equally spacious. The circulating library, also located on the Esplanade, had 7,000 volumes to offer on loan to the visitor, as well as a commodious room for the reading of newspapers. There were opportunities to buy jewellery, stationery and a wide variety of fancy goods as well as a high-ceiling 45ft long card room where gentlemen could squander their inheritance. One contemporary guidebook said that Harvey's Library 'deserves to be ranked among the first libraries in the kingdom'.

The beach had much to offer too. Accessed by stone steps or a gentle slope halfway along the promenade it was said that although as soft as a carpet in a dining room the sand was firm enough to provide a stable surface for exercise, be it by foot or on horseback, or even in a carriage. With a sweep of two miles the bay provided plenty of space for all activities. Visitors could watch the bathing machines being drawn by horses into the sea to reach the dipping spots, or they could admire the yachts and excursion boats as they sailed to and from the harbour at the centre of the bay. Portland, three miles away could be seen from the lookout station, or reached by boat in less than half an hour with a favourable wind. The protection provided by the surrounding hills rendered the sea so calm that even a raging tempest could rarely disturb its tranquillity. Georgiana and her family most probably visited the camera obscura, which stood nearby and commanded a view of the town, a distant part of the country and the sea. Around 100 yards further on stood a battery mounted with heavy guns.

The town quickly became a favourite destination although Jane Austen didn't share the general opinion of Weymouth's merits. It was 'a shocking place without recommendation of any kind on account of there being no ice in the town', she wrote to her sister Cassandra.

Thanks to Fanny Chapman's diaries we know that she, together with her aunts and Dr Cooper arranged lodgings for the Henderson family in anticipation of their arrival in July. When he saw his godson 'little Cooper and John' walking by his window one morning the doctor called the boys inside. Fanny remarked that eleven-year old 'John is very much grown and improved'. Like the rest of the country the heatwave affected Weymouth. Fanny described Wednesday 13th July as 'one of the hottest days ever felt'. They awoke one morning to find the town enveloped in 'a very thick fog' as a result of the cool sea breeze hitting the hot air. It was 'so thick that at times they could hardly see the Esplanade' but eventually it lifted and they could once again enjoy the sunshine.

During their stay Georgiana and her husband joined upwards of one hundred people for 'one of the best conducted and pleasantest parties' laid on by officers from nearby barracks. A great many tents had been set up near the lookout. At half past three they all sat down to 'a most elegant dinner...with the greatest profusion of fruit' that they had ever seen. Then 'the Belles, most of them very handsome and elegantly dressed, the Beaux all dancing without their hats in the presence of a great many people' who had come to watch the fun, even though the day was intensely hot. Fanny wrote that the scene 'had exactly the appearance of the picture of the Dutch fairs'. Everyone appears to have had a good time as she added that 'Cooper was very tipsy (as indeed were most of the gentlemen) but very good humoured and kind'. As the following day was even hotter Fanny decided to stay on shore rather than join her aunts for a fishing trip with Colonel Bastard. She accepted the Hendersons' invitation to dinner and at seven o'clock the couple escorted their guest back to her lodgings as her aunt had sent for the key of the tea caddy. 'There was a good deal of humour' as tales were told about their outing, although nothing is said about fish being caught. At least no one had succumbed to the agonies of sea sickness. During the course of their conversation the weather changed. The whole sky was illuminated by lightning. With thunder rumbling overhead Georgiana and her husband hurried back to their own lodgings. As the storm continued to rage and spread inland it collided with warmer air and the rain turned to hail. Large areas of Somerset, Dorset and Gloucestershire were affected. Hailstones, the largest with a diameter of 4", caused a lot of damage to land and property. Many individuals caught outside were injured, and in some cases killed. The storm cleared overnight and the family woke to another 'very fine day'.

53 In a capital style

We can imagine that the Red Barracks proved of particular interest to Georgiana's sons. Although it had its own parade ground the soldiers based there regularly practised their marching skills on the firm sand of Weymouth bay. Seventeen officers and around 300 men formed the King's German Legion, a unit of the British army set up in 1803 under the command of their Colonel-in-Chief, the Duke of Cambridge. These, mainly expat Hanoverian, troops played a vital role in a number of successful campaigns undertaken during the Napoleonic Wars. Dressed in their uniform of red jackets with contrasting blue collars, grey leggings and the sun glinting on the metallic badges on their military caps, the soldiers must have presented quite a sight as they marched up and down the beach and practised their drill as they shouldered their Brown Bess muskets. It is quite likely that young John and Cooper fetched their toy rifles and mimicked the soldiers they had just watched on the beach, no doubt amusing their parents with their playacting.

As well as this visual feast of military skill the officers and men exhibited as they paraded in front of the tourists, the bands of the German Legion, together with the Somerset Militia, provided musical entertainment at the Assembly Rooms. Located in the centre of the Esplanade, these lofty, light and spacious rooms enabled upwards of one hundred couples to dance with ease. Fanny wrote in her diary that she was 'sure it was cheap enough; half a guinea the gentlemen and five shillings the ladies admits them for the whole season to the concerts and promenades'. These events were overseen by a Mr Thomas Rodber. He acted as the Master of Ceremonies to ensure that the strict rules were adhered to: the balls had to begin as soon as possible after seven o'clock and finished precisely at eleven; no lady or gentleman was allowed to dance if they were wearing coloured gloves; and they could not quit their place if dancing a country dance until it was finished. On Tuesday and Friday evenings gentlemen could not appear in boots or ladies in riding habits. Swords had to be left at door and no dogs were to be admitted. No doubt these dances and concerts provided visitors to Weymouth with a pleasant diversion from the constant threat of Napoleon's forces. The soldiers, as they exercised on the sand or marched through the town, together with the country's naval fleet provided the visitors and residents of Weymouth with a sense of security.

On 10th July Georgiana and her family watched as the 33gun frigate *Alomene* came to anchor 'in a capital style' just outside the bay. The ship's captain, William Tremlett then came ashore with two representatives of the Spanish government who had come to ask Great Britain to help them in their own war with the French. Within a short period of time the captain and his crew returned to active service. Later Georgiana and Henderson heard about Tremlett's bold plan to capture two large French frigates. He had chased them for over 130 miles, but due to the ignorance of his pilot the *Alomene* ran aground allowing his quarry to escape. However, once his ship had been re-floated and repaired Tremlett and his crew went on to capture and destroy upwards of fifty French ships before their own vessel was wrecked on the rocks near the Loire in 1809.

A fortnight later an expeditionary force came to anchor between Portland and Weymouth. Wooden hull after wooden hull filled with soldiers who were on their way to the continent to fight England's enemy. The Hendersons, like many of the tourists, may have taken a small boat out to visit the moored fleet to say farewell to those going off to war, as Fanny did with one of Georgiana's friends, Mr Bussell. He was a well-respected member of the Somerset Militia, which made up part of the 9th Regiment. Many of those aboard called out loudly to him 'How do you do Mr Bussell' and 'I'm very glad to see you Mr Bussell'. The soldiers all pressed hard against each other to speak to him when he drew up alongside. He and Fanny left to the sound of a hearty three cheers and 'Rule Britannia' played upon a drum and fife. Georgiana, like many visitors to the town, was awoken one morning by cannon fire at three am. This was a signal for the men on shore leave to return to their ships as the wind had changed in the fleet's favour. It is likely that the Hendersons were in the crowd that gathered on the Esplanade to watch the fleet as it slowly but surely disappeared from view.

Six months later Georgiana and her husband heard the sad news that Sir John Moore had died. He had been in charge of coastal defences along the coast from Dover to Dungeness before being sent to Spain to help in the fight against the French invasion. During the battle of Corunna he had been fatally wounded when he was struck by a cannon ball in the left breast and shoulder, and the whole of his left side and lungs. He remained conscious for several hours – long enough to be assured that, thanks to his delaying tactics, the British forces had escaped from the battlefields. As he lay dying he said 'I hope the people of England will be satisfied. I hope my country will do me justice'. His funeral was commemorated in verse and a number of monuments were raised in his honour. At the end of this battle 900 members of the British force were dead or injured – and may have included friends of Georgiana.

54 Every mark of loyalty and respect

At this time of national emergency Henderson, like many others established and supported local volunteer forces to offer a last line of defence, if Napoleon was successful with his invasion plans. Dr Cooper joined the 2nd Somerset Militia quickly rising from the rank of Captain to that of Colonel. He was currently with his troops in Weymouth and when he was off duty he met up with friends in town, like Georgiana. No doubt she was one of the 'great...assemblage of beautiful women' who joined Cooper in his box at the Theatre Royal for the performance of two plays, the comedy *Town and Country* and the melodrama *The Tale of Mystery*. Newspapers reported that they were performed 'in a style of grandeur highly creditable to Mr Sandford the Manager, who in the part of *Reuben Glenroy* was particularly chase and never appeared to more advantage'. Mr Bennett in the role of *Cosey* 'kept the house in a continued roar of laughter' and the 'actors 'exerted themselves with much credit and received loud testimonies of applause'. The reporter continued that it had been considered unfair to make any particular comments on the performance of Mrs Berkeley in her role as *Mrs Glenroy*, as she was almost a novice to the stage. However, she appeared very correct in her parts and her person was good, but her face was not expressive. The report concluded that the orchestra 'performed with great excellence'.

Georgiana and her husband would have joined the 'numerous and elegant assemblage of Nobility and Gentry' at the Royal Hotel Assembly Rooms to hear Mr Thelwall speak on 'the unbounded ambition of the Oppressor of Europe, and the glorious struggle of the Spanish Patriots'. For over two hours Thelwall used powerful, eloquent and energetic language to deliver his message and he made such a deep impression on the audience that the newspapers reported that they 'expressed their high approbation by loud plaudits'. We can imagine that Georgiana wrote to her family and friends about Thelwall's oration and other events she witnessed during her stay in Weymouth, as well as recording them in her missing diaries. She would certainly have written to them about the arrival of His Royal Highness the Prince of Wales on Tuesday 23rd August. Accompanied by his brother, the Duke of Cambridge, he had come in his capacity as Colonel in Chief of the German Legion (formerly the Hanoverian Light Horse) to review his troops.

In anticipation of the event the townsfolk and tourists set out at 11.00am for the temporary camp which had been erected on the Downs. The Prince sent word that he had been delayed and the crowd had to wait until 3pm to witness his inspection of the Legion under the command of General Linsingen, together with the 5th Regiment of the Dragoon Guards, Lord Hinton's regiment of the 2nd Somerset, the South Devon Militia commanded by Lord Rolle, the largest landowner in Devon and a troop of horse artillery led by a Captain Duncan. The several thousand spectators cheered as the Prince, dressed in his splendid Hussar regimentals with gold spurs and stirrups, rode onto the field. When he reached centre stage he received a general salute before the bands of the several regiments played 'God Save the King'. He then inspected the whole front line of the parade before the troops passed him in review order, then the cavalry rode by in single file, saluting their Colonel in Chief as they did so. All to the musical accompaniment of martial airs. The spectacle continued as the soldiers advanced in line and each regiment fired a volley over their heads. The cavalry then charged at full speed and with great precision executed a series of manoeuvres. Afterwards the Prince had a long conversation with Cooper and congratulated him on the effective state and high discipline that the volunteers had demonstrated that afternoon. He asked that the men be congratulated on his behalf for their steadiness under arms. Few watching the review would have feared for their safety if the French did make it to England's shores.

As they returned to Weymouth the royal brothers were met with every mark of loyalty and respect. Loud cheering accompanied them along the route. The windows of the houses in Gloucester Row and the Crescent were filled with women of beauty and fashion welcoming them by waving their handkerchiefs. His Majesty's ships fired a royal salute which was returned by the yacht of George III's aide-de-camp, Lord Craven. The bay was filled with ships 'decorated with colours of all nations...and gave an additional lustre to one of the most picturesque marine views...ever witnessed', said one reporter. That evening the Prince hosted a magnificent dinner at the Royal Hotel for

Cooper and his officers. 'Every delicacy that could be procured was profusely served up', he told Georgiana when he met her, and other friends, later that evening at the Assembly Rooms, which were 'most brilliantly filled with all the rank, beauty and fashion, of the town and country' for a ball. The *Morning Post* reported that 'His Royal Highness danced with the lovely Countess Craven, who had quit the stage the previous December to marry the Earl. Mr Rodber, as Master of Ceremonies, was most attentive and obliging to all the guests. 'If we had been of the Prince's party', wrote Fanny, 'he could not have paid us more attention'. No doubt Georgiana echoed this sentiment. The evening concluded with fireworks, illuminations and every testimony of joy, and so it no surprise that the revellers did not get to their beds until one o'clock in the morning.

Further entertainment followed. After hosting a public breakfast at the Radcliffe Barracks the officers of the Hanoverian Light Horse, with their men, went to the nearby Ridgeway Hill to carry out a sham battle. Once again the townsfolk and tourists, no doubt including Georgiana and her family, came to watch the men put through their paces. The 1st and 2nd Regiment divided into two brigades, one to represent the enemy. With a display of military tactics, courage and the most perfect discipline the men once again showed their readiness to defend England from the enemy. When the demonstration had finished the men sang a German hymn. 'The number of voices had a wonderfully fine effect and appeared to delight and surprise the Prince very much', it was reported. On their return to Weymouth they attended a most sumptuous dinner given for the Royal visitors and fellow officers – including Cooper by General Charles Linsingen, who had fought in a number of campaigns as Chief of the 1st Hussar regiment. Later in the evening Georgiana and Henderson met up with their friend, who no doubt told them about the meal before they all sat down for a concert. As the Prince was in attendance it proved very difficult to find a seat as the room was so full but when Captain Gylett saw Cooper, he, his wife and a Captain Staples moved up to make room for their friend and his guests. This was another successful event with Mr Atkin's flute playing being described as 'charming' by His Royal Highness. As he was leaving the Prince took his Colonel's hand and said 'God Bless you Cooper till we meet again'. Georgiana must have been delighted to see her friend receive this public acknowledgment from their future King.

After the Prince and his party left early the following morning to visit his brother at Oatlands Fanny announced that 'Weymouth appears quite quiet'. However, the officers at the nearby barracks continued to provide a little colour for the summer visitors as they returned to their usual social round. Georgiana accepted Fanny's invitation to dinner at the end of August. No doubt the main subject of conversation was the recent royal visit and Mr Rodber, another of the dinner guests, most probably delighted in hearing the talk about the successful ball he had arranged for the Prince. They would also have talked about the demonstration of military skill and tactics they had witnessed. Little did they know that the German Legion would put this to good use and enable them to play an important part in Wellington's successful campaign at Waterloo.

55 Took the least notice

The fine dining continued after the Royal party left Weymouth. At the end of August Georgiana and her husband sat down, with sixteen others, for dinner at the home of the winemaker Morgan Geatman. Another guest, Fanny Chapman, wrote that she 'never saw a better dinner or better conducted, with a most elegant dessert and a profusion of all kinds of wine: old Hock, Champaign [sic], Madeira, Cypress and in short, everything that was good, and given with the greatest liberality'. The evening continued with games of whist and speculation and Fanny described the whole event as 'a most superb and elegant entertainment', although her pleasure was marred by Cooper's behaviour. After ignoring her all day he had condescended to ask her to eat some cheese. When she left the party, he offered to shake her hand but she only 'give him one finger' as she did not intend to put up 'with impertinence from any one, but more particularly from one whom it had always been [her] study to oblige and please'. She wasn't the only one to have her evening spoilt. Another guest and long term friend of Georgiana and Fanny, Mrs Williams 'was very mortified and mad at Cooper's attention to Mrs Henderson, who sat next to him, both at dinner and supper'.

Fanny must have been pleased to see her discomfiture as the previous month when she, and her aunt Powell, called on the Williams family home near Dorchester, 'Mrs Williams pretended to be delighted' to see them but Fanny 'knew it was only pretence. Her manner to Cooper', who they discovered had been with her for some time, 'grows more absurd and impudent every day' and Fanny continued, 'I am much mistaken if they do not understand each other perfectly'. A few days later, while enjoying tea with friends and listening to the band, 'nothing could be more happy and comfortable' until Mrs Williams interrupted the 'social party with her nosey vulgarity' and stayed as long as she reasonably could. Four days later, at a ball at the Assembly Rooms, Fanny saw Mrs Williams look 'extremely ugly and vulgar' as she was evidently mortified at seeing 'Cooper [as he] danced and danced with Mrs Cox'. No doubt Fanny took great delight in telling Georgiana and Henderson, who both looked 'remarkably well' she wrote, this news when she called on the couple for tea.

They were also present when Mr Geatman called on Fanny and her aunts and was told about Mrs Williams' behaviour, and how she had continued in bad humour as she had 'perceived how cold and distant our manners were to her, to what they used to be'. Fanny further told them that Mrs Williams had written 'a very fine letter of apology...full of lies and contradictions, professing a great deal of affection, not an atom of which she feels'. She sent a second apology but it was 'such a farrago of nonsense and lies', said Fanny. Geatman replied that 'he had not heard a word of it before and appeared very much surprised' at this report. Fanny vented her feelings in front of their guests. She told them how the lady had told a great many histories about herself and her family, not half of which were true to the Chapman's knowledge and Fanny suspected the other half were false as Mrs Williams had told some of them several times 'and they varied each time'. Fanny hoped with all her heart that Geatman would repeat every word of her account to the woman. To Fanny's surprise, but perhaps not Georgiana's, Cooper chose to take Mrs Williams' side and he could not be persuaded otherwise. In fact, he was out of humour with their behaviour and Fanny supposed that in the end his will would prevail with her aunts, 'either by slight or by coaxing', so that they would treat the lady in a proper manner. Fanny would not be so easily persuaded and was glad to have any opportunity to show how much 'she despised and disliked the woman'.

Fanny found it particular hard to stomach Cooper's behaviour as he had condemned her for the very conduct he had himself adopted. He had hardly been civil to her, spoke one word or paid her the least attention, except for his own convenience and comfort or when he wanted anything on the table. If he imagined that treating her in this manner would induce her to receive Mrs Williams 'with the same cordiality' as formerly he was very much mistaken. As if to confirm her opinion of the woman she called on Fanny and her aunts the following morning in spite of being told that they would not be able to receive her as they were already engaged for dinner. Mrs Williams cried and moaned and 'told a thousand falsehoods' which to Fanny's disgust 'at last prevailed' and her aunts treated her with kindness again. They accepted an invitation to visit the Williams' family home near Dorchester. Fanny had no choice in the matter she had to go with them. They boarded the carriage that had been sent for them but not long after they left Weymouth the coachman had to return for a replacement pair of horses, but these turned out not to be much better than the first team. When they reached Ridgeway Hill they could not manage the weight of the coach and passengers and so Fanny and her aunts were obliged to get out and walk. When they finally arrived Fanny wrote that although Mrs Williams had described her family home 'as such a perfect place', she 'never saw such a miserable patchwork business as the house at Herringston'. The Williams' family had lived here from 1513 and succeeding generations had enlarged and embellished the original 14th century manor house. Mrs Williams took them on a tour of the building where her visitors would spend a couple of uncomfortable nights 'without a convenience or comfort'. I wonder if Georgiana, who had been a friend of the family for many years and would have visited their home, shared Fanny's opinion of Herringston. Mrs William managed yet again to cast herself in a bad light as she left her guests to go to Purbeck for a few days. 'It is certainly a new way of acting, to invite company and then leave them to entertain themselves', she wrote, adding 'I suppose it is the Herringston fashion'. It was some relief therefore to call on Mr Geatman, who lived nearby, where they spent a pleasant morning, even though Georgiana was also there. 'Mr Henderson played and sung a great deal', no doubt lifting their spirits. After an enjoyable lunch it was time to return to Weymouth. While her aunts joined Georgiana in the carriage Fanny had to sit outside on the box seat with Henderson.

It would appear that Fanny's affection for Cooper appears to have intensified during this holiday in Weymouth. He, however, had set his sights on the widowed Mrs Fenwick. He sent her a charade he had composed and Fanny noticed that he was 'out of spirits and uncomfortable' as he waited on her reply to his literary riddle. Eventually 'he wrote a very long letter' and as he didn't show this to Fanny and her aunts, which was his usual practice, she suspected that he had sent Mrs Fenwick a marriage proposal. A month later, when they were all on the Isle of Wight, Cooper appeared 'very much out of spirits in consequence of letters...from Mrs Fenwick'. Fanny became aware that Georgiana, who was also holidaying on the island with her family, was 'so much engaged in attending to, and getting close to Cooper that she had no time to spare for the rest of the company' at dinner. She wrote that she 'never saw anything so awkward as Mrs H[enderson] is in entertaining her guests', so much so that Fanny's aunt had been 'obliged to do the honour of the house, the same as it if had been hers'. No doubt Georgiana was concerned about Cooper's state of mind and so she may have been paying him particular attention, but he remained 'very much depressed and out of spirits'. At the end of September, Fanny wrote that he decided 'to go into the north, in search of a wife, apparently much against his inclination'. This led Georgiana and the others to believe that he was only chasing Mrs Fenwick because she had 'a great deal of money' following her inheritance of the Bywell Estate in Northumberland with a value of £145,000 (around £8 million today). Fanny did not 'think any man can withstand that temptation' and she was 'equally sure that he cares no more for Mrs Fenwick (independent of her large property)' then he did for her. Cooper was unsuccessful as she chose to marry the Revd Septimus Hobson instead, in spite of his reputation as an alleged child abuser following his time as Chaplain to the Female Orphan Asylum in Lambeth.

A thirty-three-year old spinster living with her aunts and dependent on Cooper for the roof over their heads, Fanny wished to be his wife but 'vanity and self love' did not blind her so completely as to suppose Cooper would only marry her if she 'had five thousand a year at her own disposal'.

56 Getting close to Cooper

Georgiana and her husband were not quite ready when Fanny called for them early one morning so she agreed to wait for them at the pier. The miserable wet weather had already delayed their crossing but at 8am the Hendersons, Fanny, her aunts, Cooper and their friends Captain Roach and Mr Bussell were finally able to set sail for the Isle of Wight. Although very blustery the weather was fine until their vessel reached the Needles when the heavens opened, and it continued to rain all day. Due to the heavy swell everyone, except Cooper, Georgiana and Henderson, succumbed to sea sickness. Fanny felt so ill that she was 'obliged to lay on the deck, and in spite of being covered with sails and greatcoats she was soon wet through. Cooper thought it unsafe to continue to their destination, Cowes, and instead he directed the captain to seek shelter at Yarmouth. The passengers disembarked and were fortunate to find beds available at the inn. Once they were in their room Fanny and her aunt 'immediately undressed and got in between warm blankets for an hour and by that means escaped colds'. The discomfort she had suffered on board ship led Fanny to fancy that their accommodation, although dirty and indifferent, was in fact very comfortable.

Thankfully the weather eased overnight enabling them to re-join their boat to continue their voyage to Cowes. They landed near an unoccupied cottage and decided to examine every part of it before making their way to East Cowes where they arranged accommodation in one of the hotels. Once they had secured rooms they walked to the recently built East Cowes Castle, the home of the architect John Nash. The owner and his family were away in Ireland but one of the maids 'very obligingly' showed them over the whole house. They saw a great many men at work on additions designed by Nash for his picturesque structure. As Norris Castle was not far away they decided to walk there to inspect the finished building, as it has been incomplete on their last visit. The owner, who happened to be Georgiana's cousin, Lord Henry Seymour accepted their invitation to dinner. After an enjoyable meal they sat down for a few hands of whist, before Fanny instructed Georgiana in the rules of another trick trading card game, Loo. The evening concluded with Captain Roach singing several songs for their entertainment.

They awoke to another fine day. While Cooper and a Mr Bowen went out shooting the women and Mr Bussell took the ferry to West Cowes. Here they parted ways on the quay and we don't know where Georgiana went and whether she had re-joined the group when they saw George III's thirty five year old daughter, Princess Sophia of Gloucester, who was staying nearby. When they all returned to East Cowes Fanny's aunt Mrs Neate and the Hendersons undertook a sailing trip to Spithead. Later in the day Cooper returned in high spirits as he and his companion had bagged two brace of partridges, a curlew and a landrail – otherwise known as a corncrake, similar in appearance to a moorhen. That evening the men in the party 'were all very gay and talked on a great deal', wrote Fanny. After breakfast the following morning they all went to see the improvements made to the home of a Mr & Mrs Mackenzie before setting sail for Weymouth. However, the sight of a sloop limping back without its mast and some of its sails after a failed attempt to run through the Needles, led them to lay over at Yarmouth again. Although it was raining hard Fanny was able to report that she didn't get wet through this time, neither had she been the least sick. However, after the comfort the hotel had provided they realised that the accommodation at the inn was much worse than they remembered, and the food was 'shocking bad'. They spent the day walking all over Yarmouth before visiting the parish church of St James to see the monument to a member of the Holmes family, which they believed had been carved by the 18th century sculptor Louis-Francois Roubiliac. It was said that when Sir Robert Holmes, who had served under Prince Rupert and as Governor of the Isle of Wight in the late 17th century, captured a French ship he discovered a headless statue in the hold. It was meant to depict, and be a memorial, for King Louis XIV. The sculptor had also been discovered on board. He was on his way to France to take a likeness of his royal master but in exchange for his freedom he agreed to carve Holmes' head to add to the overlarge white marble statue which was now before them. After seeing this and other memorials in the church the party made its way back to the inn. Mutual friends who were staying nearby, Isaac Gossett and his wife Catherine, called in on them but declined to stay for tea.

The following morning after a 'very nasty uncomfortable breakfast' they set sail for Swanage. Once again the weather was unfavourable and they did not arrive until six o'clock, very cold and wet. Fanny was so sick that she had to lay down for most of the voyage. She must have envied Georgiana who did not appear to be affected by the motion of the ship. Thankfully, a snug little inn provided them with lodgings for the night. Everything was 'so comfortable, clean and nicely dressed' that it repaid them 'for all the inconvenience suffered on the voyage', wrote Fanny. The next morning Georgiana's husband and Capt Roach decided to visit the stone quarries at Tilly Whims, whilst the rest of the party went calling on friends in town. The two men watched as the quarrymen split the rock from the cliff face using only metal punches, wedges and hammers before the masons dressed the Portland stone ready for use. As agreed they all met up for the one o'clock sailing to Weymouth. However, the ship had to tack continuously as the strong wind was blowing directly against it and this, together with the 'tremendously high' sea, proved very disagreeable to most of the travellers. Fanny once again felt awful, was unable to relieve her stomach and suffered more than if she had been sick. Not surprisingly in this state she doesn't mention if any of the others were ill. It took them seven and a half hours to reach their destination. No doubt they were all glad when the ferry docked and they were able to step ashore. In spite of the sailing conditions the party agreed, over supper that evening, that their expedition had been very pleasant and gratifying.

Although she had been jealous of the affection Mrs Fenwick and Mrs Williams displayed for Cooper at least they weren't in his company on a daily basis. Georgiana, however, made a point of waiting for him to arrive when she came to Fanny's lodgings for tea, even though she had her husband with her. On Tuesday 13th September she wrote that 'Mrs H[enderson] just as imprudent and ridiculous as yesterday and Cooper encouraging her in her folly'. As Georgiana believed it was his medical knowledge that had saved Henderson's life when he succumbed to a serious illness it is not surprising that she had a fondness for Cooper. To Fanny's relief they finally left Weymouth but she must have been put out when she discovered that they had accidentally packed two of Georgiana's petticoats in their luggage and she was charged with returning them. She wrapped them up and sent them to Mr Bussell with a request that he get them back to their original owner. Although she felt that she had lost 'Cooper's cheerful society' over the last few months Fanny could only hope that now Georgiana no longer had daily access to him he would once again look upon her in a fondly manner again.

57 Not possible to refuse

Fanny didn't have Cooper to herself for long. Six weeks after returning to their home at Batheaston they were once again on their travels. This time they went to Cheltenham to take the waters and 'the Hendersons...both looking well' arrived shortly afterwards. A few days later they had arranged to meet up for a trip to the theatre but as the weather took a turn for the worse, it rained all day, Georgiana and her husband sent their apologies. 'At night [it] blew a perfect hurricane' and although 'the lightning was tremendous it didn't deter the other theatregoers. However, they did consider it too dangerous to take a chair and instead they chose to walk and, to Fanny's delight 'Cooper took care of her'. Although she thought the play the 'most disgusting' she had ever seen she did praise the celebrated eight-year old comic Master Dawson in his role as Scrub in *The Beaux Stratagem*. Cooper and Fanny's aunt do not appear to have shared her opinion as they paid for their servants to see a performance of this play. No doubt she told Georgiana all about it when they met up at the well the following morning. Unable to take her usual walk around the pleasure grounds as the continuous rain had made the ground too muddy, Georgiana paid a small consideration to the pumper and manager of the well, a Mrs Forty, in order to take her exercise in the sixty-six-foot long corridor or 'walk' as it was known that adjoined the pump rooms. Within a few days of her arrival in Cheltenham her friendship with Cooper was once again causing Fanny some concern. Thursday 27th October was a beautiful day. They met lots of friends at the well and afterwards walked a good deal. However, Georgiana and her husband were among their dinner guests, and the couple stayed on for supper when Fanny saw 'Mrs H[enderson] acting with Cooper in the same improper manner that Mrs Williams does'. She concluded with the observation that it had been 'very far from a delightful or pleasant day'. Not long after they all met up at the well and, much to her annoyance' the Hendersons insisted on walking back with them. 'There is no getting rid of them once they have a hold on one', complained Fanny. She echoed this sentiment about the couple a few days later but then to her surprise when Georgiana entertained them after dinner Fanny realised that she had 'spent a pleasanter day' than she had expected.

The social round of dinners and suppers, together with regular visits to the pump room, meant that Georgiana was often in Cooper's company. One morning she called at their lodgings only to discover that they were all out so she called again later in the day. Although the women had returned Cooper was still absent, so she decided to wait. Fanny thought that it was as if Georgiana 'never intended to go away' and 'she waited in hopes of seeing Cooper again' but 'she was disappointed'. Fanny found plenty of occasions to record her dislike, such as the occasion, when in spite of the heavy persistent rain, Georgiana called at their lodgings and stayed two hours under the pretence of 'copying poetry'. The aunts invited her to stay to lunch but she replied she did not eat at that time, however she changed her mind when Cooper came down. Fanny 'fancied' that Georgiana thought 'we should go and leave her alone' with him but they 'completely disappointed her and would not move'. Georgiana then arranged to meet him at the pastry cook's but to her dismay he brought Fanny and her aunts with him. She invited them all to dinner later that day. One of their other guests, and an old friend of both the Hendersons and Cooper entertained them with some music after the meal but unfortunately this gave Fanny another opportunity to deride her hostess. 'Mrs Henderson' she wrote, 'fancied she played also but it was so very bad after watching Mrs Porcher, that it was shocking'. On another occasion when they met at the well Georgiana and her husband insisted on walking with them to their lodgings 'for when she gets hold of one, there is no shaking her off', wrote Fanny. They met again that evening for supper at Mrs Penning when she was once again annoyed at her rival's behaviour: 'Mrs Henderson continued to sit so very close to Cooper she was almost in his lap'.

Cheltenham certainly provided some distractions. Cooper 'found a Ladies Pocket' on his way to the well. He carried it openly in his hand but when no-one came forward to claim it he took back to his lodgings where, in the presence of Edmund Bastard as his witness, he emptied it and discovered 'a purse containing three guineas, a half crown, shilling and sixpence, a pocket book, which they did not open and some receipts which proved to belong to Lady Anstruther', wife of the former Chief Justice of Bengal. Cooper sealed it up and sent it back to her by way of Bastard who was a friend of the family. Fanny felt slighted once again when they were all awoken to news of a fire in one of the new houses in the Crescent. Cooper was so eager to witness it that he wouldn't wait for her to go upstairs for her bonnet. 'Dependants must put up with unkindness and slight' she wrote. The firefighters managed to put the fire out before it spread to the rest of the terrace but the building itself was completely destroyed.

Eventually it was time to leave Cheltenham. On a very disagreeable morning in early December they said their farewells and set off for Batheaston. Cooper was very out of sorts and barely spoke during the long miserable journey home. By the time they reached the Cross Hands on the edge of the Cotswolds the early mist had turned into a fog so thick they could barely see twenty yards in front of them. The 14th century inn, where they stayed for the next two hours, provided them with 'some excellent mutton chops and the best bread and cheese'. While they waited for the moon to rise to help light their way Cooper arranged with the innkeeper to buy some of his stock of the cheese he had so enjoyed with the meal. On their arrival they discovered that Edmund had sent them four of the finest pineapples and Henderson a barrel of oysters for Cooper's birthday dinner the following day. That evening passed 'tolerable pleasant and cheerful' wrote Fanny with the usual games and music, and the party did not break up until one a.m. Henderson gave his friend a pocket book as a birthday present. The next day he returned with fans for Fanny and her aunt. She would like to have refused the gift but it would have been impolite to do so.

The Hendersons had also left Cheltenham and were now spending a little time at Bath before returning to Abbey House. Georgiana had said that she would travel back with Cooper after his dinner with Lady Louisa Lennox, a former favourite of George II, as she 'had so much to do' and wouldn't be able to come earlier, but Fanny's aunt said she would wait and Fanny thought that this 'was a disappointment…for the lady', and possibly for Cooper too she added. Georgiana was staying with them for a few days as her husband had business to deal with in London. She was late coming down to breakfast on her first morning with them and Cooper 'made such a fuss and laughed so much' that she was determined to get up before seven in future. In good humour he then walked into Bath with Bastard but on his return, a little after five, he was 'extremely out of temper' and, Fanny wrote, remained so all through dinner and he then found fault with the tea. To her relief his mood improved after he played several card games but then she saw that this was more to do with him ogling 'Mrs Henderson, which she returned with interest'. Although she got up early the next morning, as planned, Georgiana 'did not come down till she thought Cooper was down' as well. As only Bastard joined her for a walk in the garden she went back inside after only a quarter of an hour. Fanny decided this was because their guest must have thought 'it was not worthwhile to walk for health and exercise alone'. She was disappointed when Cooper made her give up her seat for Georgiana in the carriage sent by Mr Wiltshire to take them to Shockerwick for the day. The weather deteriorated by the time they returned. The heavy rain turned to snow and the wind 'blew tremendously' throughout the evening and for most of the night. The temperature dropped and turned the waterfall in the garden into a sheet of ice. Georgiana was up early again and Fanny found her in the dining room writing but she suspected she was really waiting for Cooper, but to Fanny's delight he only stayed with her for a minute. Although there were heavy frosts they still walked into Bath on several occasions until it became 'excessively cold' and began to 'snow very fast', and they had to stay indoors. While the others played several rounds of whist Georgiana made some 'otto of roses'. She then filled three little bottles with this essential oil before fitting gold chains so that they could worn around the neck and then presented them to the women. Fanny wished with all her heart that she had not been given this gift and her unhappiness was made even worse when she watched Georgiana as she 'made fierce love to Cooper' at dinner. This may not have been as intense as Fanny makes it sound as she was jealous of any women that received attention from Cooper. As Henderson couldn't be there he sent his host 'a very nice stilton cheese'. However, when he returned to Bath he found his lodgings 'empty and very uncomfortable' but Fanny wrote that this 'did not at all distress his amiable wife who, provided she can be with Cooper, does not care what becomes of her husband and children'. Although Christmas Eve was a miserable day with both rain and snow Fanny was in a good mood because Georgiana had gone back to Bath to be with her family. However, this joy was short-lived as the couple and their son called on them at Batheaston on Boxing Day, and Georgiana persuaded Cooper to advise her husband that they should stay in Bath for another month rather than return to Chertsey, as planned.

58 Vulgar and disagreeable as usual

On Tuesday 3rd January 1809 Georgiana and her friends awoke to 'quite a white world'. Snow had fallen heavily throughout the night blanketing the ground. A rapid thaw then quickly set in before a period of continuous heavy rain. Fanny wrote that her aunt was 'very unwell with a violent cold in her head'. 'It was 'so different to the Christmas's' we used to pass at my uncle Appleton's and Lambridge', she lamented.

The long dark evenings during the worse weather were passed in convivial company. As well as musical interludes Georgiana and friends played various card games and rounds of chess. They also tried their hand at solving some of the charades devised by Cooper, like:
> What I believe you have often times done
> Yet what you did not, for you did it in fun
> When you did ill, you were known to do well
> But what you did do, I fear I can't tell

The answer is 'amiss'.

Georgiana heard that her friend John Wiltshire had taken a nasty tumble. The snow combined with continuous rain had made the ground treacherous and his horse slipped and fell on its rider. She made several visits to Shockerwick House to see the invalid who had been confined to the 'sopha' in order to rest his heavily bruised leg. Georgiana broke one of her visits to take lunch with Cooper at Batheaston Villa. Fanny, not unsurprisingly, was put out by her presence. 'Mrs H[enderson] as vulgar and disagreeable as usual' she wrote, although she doesn't elaborate on her comments so we can only assume that Cooper was paying his guest too much attention in Fanny's eyes.

Shortly afterwards the weather turned intensely cold, so cold that the heavy rain 'froze as it fell so that the ground was a sheet of ice'. Then it snowed, and snowed heavily for some time, before an extremely fast thaw set in, followed by more heavy rain showers. As the water flowed downhill it carried with it sand and mud which choked the little brook causing it to flood near Batheaston Villa. As it started to flow under the doors the residents sprang into action as the lower part of the house was in danger of being under water and all the carpets spoilt. With some difficulty they managed to stop it 'running into the drawing room [and] at last succeeded in returning it into its proper channel'. The water was six foot higher than it had ever been according to the oldest person in the village. The roads and bridges became impassable. Georgiana heard that two horses from one of the stages drowned but thankfully, by an immense effort, the passengers managed to escape from a watery grave. The flood also affected Bath. Seven people died when three houses in Bedford Street were washed away. The basements of many properties, particularly those in Great Pulteney Street, were inundated. Georgiana's missing diaries would have reported the immense damage she witnessed, as well the loss of all the cattle and hay swept away between Bath and Bristol.

Although they had woken to a violent storm they discovered that the flood waters decreased rapidly making it possible for Georgiana to check on her friends at Batheaston. She and her husband stayed for dinner and supper, then played several rounds of Casino, with Cooper, Fanny and Mrs Williams, who had also come to check on the family. This card game had come into vogue at the end of the 18th century. Although Fanny won three shillings she said the day was 'as disagreeable as it could be', no doubt due to the presence of her two perceived rivals.

Mrs Chalie had to send out messages saying that as a result of the weather she had postponed the ball until the following evening and when it finally took place, she had been too ill to attend so the Misses Gladstones took on the role of hostesses for the evening. However, so many guests sent their excuses whether it be because of the bad weather or the floods that there were only nine gentlemen to escort the fifty women dressed in their finery for the event. We don't know if Georgiana and Henderson were to be counted in this number.

During a lull in the weather Cooper paid a visit to the home of one of Georgiana's friends. On his return 'he talked of nothing the whole evening but of the "princely style" in which Mr Bastard lived, not even inferior to the Prince of Wales', Fanny moaned. A Tudor mansion built in the reign of Henry VII by Thomas Pollexfen (pronounced Poulston) Kitley House had remained in the family until the early 18th century when William Bastard married Anne Pollexfen. It is said that their grandson, John Pollexfen Bastard, indirectly inspired the nursery rhyme 'Old Mother Hubbard' when he told his wife's sister Sarah Catherine Martin, who was staying with them at the time to 'run away and write one of your stupid little rhymes'. Georgiana most probably felt particularly close to his uncle Edmund Bastard MP who, like her, married for love. He eloped to Gretna Green to marry Jane Pownoll, three years after her father died. Perhaps the executors of her father's estate did approve her choice of husband. Her father had been a distinguished naval officer who helped capture a Spanish frigate which they discovered was transporting a valuable cargo of bags of dollars, gold coins, ingots of gold and silver, cocoa and blocks of tin. Their prize was valued at around £78 million at today's prices, and Pownoll's share of the bounty came to nearly £65,000 which equates to £9 million. Cooper, like Georgiana, would have seen the model on the landing at Kitley House of the captain's last command, *HMS Apollo*. Whilst patrolling the North Sea Pownoll engaged with a French privateer. After an hour of intense firing he was hit by a cannon ball and killed. It was said that the ship's company had lost a father and the navy one of the 'best officers under every line of description in the service'. John Bastard, who was in the service, was promoted in honour of his grandfather's contribution to the navy.

Much to Fanny's discomfort Cooper 'was not in good spirits and evidently uncomfortable at leaving the magnificence and grandeur of Kitley to come to a hum drum family circle'. He also came back with the determination to sell Batheaston Villa Fanny believed 'at the instigation and repeated solicitation of the elder Mr Bastard'. 'Thank goodness', she said when she heard that William Bastard was leaving town. Cooper suggested that he could let the Villa and if he could get £450 a year then he would have £1500 a year to spend 'but I can't afford to marry on that', he told Fanny.

'Marry, you don't want to marry'
'Yes I do', he replied
'You would not marry except the lady had a large fortune'.

'No I could not afford to do so without, but if I had ten thousand a year I would ask you to marry me'.

Even though he claimed that he made this statement 'upon my honour as a man' and as much as she wished it Fanny didn't believe him. His behaviour over the next few days proved her right. A tempest raged so violently that Cooper did not think it was safe to go out, and this did nothing to help his temper. He 'took the least notice' of Fanny 'except to desire' her to pass him the inkstand and when he discovered there was very little ink in it, he became even more disagreeable. Finally, the wind eased and they joined Captain Graves and Morgan Geatman on a trip into Bath. However, the wind strengthened again and it blew such a hurricane that they had the greatest difficulty in boarding the coach. In spite of the deep snow Henderson called at the Villa to tell them that the couple planned to stay in Weymouth in the same month as Cooper. Fanny suspected that this decision was made at Georgiana's instigation and she was surprised that the men didn't have enough 'sense to see her folly'.

The bad weather continued into February and with Cooper away Fanny was left not only to look after her aunt, who had gout and could hardly put her foot to the ground, but also to deal with potential buyers. 'A person calling himself Sir Hugh Bateman' came to inspect the villa on a Wednesday instead of the advertised day. When the maid informed him of his error he told her that 'he could not come on any other day but this and it was very hard he could not see the house when it was to be let'. The maid told him that as well as being the wrong day the ladies were at home and 'engaged in prayers'. This didn't stop Sir Hugh and he forced his way into the drawing room. The maid told one of Fanny's aunts about the intrusion and she came out into the hall and asked to see his ticket. He replied that he didn't know it was necessary. 'No one could be admitted but on Thursdays and then not without a ticket from Mr Clarke', she told him, 'if she deviated from the rule laid down she should have constant interruptions which were very unpleasant'. She was so determined that Sir Hugh wished her good morning and left, only to return the following day with his wife and two daughters.

59 She might have the pleasure

Georgiana and her family arrived in Weymouth on 5th June 1809 'to stay as long as the Colonel does I presume', wrote Fanny. She and her aunts joined them a month later. Mr Bussell met them 'in the kindest and most friendly manner, as he always does. Not so the Colonel', she complained he was very distant and 'not at all glad to see us'. To her dismay 'Mrs Henderson…runs in and out of the house like a puppy', but Georgiana couldn't stay long on these visits as she needed to comfort her son John who had been kept indoors after he 'dislocated his elbow'.

A month later Georgiana, with a Mrs Simmons, called on Cooper who had invited the two women to dinner at Broadmayne, a village about six miles away. 'The great disappointment and annoyance of Mrs H[enderson] who was quite in a pet' when she discovered that he hadn't got dressed for the appointed hour amused Fanny. He asked Mr Bussell to take his place and he would make his way there later. By the time they all returned Fanny, to her annoyance, saw that Cooper had managed to improve Georgiana's mood. Not long afterwards Georgiana became unwell and was housebound. Through common courtesy Fanny and her aunt visited the invalid on several occasions to sit with her. To their surprise on one of their visits they found Cooper in her company and, she wrote, 'he took great pain as well as Mrs H[enderson] to tell us that he had not been there long'. A week later Cooper was sent for and Fanny thought this was 'rather an extraordinary manoeuvre for a woman alone to do'. He stayed with Georgiana for about half an hour but we don't know if this related to her health or she wanted to see him about another matter. She recovered over the next couple of days and was able to join Sir John and Lady Hawkins, the two Misses Smith, Major Durbin, Mr Bussell, Mr & Mrs Porcher, Rebecca Workman, Mr & Mrs Jacobs, Miss Whytel, Mrs Neate and Mrs Powell for a dinner to celebrate Fanny's 30th birthday. Fanny wrote that it was 'a tolerable pleasant day', Lady Hawkins looked lovely and Mr Bussell 'made fierce and open love to Miss Smith'. All but Georgiana, who 'would have staid all night', left before supper. Cooper and his sister-in-law settled down to play five games of chess, which didn't finish until one am, and 'Mrs H[enderson] was very loathe to leave while they were playing'. Fanny concluded her entry with the comment that it was 'not near so happy a birthday as last year'. When Mrs Williams came to tea Cooper's behaviour was 'very extraordinary!! not to say indecent' Fanny recorded. She had come to deliver an invitation to them all to come to dinner at Herringston. On the day fifteen of them sat down at a table not large enough for twelve. Georgiana, like Fanny, 'had not room to move' and they were obliged to cut their meat and then sit sideways to put it into their mouths. Fanny thought all the children were very much improved and she reported that Mrs Flinn looked so much better and is 'likely to live longer than Mrs Williams wishes'. It was such a beautiful moonlit night that after they dropped Mr & Mrs Porcher at their home Cooper and Georgiana decided to leave Fanny and her aunts to continue their journey in the carriage, whilst they walked the rest of the way to their lodgings.

Cooper not only enjoyed the delights of Weymouth he also took pleasure, as we have seen, in flirting with the married women in his friendship circle. Fanny watched as he coaxed and caressed Mrs Williams out of a very ill humour which had been brought on because she was not seated next to him at the card table. Several days later he held a large dinner party where he served 'the best haunch of vension'. The women then adjourned to the parlour to play several hands of whist while they waited for the men to finish their port. When they did appear some were 'very drunk and some middingly so', Cooper was one of the former and it made him behave towards Fanny in a much kinder manner than he had since their arrival in the resort. One of the other guests, a Mr Grimes, fell asleep on the 'sopha' [sic] as a result of his over indulgence, and was later found in the same condition on the stairs. On another beautiful evening, Fanny wrote, the two rival Queens sat on either side of Cooper though 'Mrs W[illiams] was in the dumps because he did not play the same tricks with her as he did Mrs H[enderson], who sat almost in his lap'. However, later at supper both 'the rivals were much mortified when Cooper chose not to sit with either of them'.

The army were still in residence and Mrs Porcher took Georgiana, Fanny and her aunts, to see the 2nd Somerset regiment practising their manoeuvres at Radipole Lake in the heart of Weymouth. Even though it was an intensely hot day the men 'perfomed very well'. While Fanny and her aunts made their way to the riding school to watch the 16th Regiment demonstrating their skills, although they didn't stay long as Fanny 'expected every moment the horses would get loose and run amongst them, Georgiana and Mrs Porcher returned home. Even the Quakers provided entertainment for the tourists. At the beginning of August several of Georgiana's friends joined Fanny and her aunts and a very large crowd to witness a meeting. Although there were fine speakers only two women were inspired to stand up and testify. One spoke very well and the other very badly in a terrible crying tone and she 'stopped every two or three words, as if she had lost her breath'.

When Cooper sent word that he would not be able to dine with the Hendersons as Lady Smith was still very poorly, Georgiana called on Fanny and her aunts to tell them that the dinner would be delayed until, Fanny surmised, Cooper could attend. Then Georgiana became concerned that they accepted the postponement too quickly and the women may have thought that she didn't want to see them without Cooper. Then she 'began to palaver in her sycophantic manner of her sorrow at not seeing them'. She then 'pretended to persuade' Fanny's aunt to go back with her but she 'steadily refused and at last [they] got rid of her'. When she discovered that they were having their breakfast when she called on them one morning Georgiana came back later on her own, 'to have a little private amusement with Cooper before he went away'. Later he took his leave of them all and Fanny was pleased to find that he treated her 'with tolerable kindness' but not she noticed 'with half the affection he did with Mrs Henderson'. She watched as he rode to the turnpike accompanied by Georgiana and her husband. The couple lingered until Cooper was out of sight and Fanny thought 'she never wishes to see her husband'. She took great delight in hearing from a Captain and Mrs Simmons 'a great deal about Mrs Henderson's improper conduct in the Winter...and they did not spare her at all'. Frustratingly Fanny doesn't record any of this gossip and so we are unable to gain an insight into Georgiana's behaviour. It may all have been sour grapes as they didn't like her close friendship with Cooper.

Georgiana and her family were still in Weymouth for the celebrations held to mark the forty-seventh birthday of the Prince of Wales. After watching a number of events on the beach they made their way to Harvey's Library for a 'Vocal Concert'. The singing was 'delightful' although the proceedings were disturbed by a Mr Deveral who arrived late and in a very tipsy condition. He then sat down next to Major Durbin and spoke in a very loud voice. After the concert they returned to their lodgings to watch the 'very good fireworks' which were let off opposite their windows. A week later the Hendersons held a dinner party and, as well as Fanny and her aunts, the guests included Lord Hinton, Major Durbin, Mr Grimes, Mr Atkins, Mr Bussell, Mrs Allen and her two daughters. Fanny hasn't said what they had to eat or drink but she does record that one of the Misses Allen was 'the most coarse, inconsequential, affected piece of goods'. Georgiana and her children joined the families of Captain Scot and Mr W. Williams, together with Henry Porcher, for a trip to the theatre to see *Laugh When You Can* and *Bluebeard*.

A few days later Henderson became unwell so, to allow him some peace and quiet to recover from his illness, Georgiana took the children aside and dressed them up as different characters. She then took them in their masquerade costumes to show their friends in the town. Fanny thought young John made an excellent housemaid.

Because 'Mrs Henderson was of the party and is always forcing herself wherever we are, that the world may believe she is very intimate and a great favourite with us' Fanny decided not to join her aunts and the others when they decided to walk to Gloucester Lodge. This red brick house with a sizeable garden that had been built sideways onto the esplanade was the summer home of George III. Two of his daughters were coming to stay there while Georgiana was in Weymouth. Fanny chose to remain at home instead and practice her shoe making.

Cooper returned to Weymouth at the beginning of September. Fanny, her aunts and their guests George Shirley and Mr Bussell continued playing the card game Quadrille, when he arrived and did not trouble themselves to stop when he entered the room. He kissed the women 'so very coldly, that anyone seeing him would have supposed he had been only a slight acquaintance', mused Fanny. Their days continued to be filled with visits, balls and suppers – and an occasional trip on the water. During their stay Fanny heard that a gentleman had agreed to buy Batheaston Villa on Cooper's terms and on hearing this news she felt a sharp pain in her side and she had to go straight to bed. After this she had even less time for Georgiana when she found her and 'four of her stupid brats' waiting for her to return from her morning walk. She went straight upstairs and left her aunts to deal with the visitors. She managed however to be polite at dinner when Georgiana sat down with them and their guests. Cooper must have been aware of Fanny's mood as he whispered to her that if he had fifty thousand pounds he would try to persuade her to share Bath Easton with him, but she didn't believe a word he said. Georgiana continued, most probably unintentionally to cause Fanny grief when she joined Cooper on a visit to the home of Mrs Williams at Herringston. He told them he would be back later that night, needless to say he did not appear instead he sent a note to say he would return the following morning. She was sure that Georgiana was responsible for delaying him so that they travel alone on the journey back to town. To add to her misery she became unwell with a bowel complaint and felt so cold that she ordered the fire to be lit. 'Feeling very indignant' she did not welcome him home. 'After passing eleven weeks there as unpleasantly' as she could remember Fanny and her aunts finally left in the knowledge that Georgiana would be waiting for Cooper's return to Weymouth without them.

Georgiana appears to have enjoyed a happy marriage with Henderson. He had provided her with a very comfortable lifestyle, a fine house and five children. Fanny however paints a very different picture of her as flirtatious and having a very close friendship with Cooper. He had a reputation as a womaniser and enjoyed female company. Fanny wanted him for herself and so was jealous of the attention he paid to other women. It is tantalisingly to think that Georgiana's long lost correspondence and dairies may throw light on the nature of her friendship with Cooper as well as others.

60 Nothing unpleasant makes a lasting impression

Fanny thought Cooper 'out of spirits and evidently sorry at having been persuaded to sell the villa'. He was so 'very low' he 'could not help shedding tears when he got into the carriage' making her think that he regretted the decision 'to sell this sweet place tho' he is that kind of disposition that nothing unpleasant makes a lasting impression on his mind'. When he met up with Georgiana in Weymouth he told that he had been busy making a start on sorting out the contents of the Villa before the new owner arrived. He had gone through old bills, some of which dated back nearly a hundred years, and then burnt them. Before he left the Villa he instructed the women what was needed and gave them some uncut Brazil diamonds, half guineas and silver coinage that had been the property of their sister and his late wife, from whom he had inherited Batheaston Villa together with a large fortune. Before their marriage she had negotiated a settlement to retain her inheritance but within six months she revoked this agreement and made him sole beneficiary. Following her death in 1802, her two sisters and niece who had been living with them, agreed to make no claim on her estate if he continued to look after them.

While Cooper enjoyed the delights of Weymouth the women were left to clear the villa ready for the new owner. They cleared the store rooms, organised things for valuation and identified the fixtures that the buyer wanted to keep. Everything else, the music, shells and curiosities that were scattered throughout the building, etc., were packed up. Then Fanny went through the plants in the greenhouse only to find that 'nearly half of them had died or by been sold by the gardener'. They also had to look for a new home for themselves. They viewed several nearby properties including a miserable cottage at Bathford, a place near Midford Castle on the other side of Bath and an old-fashioned house with beautiful grounds that they really liked but thought they wouldn't be able to afford the rent.

On 16th October 1809, or 'black Monday' as Fanny described it she 'walked around the garden and took leave of it' and then 'into all the rooms where [she had] passed so many, many happy hours, there was not one that did not recall some delightful recollection', she mused. 'In all human probability' it would be the last time she would ever see the villa. As soon as they finished breakfast Fanny and her aunts got into the coach 'which was packed as full as it could be' and they travelled to their new lodgings in Henrietta Street in Bath. On that same day Cooper held 'a very large and gay party...which did not break up until four o'clock in the morning'. Although she hadn't been included Fanny was sure that the Hendersons would have been there. She also said that it would have been better for Georgiana if she had stayed where she was 'to save appearances' rather than move to lodgings next door to Cooper but she added, 'it is evident that she is not of the same opinion and sets the opinion of the world at defiance'.

It is likely that Georgiana had returned to their London home by the 25th October to take part in the celebrations marking the Golden Jubilee of King George III. Church bells rang in every town and village, flags flew from every mast and guns were fired to mark this rare event in England's history. Troops and voluntary forces marched through the streets and services of thanksgiving were held in every church as well as St Paul's Cathedral. In the evening Georgiana would have taken her young family into the City to see the illuminations at Mansion House – an oak leaf, thistle and shamrock were picked out alongside the royal cipher and crown. Everywhere they looked was ablaze with colour. The exterior walls of the Bank of England were lit up and there was a beautiful promenade at the Post Office where they could walk 'in an arbour of variegated lamps'. The shops, auction rooms, libraries, theatres, clubs and private houses were festooned with special Jubilee candles. Georgiana would have dressed their home in Montague Street with patriotic pictures and portraits of the King. The sky was so filled with exploding fireworks that it turned night into day. George III celebrated his special day with his family at Windsor where a private service was held before he attended a grand fete at Frogmore.

Georgiana would also have witnessed the funeral of the King and the subsequent coronation of the Prince of Wales as George IV but we have no personal account of these events. It would appear that now she was no longer part of Cooper's everyday life Fanny had very little contact with Georgiana although she does record a visit to London in

May 1810 to visit another Mr Henderson, a dentist in Charlotte Street. Her aunt had two teeth removed and had to go back the following day to have her gums hardened. While they were waiting they heard a gentleman having a 'tooth taken out' and he 'cried out so loud' that it made Fanny quite nervous for the rest of the day. She didn't wonder at his cries when she saw that he had 'the longest tooth' she had ever seen had been extracted. On a third visit the dentist didn't have time for them so they called at Montague Street only to find, to Fanny's relief, that Georgiana was out. However, a week later she, and 'two of her brats' called on them at their lodgings to issue an invitation to dinner. As they were busy on the day suggested it was agreed that they would attend the following day but when they arrived at Montague Street they discovered that Henderson was out and it was only Georgiana and her eldest son who would be eating with them. Afterwards they were given a tour of the house which Fanny had to admit was 'an excellent one'. Georgiana called on the women on several occasions and then, on the day they were due to leave, she and Henderson came and sat with them until it was time for them to board their coach to Bath. Georgiana asked them to deliver a parcel to Cooper when his sister-in-law took him the 'two pair of handsome wine coolers' they had bought as a gift for him. On the following New Year's Day Henderson sent his friend, 'a very bad cod fish and some excellent oysters' and 'a stilton cheese'. As the diaries of both Fanny and Georgiana are missing we don't know if they continued to be in contact particularly when the women moved into Henlade House in Taunton, over fifty-five miles from Bath. We can imagine that they all celebrated, in varying degrees, Cooper's third marriage to the daughter of Sir George Baker, Physician to King George III and, seven years later, his funeral following his death at the age of 63 in 1828. Cooper didn't forget Georgiana. In his will he left instructions that she should receive a ring in token of their friendship. Mrs Williams was also bequeathed a ring. His godson, Cooper Henderson received a bequest of £300 with interest. This is the last known reference to Georgiana and her family in relation to John Hutton Cooper and Fanny Chapman.

61 A canary in a cage

Georgiana's sons, like their contemporaries, were sent away to boarding schools for their education. From a surviving letter we know that seven-year old Charles Cooper was attending a small school near Brighton. 'Dear Mama,' he wrote, he was happy to report that he was quite well and he was 'looking forward with pleasure to the time' of her return from some unknown destination. In another letter, written four years later, he apologised for taking so long to write but he had seen and heard so little that he couldn't keep his promise to write to her every week. In this letter he told her that Mr Tilt, where he was staying, had 'a great number of rabbits at his farm' and they had two of them for their dinner. On another day there was great excitement as the hunt passed by. With other boys he had followed the huntsmen and hounds and they were 'in at the death'. He also told his mother that one of the boys had a couple of dormice but they were 'such sleepy little creatures they do not keep awake five minutes at a time'. Another one let his bird out of its cage but it flew away and 'so it was all dickey with him', he wrote. The school room he added had been recently papered and wainscoted, and a board with some Latin sentences on it had been put up, but other than that he had nothing to report and makes no comment on his lessons. In conclusion he asked his mother to pass on his love to all at Montague Street, his grandmother as well as his brother John when she next wrote to him at his school.

Four years later we find that Charles Cooper was now a boarder at Winchester College, following in his brother's footsteps. Founded in the 14th century and modelled on Eton it offered a classical education under its Headmaster Revd Dr Henry Dison Gabell. On 12th March he wrote apologising to his mother for the shortness of his previous letter 'which I would certainly not have sent if I had been able to have written a better'. Although he was only using a single sheet of paper to save on postage he had so much to tell her that after filling both sides, except for the space for the address, he then turned the sheet 90° and continued writing, overlapping the text underneath, but he still had more to say so he then wrote diagonally across the paper so that there were three lines of text crisscrossing both sides of this single sheet. Aware that his mother might struggle to read his letter he suggested that she put 6s 8d in the pocket of her older son 'John the lawyer' to decipher it for her. As promised, he then gave her an account of college life although 'it would be very arduous undertaking' and he was afraid that 'when the history' was finished his mother wouldn't understand it. As a Commoner he never saw the College boys except when they mixed in class or went into the hills. The Commoner's court, he told her, was 'a beastly place'. The Headmaster's house was on one corner and Mrs Bell lived in a building on the opposite side. She used to hand out jugs of milk through a hatch in her door but, Charles Cooper told his mother, it was so bad that he never drank any of it for breakfast. A gate in the wall of their playground was unlocked at 12pm to let the boys out into College Street for an hour. From the court they could access the Hall which was lined with their toys. He was regularly told that he was one of the luckiest fellows as he got his toys so soon after he arrived at school. The knife and fork had proved a great luxury at dinner, he told his mother and then he asked her to send him a filtering coffee pot. However, as this would need to be kept with his toys it would need to have a small spout and handle. He also asked her for some common coffee, coarse sugar and a small amount of tea, provided it was not too expensive.

He then outlined a typical school day. First he had Vulgus and once he had finished these Latin verses he had to take them to his tutor for correction and signature, then with nothing else to do he prepared for his afternoon lesson. Dinner at 1pm was 'the most uncomfortable meal you can imagine' he complained to his mother. At 4pm the hatch opened to serve the boys bread and cheese. Charles Cooper was very happy to add the cheese rejected by many of the boys to his own plate as he had developed a taste for it at family meals. Later the table was covered with coffee, tea, barrels of oysters, meat pies, plates of meat and private cheeses. 'Many who mess in the morning do not in the evening' he informed her, as they all couldn't all get a place on the fire to boil their water. This was a time he could talk freely with the other boys and during his conversations he discovered that many of them knew his mother, so he said he would send her a 'printed roll' of their names. He also had to report that when a group of them were called to the hatch one of the boys 'kindly stood' on his foot and he later discovered that the skin of his 'Great Toe' had been completely taken off. He didn't think it was serious and only went to the doctor a couple of days later, when it started to hurt and he found more blood than usual in his stocking. Sent to the very snug sick room where he joined six or seven other boys with various ailments but by the fourth day of his confinement it was only him and a 'very nice fellow' and then he was on his own. Naturally his thoughts had turned to home which, he assured his mother, he would 'never forget'. Towards the end of this long letter he asked her to remember him to his former art teacher, the well respected watercolourist Samuel Prout who he would 'never be able to repay his attention and thank him sufficiently' for the trouble he had taken in teaching him to paint and etch. No doubt the whole family would have been delighted to hear the news that the artist was appointed Painter in Watercolours in Ordinary to King George IV ten years later, and then to Queen Victoria. He also asked his mother to remember him to her friend Moxley who, he supposed, 'had worn out his back in answer to the applause he received nightly at the Apollonicon'. This extremely large automatic machine had around 1,900 pipes and 45 organ stops and used a technique similar to a barrel organ to replicate the sound of an entire orchestra, and it only required a few people to operate it. The Duke and Duchess of Kent were 'graciously pleased to express their highest approbation' after attending, by invitation, the first performance of this new instrument at the West End premises of its inventors Flight and Robson. In this same year, 1817, Georgiana took her youngest son to the first public performance of the Apollonicon before he left for his new school. This was the only concert and public recital organ in London for nearly a quarter of century and Lord Bryon's mistress Claire Clarmont was particularly enamoured by it. She attended three performances in 18 days to hear Alfred Moxley play Bach fugues and Haydn symphonies.

Now released from the sick room Charles Cooper told his mother that he had an excellent appetite and, although he had been originally placed with the worst possible tutor, he would now be under the tutelage of Mr John Williams, 'the cleverest' of the three teachers. In a shorter letter written six months later he told her to tell his mother he had been very pleased to receive her letter as he feared 'they might have drowned following their recent visit to France'. He hoped that they had enjoyed their tour around Rouen and Eau and he imagined that his sisters had 'looked at the dark blue sea' as they waited for the ferry at Calais in anticipation of the 'great discomfort of their stomachs'. No doubt, he added, they had found Montague Street very dull after 'the bustle and gaiety of the Boulvard, Elysian Fields, etc'. As to life at school Mr Williams had left but, he thanked God, his replacement was 'a decent young man named Francis Swanton'. Another master by the name of Urquhart was getting married to one of the Bishop of Hereford's daughters but he didn't know if 'she had much of the needful or not'. This news had turned Charles Cooper's thoughts to his sisters who he supposed were 'now looking for hubs'. Did his mother know if the Queen would live or die? He had to ask questions, he told her, as shut up in a yard he felt like 'a canary in a cage [that] cannot tell his friends what it thinks of the country'. Signing off as 'Your ever affectionate Son', he asked her to 'write soon remember me to all'.

These few surviving letters convey the affection that the children felt for their mother and suggest that Georgiana was happy in her situation.

62 Beyond the power of description

With Napoleon's defeat at Waterloo in 1815 the British could once again visit the continent and Henderson would have taken his sons on a Grand Tour to complete their education. Georgiana and her daughters would have attended the balls and parties held to celebrate England's victory against the French. Dressed in her finery Georgiana and her husband made their way to what was considered one of the best mansions in Portland Place, for a ball organised by Mrs Gosling. The couple would have been among around the 300 or so guests who climbed the magnificent staircase, brilliantly lit by chandeliers and lustres, to the first floor ballroom. During the course of the evening the musicians played a waltz. No doubt at the age of 44, and as a mother of five children, Georgiana found it delightful to join her husband in this dance which had initially scandalised society due to the intimate nature of the waltz which required dancers to hold each other close. When they wanted a break from the dancing they could adjourn to one of the three adjoining drawing rooms with floor to ceiling mirrored panels, or walk on through to the fourth room considered one of the prettiest boudoirs in town fitted out, it was said, 'with extraordinary taste' which had been appropriated for those who wished to play cards. At two o'clock everyone was summoned to the supper room where 'every delicate ornament was used to give zest to a most excellent banquet consisting of every delicacy'. An hour later they returned to the ball room where the dancing 'was kept up with proper spirit until six o'clock' in the morning.

Another ball Georgiana would have attended was that held by the Spanish Ambassador, His Excellency the Duke San Carlos at his grand house in Portland Place, to mark the marriage of King Ferdinand VII. With 'his amiable and accomplished Duchess' the Duke welcomed his guests, including the Prince Regent and members of the aristocracy, in their grand drawing room where they had placed a portrait of the absent Spanish King in the centre of a splendid throne. Rare and choice plants in flower were displayed in the window recesses and other parts of the reception room. 'Exotic plants from Botany Bay' decorated the grand staircase and the railings were covered with evergreens…with baskets suspended on each side…containing the rarest plants that could be procured. The whole had the effect of ascending an illuminated grove', said one guest. Dancing began with quadrilles at eleven o'clock and continued with supper served in the lower rooms at a quarter past one. The whole exterior of the mansion was brilliantly lit with variegated lamps and several engines and firemen were on standby in case the lamps and candles caused any accidental fires.

These pleasant activities were interrupted in November 1819 when tragedy struck the family. Georgiana's middle child, twenty year old Jane Catherine was struck down with 'a most distressing and painful illness...her complaint...pervaded the whole exterior of her body and then 'from some cause or other was driven inwards, or as it was technically termed "translated" to the Heart', as Henderson described it to his old friend Dr Thomas Monro. During the five weeks that she suffered her pulse 'had never been below 120°, often 140° and near the end it registered 150°'. As well as this rapid heart rate she suffered from pain in her joints, shortness of breath and a persistent cough which exhausted her until she had no strength left to fight the infection. Her doctors had used bleeding, purgatives and medicines to promote perspiration. but she did not respond to any of the remedies. 'At last Nature was exhausted and our beloved and ever to be lamented Child calmly resigned her last breath, and with it as pure a soul as ever was possessed by mortal went to her maker', he wrote to Monro. Their only consolation was that they couldn't believe that anyone 'nearer perfection' was 'ever created' and they had to trust that she was 'now where there is eternal happiness!' In order to understand why she had such a fast pulse during the course of her illness an eminent surgeon opened up her body and discovered that Henderson's daughter had succumbed to 'Rheumatic Gout' brought on by a bacterial infection. Today we know this as rheumatic fever. They were completely unprepared for this terrible blow and were naturally plunged into grief and affliction beyond the power of description. Henderson concluded his letter with the wish that Monro and his family would 'enjoy every possible happiness and be strangers to sickness or sorrow'.

Twenty four years later Georgiana would be mourning the passing of her seventy-nine year old husband who had died from old age, or 'decay of nature' as it was described on his death certificate.

Henderson had ensured before he died that he had made ample provision for Georgiana but as a token of the regard he had for his wife he also left her an annuity of two hundred pounds a year. The rest of his estate he left to his eldest son John as arrangements had been made for his other children. Within two years Georgiana had to arrange another funeral, this time for her youngest daughter Harriet. She died after she threw herself over the banisters of a flight of stairs at Montague Street. The doctors declared that she had carried out this act 'while insane'. It may have been depression that drove her to take her life. This might have been a family trait as Charles Cooper in one of his surviving letters to his mother had written about 'John's melancholy fits', or possibly she never recovered from an overwhelming grief at the death of her father. We shall never know.

Georgiana lived for another seven years before she died at the same age and from the same cause as her late husband. She then joined him in Catacomb B of the fashionable necropolis for the great and the good at Kensal Green. Her will clearly shows the resentment she still bore her parents, even though four decades had passed since their deaths. She writes 'a Jane Catherine Keate, my late mother deceased...did in exercise of the power given to her by the will of her then late husband George Keate' instruct her executors to sell the Keate estates to raise money to cover the cost of her bequests. Parliament subsequently passed *An Act authorising the Trustees...to sell...land and tenements in Spitalfields* in response to her instruction. This sale raised a sum the equivalent of around £220,000 today, and after honouring her bequests the executors invested the remaining monies, together with the rents collected from other properties, into a trust for Georgiana's children – but only to those children that she bore by any other man than John Henderson. So even their children were blighted by their mother's disregard of her parents' feelings at the time of her marriage. If her daughter had not fulfilled this requirement then the executors were to direct the bequest to the son of the Keate's oldest friend, Robert Le Geyt of Canterbury. After laying out this history in her will Georgiana then dealt with her own bequests in one short paragraph. Any property and assets that she owned at her death were to be divided equally between her surviving children.

63 The entire field of art

What of Georgiana's surviving children? John, the eldest, continued to live in the family home in Montague Street. Like his grandfather and father before him he studied law and graduated from Balliol College, Oxford, and like them he never practised his profession. Instead he pursued antiquarian interests. He added Venetian glass, Chinese and Japanese bronzes to the rare objects he had inherited from his parents, such as the pair of enamelled silver snuffers which were once the property of Cardinal Bainbridge, Archbishop of York who was the immediate predecessor of Cardinal Wolsey together with a tortoiseshell snuff box which had an exquisite portrait of the French aristocrat and favourite of the royal court, Comtesse de Grignan on the lid. Both of these items had been acquired by Georgiana's father and their appearance in the Henderson household suggests that, in spite of her parents' animus their executors thought that their daughter could have items that she would have known from her childhood. John's collections placed him in the orbit of London's learned societies. He regularly loaned items for display and discussion to meetings of the Society of Antiquaries and the Archaeological Institute. The museum keeper, scholar and eminent Victorian collector, Augustus Wollaston Franks took the credit for persuading his close friend to leave nearly 900 items to the British Museum. Although this bequest did not 'represent the entire field of art' which Henderson had studied it did mean that gaps in the museum's collection were filled in a most satisfactory manner. The National Gallery was invited to take their choice from the Old Masters, portraits, watercolours, drawings, and works by modern artists which graced the walls of Montague Street. A large part of his antiquities collection went to the University of Oxford.

Perhaps inspired by his mother's artistic skill John took a great interest in the Royal Female School of Art, which had been founded in 1842 with the aim of training 'young women of the middle class to obtain an honourable and profitable employment', instead of painting purely as a pleasant pastime. As well as paying the one guinea (£1 1s) annual subscription John served as a Trustee and Treasurer for many years, and provided additional prizes for the juvenile class section of the annual competition. He presented the School with a volume of photographs he had published showing examples of the bronzes, china and other rare objects he had in his collection. The School's future, which had been uncertain, was secured when he left a bequest of £100 following his death at the age of eighty-one in 1878.

Little is known about the oldest and only surviving daughter. Named after her mother Georgiana continued to live in the family home in Montague Street where she most probably acted as hostess on formal occasions for her bachelor brother. An amateur artist herself, her view of Venice could be found in the collection of her nephew, and she continued to pay her annual one guinea subscription to the Royal Female School of Art until she died at the age of eighty-three in 1881.

Charles Cooper was the last of her children to outlive Georgiana. In a case of history almost repeating itself he fell out with his father over his choice of bride. He had fallen for the sixteen-year-old daughter of a Thames lighterman who may have been working as a maid in the Henderson household, or for one of their nearby neighbours. The couple eloped to Gretna Green and were married on 3rd November 1829. With the deed done Henderson arranged for a second discreet wedding in London which was held on Christmas Eve that same year. After the marriage Henderson gave his son a small allowance and told him to leave London. The newlyweds found a small house in Bracknell in Berkshire that suited their purse. As Charlotte had no dowry to offer her new husband Charles Cooper turned to painting to supplement his income. However, in later years Charlotte, as the only living family member, inherited large tracts of land in Canada from a very distant cousin, Colonel John By. This military engineer built the 125 mile long Rideau Canal and founded Bytown, renamed Ottawa which became the capital of Canada. Nine months after their first wedding Charlotte presented her husband with a boy they named Charles Cooper. Two years later she was pregnant again and they moved to a larger home nearer London, near Kensington Turnpike. With great skill and an eye for composition Charles Cooper was able to conjure up images of the mail coaches, gigs, wagonettes, chaises and phaetons that passed his door each day. His paintings showed vehicles travelling through the slumbering countryside on a moonlit night, or battling the wind and rain, or struggling through heavy falls of snow with the outside passengers huddled together, no doubt longing for a short respite at a warm friendly inn where they could get something to eat and drink while the ostlers changed the horses for a fresh team produced a decent income for the artist as they appealed to connoisseurs. Charles Cooper was able to move his growing family to No.3 Lambs Conduit Place, a short distance from his childhood home in Montague Street. Hopefully Georgiana and her husband were reconciled with their son, particularly as he had named his second child after them, John Keate Shepard Henderson (born 1833). Seven more children followed: Charlotte (1835), Kennett Gregg (1836), Robert (1838), Mary (1840), Roderick William (1841), George By (1845) and finally Henry Cooper (1848). Sadly, their son Robert died at the age of three and a half from an unknown brain disease. The last two boys were born after their grandfather died but Georgiana would have known all her grandchildren before she died in 1850. With his share of her estate Charles Cooper was able to move his family out to Lower Halliford, Shepperton where he had leased a hip roofed eighteenth century house on the north bank of the Thames. Their new home was large enough to accommodate his large family, a governess, nurse, cook, housemaid, coachman and indoor servant. Charles Cooper now settled into the life of a leisured gentlemen but within a few years his wife Charlotte died from cancer. She was only forty-five years old. Their twenty-three-year old daughter took over the daily running of the house although she didn't have to worry about the older boys who had moved out and were leading their own lives, Charles Cooper junior had set himself up as a dentist, John Keate Shepard had joined the Royal Welsh Fusiliers where he rose to the rank of Lieutenant and his brother Kennett Gregg became a Major-General in Her Majesty's 60th Regiment (Rifles). The younger boys had been sent as boarders to Westminster College. Although ten years older than his wife Charles Cooper lived for another twenty years and died at the age of 74 in 1871. He was buried alongside Charlotte, his son, parents and sister in the catacombs at Kensal Green and his children erected a brass tablet in his memory in St Nicholas' Church, Shepperton. Britain's longest serving lifeboat which took part in the evacuation of Dunkirk was named after him too.

Most of Georgiana's grandchildren lived into their 60s and 70s but only two of them married. Kennett Gregg had one daughter who died a spinster. Roderick William had two sons and a daughter Marie By.

She married George Tertius Seabroke in 1907 and their children provide the only surviving line of descent from Georgiana.

Acknowledgements

I would like to thank Lucy Pesaro for bringing Georgiana's diaries to my notice, Georgiana's only surviving descendants Peter and George Seabroke for their support and interest, Charles Lane for his help with Charles Cooper Henderson, George Rosenberg for telling me about the references to Georgiana in his great aunt's diaries. I would also like to thank my literary friends at Shenley Writers and Watford Writers for their help and support, together with my family and friends, and everyone who has encouraged me over the years.

About the author: Susan Bennett initially undertook the research which has led to this book for a Research MA awarded by Birkbeck College on *The artistic life of Georgiana Jane Henderson (nee Keate) (1771-1850),* and her dissertation was subsequently published by VDM Verlag Dr Muller in 2004.

Former RSA Curator/Archivist for nearly 25 years she is now Honorary Secretary and Editor for the William Shipley Group for RSA History (www.williamshipleygroup.btck.co.uk)